RAILROADS

Daniel L. Overbey

RAILROADS

The Free
Enterprise
Alternative

Q
QUORUM BOOKS
WESTPORT, CONNECTICUT ● LONDON, ENGLAND

Library of Congress Cataloging in Publication Data

Overbey, Daniel L. (Daniel Leon)
 Railroads, the free enterprise alternative

 Bibliography: p.
 Includes index.
 1. Railroads—United States—Management.   2. Rail-
roads and state—United States.   I. Title.
HE2741.O94   385'.068   82-7503
ISBN 0-89930-031-6 (lib. bdg.)   AACR2

Library of Congress Catalog Card Number : 82-7503
ISBN: 0-89930-031-6

First published in 1982 by Quorum Books

Greenwood Press
A division of Congressional Information Service, Inc.
88 Post Road West, Westport, Connecticut 06881

Printed in the United States of America

10 9 8 7 6 5 4 3 2 1

To Gail

CONTENTS

FIGURES

TABLES

PREFACE

The financial outlook for the railroad industry is the brightest it has been in many years, due largely to recent deregulation efforts and changes in the federal tax laws. It is not the best time to offer a treatise on the fundamental problems of the railroad industry. Still, those problems remain even if events in the past few years have made them somewhat more tolerable.

Prior to deregulation, only two policy options were available: the status quo of regulated private enterprise or nationalization. It was a question of choosing the lesser evil. Deregulation—actually a reduction of regulation, not its elimination—is an extension of the status quo in that much regulation is retained. Deregulation shows the potential for keeping railroad problems within acceptable limits. A number of knowledgeable people have doubts, however. The Interstate Commerce Commission has yet to develop a method for setting maximum rates acceptable to shippers, railroads, and the courts. Actions by some railroads have prompted calls for a reversal of recent trends and an increase in regulation. If the deregulation efforts should prove less than successful, the original options of old-style regulation or nationalization remain. The Free Enterprise Alternative offers a new option.

The Free Enterprise Alternative also offers an alternative approach to rail transportation. Simply put, it shows that a railroad need not always act like a railroad to be successful. By starting with what is routine in the other modes and not with what the railroads have always done, a new spectrum of markets and service possibilities emerges. This different perspective is useful in and of itself.

The Free Enterprise Alternative identifies those structural elements which have led to the success of the highway, water, and air transport modes—the same elements which have led to the relative decline of the railroad industry. It applies the desirable elements of those structures to the rail mode.

The ideas basic to the Free Enterprise Alternative, such as joint use of the fixed way and competition among carriers, are not new. They have been the subject of considerable study and exploration by many individuals, as the following chapters attest. I hope this presentation does justice to all of the individuals who have helped foster the Free Enterprise Alternative.

Daniel Leon Overbey

ACKNOWLEDGMENTS

I wish to thank Dr. Henry Malcolm Steiner and Randall W. Kirk of the University of Texas at Austin, Texas, for their guidance. I also benefited from the example of Charles P. Zlatkovich, of the University's Bureau of Business Research, who presented new and daring ideas in rail transportation.

Charles Stafford, Doug Johle, and many other friends helped me learn the railroad while I worked as a telegrapher-clerk at Taylor and Austin, Texas. At the Frisco Railway's Market Research Department in St. Louis, Missouri, I was privileged to work with a number of dedicated marketing professionals, among them Bob Rodefeld, Ron Cook, and Dick Lewis.

My gratitude is extended to the authors whose works I have referenced, especially John G. Kneiling of *Trains* magazine. He said what he felt should be said, whether it flattered the rail industry or not. His honesty has revealed many new opportunities for the railroads.

I wish to thank my parents, Leonard and Meta Overbey, my brother Dennis, and my sister Ramona. My first twenty years were spent in and around our family's service station, which provided both an education and an unshakeable faith in free enterprise and competitive markets.

Most of all, I thank Gail Ann Urhahn Overbey, my wife. She accepted the loss of many evenings and weekends to this project and saw the manuscript through innumerable revisions. Without her help, this book would not have been possible.

RAILROADS

1 | DEVELOPMENT OF THE RAILWAY

In October of 1603 or 1604 Huntingdon Beaumont built one of the first railways known to history. It was built to serve his coal mine near Nottingham, England. This and other early railways consisted only of rectangular wooden beams "laid end to end over roughly-levelled ground, over which teams of horses drew the loaded waggons."[1] The use of wooden rails kept wagons from sinking in the mud and greatly increased the load a given number of horses could pull. Although such rails had doubtless been used earlier to bridge muddy or soft spots in roads, this was one of the first times they were used as part of a permanent transportation system. The railway had been born.

A legal development which complemented these early technological developments was the extension of the power of eminent domain to the railways. The first railways, located in Britain, were owned and operated by coal mines. To operate the railway over property not owned by the coal mine, the railway had to purchase "way-leaves" from the landowners. As the price of coal rose, so did the cost of the way-leaves. The mine owners sought a less costly method for obtaining such privileges. By converting the private railway into a public thoroughfare, the railway—like the canals and turnpikes—could invoke the Crown's power of eminent domain and thereby secure rights of way at a lower cost. In return for this privilege, the companies had to accept a greater degree of governmental regulation, most often in the form of charter restrictions. The result was a dual usage of the railway: used both for the private purposes of the owner company and for public transportation.[2]

The culmination of these legal and technological developments was the Surrey Iron Railway, opened to the public in May of 1801.[3] It was the first purely commercial railway—built solely for public use and not owned by a canal, coal mine, or other interest. Its promoters advertised that "the carriages fit for a railway may also be used in the streets of a town, or on a common highway."[4] Individuals could drive their own wagons over the railway upon payment of a toll, and the railways provided an alternative to common roads. It also should be noted that this, the first purely commercial railway, came after almost two hundred years of railway development.

DESCRIPTION OF EARLY RAILWAYS

The first railways used horses to pull wagons over wooden or stone rails. Early railways had several names: railroad, railway, Newcastle road, waggonway, tramroad, or dramroad. The first railways differed little from highways. They depended on the wagon driver to keep the wagon on the relatively wide rails. Eventually flanges were used to help guide wagons, and their application created two distinct types of railways: plateways and edge-rails.

Plateways were the oldest type of system, utilizing a smooth wagon wheel and a flanged rail. The flange was originally more of a curb, providing the driver with only minimal aid in steering. In time, flange gauge and other dimensions were made closer to those of the wagon wheels, resulting in almost complete guidance. An "L"- or "U"-shaped rail was often used. The flanged rail first appeared in 1756, used on the Eddystone lighthouse railway in England.[5] One of the plateway's major advantages was that, by using flanged rails and smooth wagon wheels, the same vehicles could use both railroads and highways.

Edge-rails developed later when "by a real inspiration of genius, the flange was transferred from the track to the wheel; and the modern railway was born."[6] The edge-rail was slow to gain popularity, primarily because it required flanged wheels which limited the wagons almost exclusively to railway use.

Commercial railways grew in number and size. Privately owned but open to public use, they grew until a national system seemed within reach. Canal companies built many miles of railways to feed and connect the waterways. Complete integration, however, was not possible due to the lack of standardization. Many lines had progressed to the use of edge-rails, which required flanged wheels of a more exacting design and placed restrictions on the vehicles which could use the railway. Some railway companies saw this restriction as an advantage as it gave the company greater control over those who used the line, something of no little concern on heavily travelled lines. Those lines which operated more like turnpikes found plateways desirable, since the smooth-wheeled wagons could operate on both highways and railways. When operated in this manner, railways competed directly with common highways and turnpikes. Both types of railways flourished in England during the late 1700's and early 1800's.

Opening a privately owned railroad to use by the public necessitated the establishment of rules. Identification of wagon ownership was frequently required, typically by having the owner's name painted on the wagon's side. The names were used to assess tolls and enforce rules. Weight limits, speed limits, and wheel dimensions were commonly specified to protect the roadway from abuse.[7] Operating rules were similar to those of highways: opposing wagons took to the left at passing and double tracks. On some lines loaded wagons had priority over empty ones; on other lines wagons moving in a certain direction had priority. Drivers were prohibited from parking their wagons on the railway, as occasionally happened near pubs.[8]

In time, large shippers began "ganging" the wagons into trains. Several men were needed to run such a train, driving horses and braking the wagons. In some instances the trains were separated at terminals with teams and drivers delivering individual wagons over common highways. Unlike highway practice, railways usually had the horses pull in a single file due to the narrow distance between the rails.

Tolls were collected by the railway, using toll houses equipped with gates. Tolls were usually paid in cash, although regular customers were occasionally given credit accounts. Ton-miles served as the basis for tolls on many railways. The wagon's weight was obtained by using large scales; the mileage was determined by trackside milestones. Where railways were owned or operated by canal companies, a common toll structure was used.[9]

The shipper's freight bill consisted of two parts: (1) a charge by the wagoner for providing the transportation service; and (2) the railway toll. The wagoner paid the railway toll and was reimbursed by the shipper. Later, as the railway companies themselves began to operate wagons over their own railways, the two charges were combined. It was still common practice, however, to provide a schedule of tolls for those who might wish to use the railway for their own wagons. The charter of the Baltimore and Ohio, an early American railway, had such a provision.[10]

Many English and American railway charters included a limitation of profits. This was seen as a proper governmental action because the charter gave the railway the power of eminent domain—a monopoly over the route specified in the charter. Profit limitations were in order, since the monopoly vested a degree of public interest in the railway. The profit limitation was often related to the cost of building and operating the railroad or to the amount of invested capital.[11]

DEVELOPMENT OF LOCOMOTIVES

An important step in the evolution of railways was the development of steam-powered locomotives, which took place in England during the early nineteenth century. H. S. Haines describes this "momentous change" as "the most important advance in the material civilization of mankind since the discovery of the usefulness of fire."[12]

Many experiments were conducted with steam-powered vehicles on both railways and highways. In 1804 Trevithick successfully operated a steam-powered railway locomotive which utilized a toothed driving wheel. Later experiments by Stephenson and others determined that sufficient adhesion for pulling a train could be obtained by using a smooth wheel, and the steam locomotive became a reality.

Just as the development of steam locomotives depended on improvements in iron-making, so did the development of the iron rail. Iron gradually replaced stone and wood as rail material, although a few small English railways used wood or stone rails into the twentieth century. Iron rail facilitated steam-locomotive development by carrying heavier loads than could stone or wood. Although iron rails and steam locomotives were complementary, it should not be taken that one required the other. Some railways used steam locomotives on wooden rails; others used horse power on iron rails.[13]

The first commercial railway to use steam locomotives was the Stockton and Darlington Railway, opened in 1825.[14] This British railway used steam power and edge-rails and marked "the beginning of a new age in railway development, for although at the beginning part of the line was horse-operated, part was worked by locomotives."[15]

Once again, though, technological progress came by evolution, not revolution. In the United States, as in Britain, steam and horse power existed side by side for many years. A report by a U.S. civil engineer to President Jackson recommended that the Charleston and Hamburg railroad be adaptable to both horse and steam power.[16] The Baltimore and Ohio Railroad used both types of power and gained a niche in history by racing its steam locomotive *Tom Thumb* against a horsecar. Although the horse won the race, steam power soon won the railroads.

NOTES

1. Bertram Baxter, *Stone Blocks and Iron Rails*, p. 20. This excellent research work provides a detailed, well-documented description of early English railways and their development.
2. Henry S. Haines, *Railway Corporations as Public Servants*, p. 24.
3. Baxter, p. 27.
4. Ibid., p. 46.
5. Ibid., p. 45.
6. Haines, p. 10.
7. Baxter, p. 81.
8. Ibid., p. 89.
9. Ibid., pp. 92–93.
10. Haines, p. 27.
11. Lewis Henry Haney, *A Congressional History of Railways in the United States*, p. 44.

12. Henry S. Haines, *Problems in Railway Regulation*, p. 264.
13. In 1820 John Birkinsaw patented a process for joining rails in lengths up to eighteen feet to improve the ride and reduce maintenance costs. He also proposed "longer rails by welding them together." Baxter, p. 53.
14. Haney, p. 15.
15. Baxter, p. 28.
16. Haney, p. 27.

2 || A PRODUCT OF NECESSITY

During the 1830's a tremendous change took place within the railroad industry. Much like the caterpillar changing into a butterfly, the scattered tramroads of an earlier decade quickly evolved into an industry of national prominence. Steam replaced horse power; rails of iron replaced stone and wood. Railroads left behind their old competitors, canals and turnpikes, to take on a new role in transportation.

It was at this point that the development of American railroads ceased to parallel that of their British counterparts. In Britain, railways competed with and complemented existing canals and highways. In the United States they "provided means of communication where there were none before save Indian trails."[1] When Parliament considered a proposed railway charter, existing competitors forced close examination of its benefits. The only force acting on the American legislators was the people's cry for more transportation improvements—meaning railroads. As concluded by Haines, "Practically the only preliminary restriction in the early charters was in the provision for expropriating private property for railroad purposes."[2]

CONGRESS AND THE RAILROADS

Aside from granting charters, Congress was little involved in early railway development. This was due in part to the philosophy that internal improvements were a jurisdiction of the states, but it was also due to the fact that the federal government was involved in few things at all. America's early railroads were local affairs, with residents furnishing capital directly or through local governments. Both business judgment and civic pride were factors, sometimes with more of the latter than the former. State governments granted charters and, occasionally, provided financial aid to local railroads. The philosophies of laissez faire democracy and states' rights were justification for the lack of federal involvement, though not for long.

The framers of the Constitution recognized commerce as the tangible bond uniting the states. Commerce grew with the nation, as did demands for transportation projects of a national scope. By the time Congress began seriously to consider such projects, canals and turnpikes had been joined by railroads as viable transportation projects.

The American public and its Congress tended to view highways and railroads as mutual substitutes during the early nineteenth century. Steam power had been applied to railways, canals, and highways with varying degrees of success. Because of the problems with vehicle weight, highway applications such as steam tractors met with little success. In England smooth-wheeled steam locomotives were used with some success on plateways, but even in those applications the railroads were later converted to edge-rails or else faded from existence.[3]

A strong effort was made in 1836 to substitute a railway for the proposed Cumberland (or National) Road. It was argued that "the progress of steam transportation had been so great since 1820 that common roads had become only of local importance."[4] But the Cumberland Road was built as a road. The amendment to change it to a railway "did not fail because a railway was believed to be inferior to the macadamized road. Indeed we are warranted in concluding that by this time the railway had practically superseded the road as a national improvement."[5]

As indicated by the defeat of the Cumberland Road amendment, there were a number of people who opposed the early railways. Foremost in this opposition were the owners of canals and turnpikes. Unlike England, where canal owners promoted railway-canal integration, American canal companies generally saw the railways only as competitors.

Many people—including not a small group of federal legislators—philosophically opposed railways on the grounds that railways were undemocratic. Proponents of the Cumberland Road wanted common roads for the "plain, honest men" they represented. "No toll, no monopoly, nothing exclusive,—a real 'people's road!' "[6] During this era of Jacksonian democracy, railroads were regarded with suspicion as moneyed powers along with banks and any big business enterprise.

> Like banking, the railway business required considerable capital, a corporate form, and, more particularly, it required restrictions and limitations upon the manner in which it could be set up and used. It was a monopoly in the sense that canals and turnpikes were not.[7]

The railway was relatively new to the United States, whereas canals and turnpikes had long been familiar to Americans. An important factor was that anyone could operate his own vehicle on turnpikes or canals, but could not do so on railways. Permanence was an advantage of canals. The comparative ease with which a railroad could be built was, to some, a disadvantage.

It was urged that canals were superior "as a public work" and that railways were undemocratic. At the same time, it was clearly seen that railways were liable to cutthroat competition, and that a "parallel line" might involve the original and itself in common ruin. The fear was expressed that railways might be built too fast, and that, being abandoned, they would decay. Canals would be more permanent.[8]

During the railway industry's infancy, common roads were often little more than enlarged footpaths. Turnpikes were of a better design, some using gravelled surfaces. The cost of building and maintaining a turnpike—even one of improved design—was less than that of a railroad, particularly in hilly country. The reason lay in the railroad's need for gentle grades and greater exactitude in laying and maintaining the track.

By its nature a railway was less flexible in operation than was a turnpike or road. Even when equipped with turnouts and side tracks, railway wagons had to stop and let those going the opposite direction pass. Double track lines solved this problem, but their cost was too great except on lines with heavy traffic. With double track, all wagons going in the same direction were still restricted to the same speed.

Well-graded railways allowed each horse to pull far more freight than it could on a turnpike, but this was of little benefit to the individual wagon or carriage driver for whom the cheaper turnpike would serve just as well. For the large shipper, a railway was of advantage only if the shipments moved between points on or close to the railway. Railway efficiency mattered little if teams and drivers had to be supplied to make final delivery over highways, particularly where the railway distance was relatively short.

Even at this early age, railway economies of scale in operations favored high volume shippers. For the individual wagoner the inflexibilities of operation often outweighed the efficiency advantages of the railway. Turnpikes and common roads were more suited to use by individuals.

THE RAILWAY'S MONOPOLY

During the 1830's and 1840's the steam locomotive rapidly achieved supremacy as a means of motive power on American railroads. Horsecar lines continued to serve some places, particularly in cities as predecessors of the electric trolley, but their use was limited. "Railroad" had become synonymous with iron rails and steam locomotives.

The steam locomotive brought major changes in railway operation. "Well down to 1830 it was commonly thought that anyone might put his vehicle upon the railway company's track or 'way' and travel in much the same manner as upon an ordinary road."[9] But such an operation was predicated upon the use of horse power.

When the railway began to be used for the transportation of goods and passengers, the vehicles were still drawn by horses. It was therefore looked upon as a highway, like a turnpike road, though different somewhat in construction. Efforts were made to utilize it in the same way by collecting tolls from all comers who would adapt the wheels of their vehicles to the rails. But the substitution of the locomotive for the draught horse compelled the assembling of the vehicles in trains and brought the control of their movements directly under the railway management.[10]

The introduction of locomotives made it necessary that the motive power should be placed exclusively under the management of the railway company, although private wagons are still hauled in the company's trains, loaded with minerals, which are the property of the owners of the wagons. The general carriage of persons and goods was, however, conducted directly by the railway company.[11]

. . . With this concentration of the maintenance of the roadway and the control of the train service under one management, the mission of the railway began as an entirely new method of land transportation.[12]

The rapid technological advances of the 1820–1840 era forced a dramatic change in the railroad industry. Iron edge-rails proved superior to plateways: edge-rails were not prone to problems of dirt or snow accumulation, and iron edge-rails could carry a much heavier load while reducing friction between wheels and rails. This complemented the steam locomotive, which could pull longer and heavier trains than could horse teams.

Steam locomotives and iron rails encouraged bigger trains and a larger scale of operation. In the absence of rapid communication—the telegraph was not introduced until about 1852—train operations were governed by written schedules which demanded strict observance. These factors led railroad companies to operate their own trains, providing both the fixed way and carrier service. Train operations were soon restricted to only the railroad company's trains, excluding all others. Because communications technology had not progressed enough to allow a flexible traffic-control system, joint use was sacrificed to obtain greater efficiency. The railroad company became the sole provider of train service.

The changes of the 1820–1840 period resulted in a new railroad industry structure. Instead of the earlier style of tramroad operation—open to all, minimally controlled, local, small in scale, competing with turnpikes for wagon traffic—a new railroad emerged. It became a major artery of national commerce.

It was accepted practice in 1840 for a railroad company to conduct all operations over its line and exclude others from using it. Company employees ran company trains over company tracks under company direction. Privately owned cars were handled in the railroad's trains, but at the railroad company's discretion and rates.

The new industry structure was indeed a monopoly: not one created by some sinister plot, but rather one which grew from the efficiencies inherent in railroad technology at that time. The monopoly was the result of "the exclusive right to use the railway which the company owning it possessed."[13] It is important to note that this monopoly applied to the use of the railroad and not to any specific region or city.

During the latter part of the nineteenth century "monopoly" was used in a different context, referring to cities and areas served by only one railroad. When a competing railroad was built, the first railroad's monopoly over the city was broken. Although the city received competitive service from the two railroads, each railroad still had exclusive use—a monopoly—of its own tracks. The city was given competitive rail service by having two monopolies compete for its business. Those localities served by a single railroad were monopolized, because (1) they were served by only the one railroad *and* (2) that railroad did not allow any other person or company to operate trains over its tracks. It is the latter fact which differentiated the pre-1820 tramroad from the new railroad of the 1840's. Although railroad company charters continued to refer to turnpike-type operations, "this possibility was but a legal theory" and had no effect on the new railroad industry.[14]

By 1840 America had some 2800 miles of railroad compared to 23 miles a decade earlier.[15] The railroad had taken on a new form, a new structure. Advances in railway technology and the consequent changes in railway operation met with general approval. The industrial revolution was getting up steam, both literally and figuratively. The railroads were often hard pressed to keep up with the demands placed on them. Railway technology was soon so far in advance of any other means of transport that driving a horse-drawn wagon on a railroad track was only a laughable—and highly dangerous—prank.

The railroads were at the threshold of their "Golden Age," armed with a new structure, one which would serve the industry for over 130 years. By 1970, however, many were questioning the viability of that structure.

NOTES

1. Henry S. Haines, *Railway Corporations as Public Servants*, p. 17.
2. Henry S. Haines, *Problems in Railway Regulation*, p. 266.
3. Bertram Baxter, *Stone Blocks and Iron Rails*, p. 33.
4. Lewis Henry Haney, *A Congressional History of Railways in the United States*, p. 69.
5. Ibid., p. 74.
6. Congressional Debates, 1835–1836 (H. of R.), p. 4495, quoted in Haney, p. 81.
7. Haney, p. 81.

8. Ibid., p. 60. It is interesting to note that this fear of railroad overbuilding was expressed at a time when many parts of the country had no railroads and long before the 1880–1890 period of railroad overbuilding.

9. Haney, p. 82.

10. Haines, *Problems*, p. 8.

11. Haines, *Railway Corporations*, p. 26.

12. Haines, *Problems*, p. 8.

13. Haney, p. 77.

14. Ibid., p. 82.

15. U.S., Bureau of the Census, *Historical Statistics of the United States*, Series Q321, p. 731.

3 DEGREES OF STANDARDIZATION

During the latter half of the nineteenth century the railroads matured as an industry of national stature. Numbering in the thousands, railroad companies pushed back frontiers in all parts of the nation. In doing so they were forced to rely largely on their own separate ingenuity and resources in solving various technological, operational, and organizational problems. This self-reliance resulted in a great multiplicity of designs and procedures. With the criss-crossing of the continent, the individual lines found themselves becoming more and more interdependent. Conflicting standards and policies resulted in service deficiencies and higher costs. Within a thirty-year span the railroad industry resolved the major differences and established procedures for addressing future problems. This was quite possibly the greatest exercise in industrial statesmanship and self-discipline the nation has ever witnessed, resulting from the demands of the railroads themselves and not from outside authorities.

INDIVIDUALISM A NECESSITY

The extent of standardization in the United States today is taken for granted—a fact of modern life. New Jersey light bulbs fit California sockets. A motorist can drive almost anywhere and find parts for his automobile. Railroad cars and locomotives routinely cross the country in interrailroad service.

Such was not the case during the mid-1800's. The lack of transportation and communication facilities eliminated the need for national standards. Each community had its own time, setting noon at the time the sun was directly overhead. The concept of interchangeable parts was still a new idea with only limited application.

Both freight and passengers changed cars when changing from one railroad to another. Each crew on a railroad had its own locomotive and caboose, and the equipment stayed on its assigned run except when going to the division shop for repairs. It was rare for one railroad's locomotive to operate over another railroad's track.

In such an environment there was no need for interchangeable equipment. The assortment of track gauges used, varying from two feet to five feet, prevented interchange in many cases. With the passing of time, through freight and passenger routes began to appear. Cars and even entire trains were purchased jointly by several railroads and operated over a through route utilizing segments of each railroad. The development of through routes led to more general interchange agreements between railroads, which in turn led to standardization in other areas.

STANDARDIZATION EFFORTS

Standard Time

The first and most obvious object of nationwide standardization was time.[1] Variances in local time were of little importance until the railroads and telegraph systems significantly reduced the time required for travel and communications. The use of local times played havoc with schedules. It was not uncommon for a depot to have several clocks, each set at a slightly different time: one for the city's local time, and one for each of the railroads' times.

A special convention of railroad representatives met in St. Louis in 1872 to discuss the chaotic time situation. It was recommended that four time zones be adopted to cover the nation, and the resolution was approved the next year. This momentous decision prompted the Congress to authorize the President to hold an international convention and extend the system of time zones as a worldwide standard. The international convention met and adopted the time zone concept in 1884.

Standard Rules

The results of the General Time Convention in dealing with the time problem led to its retention as a continuing forum for resolving railroad problems. In addition to its efforts at coordinating train schedules and connections of various railroads, the Convention's attention was directed at "the development and solution of problems connected with railroad management in the mutual interests of the railroad companies of America."[2] The first area subject to study was that of train operating rules.

The *Standard Code of Train Rules*, adopted in 1886, was as great a step forward in its own area as was standard time.[3] Most railroads had rule codes at that time, but the *Standard Code* was created from the best of those codes. Having the approval of the newly formed American Railway Association, the *Code* was recognized as the best of modern practice by the courts in damage cases. Many of the rules were quite simple, but significantly reduced accidents. One example was the rule requiring trainmen to use only accurate, approved watches for timekeeping. Another was the double train order, issued in the same exact words to all trains meeting at a common point. The *Standard Code* incorporated many safeguards and substantially improved the safety of railroad operations.

Standard Gauge

American railroads varied in gauge (width between rails). A few lines had gauges outside the normal two- to five-foot range, but most fell within this range. Narrow gauge railroads were promoted for their lower cost, particularly in mountainous regions. Wide gauges offered stability and increased carrying capacity. Over time many railroads in the North and Midwest adopted the British standard of 4 feet 8½ inches. Southern lines moved toward a 5-foot standard, while a growing network in the Rocky Mountains and Southwest were using 3 feet. In 1886 the nation's railroads agreed in convention to adopt the 4-foot 8½-inch gauge. During that year over 13,000 miles of track in the South were converted to the new standard gauge. A number of the 3-foot lines also converted, but a few did not and retained the narrow gauge until they were abandoned years later—bypassed as through routes.

Janney Couplers

With the adoption of standard gauge the practice of interchanging cars between railroads flourished, and demands arose for standardizing certain safety appliances on railroad cars. Hand brakes, roofwalks, and handholds (grab irons) on the sides of cars were among the items subjected to standard dimensions. One of the most important advances was the acceptance of Janney (knuckle-type) couplers as standard.[4]

Prior to 1875 the most commonly used coupler was the link-and-pin. The link-and-pin had derived from the chains first used to hold wagons together. The link-and-pin, however, used only one link to minimize the slack action (buffeting) between cars. The link was held to each car by a metal pin. Brakemen were required to go between the cars and hold the link while the cars were pushed together. Once the two cars were close enough together, the brakeman dropped pins through holes in each car's drawbar, fastening the link in place. Many brakemen lost fingers and hands; many were crushed between cars when drawbars were misaligned.

The Master Car Builders Association (MCBA) in 1874 recognized the need for an automatic coupler, one which coupled itself without having brakemen move between cars. Several designs for such a coupler existed, but none had been adequately tested in service. The search for a suitable coupler continued until 1887, when the MCBA recommended the Janney type of knuckle coupler. Two years later the Janney design became the MCBA standard coupler.[5] The knuckle coupler closed on impact with another coupler and remained closed until opened by movement of a handle located at the side of the car.

Air Brakes

A factor in the adoption of Janney couplers was the move toward application of air brakes for general service freight cars. Although still in the experimental stage during the 1870's and 1880's, it was apparent that some form of power braking would be used in the future. Link-and-pin couplers could not withstand the forces generated by such braking. After much testing the Westinghouse air brake was proven reliable, and many railroads began to apply it to passenger trains. It was subsequently applied to freight cars and adopted as standard equipment by the railroads. In 1893, the young Interstate Commerce Commission required by law the use of air brakes and automatic couplers on all trains engaged in interstate service. As with other standards of this period, federal and state regulation followed the lead of national railroad organizations, serving primarily as an incentive for laggard companies to move up to standards set by the better-run railroads.

STANDARD, YET INDIVIDUAL

It might appear that railroads in the United States were highly standardized by 1890. In certain respects they were, but much individualism remained from earlier years. Signal systems varied widely. Locomotives were designed and often built in the railroad's own shops. Each railroad set its own standards for right of way clearances, stations, bridges, tunnels, and grades. Operations conformed to the basic Standard Rules, but railroads added individual rules to suit their own needs. Many substantial differences remained between railroad companies. The railroads had recognized themselves as an industry, however, and had made important steps toward creating a truly national network of rail lines.

NOTES

1. Van H. English, Dartmouth College, *The Encyclopedia Americana*, International Edition, Volume 26 (New York, 1971), pp. 758–759.
2. Rules of Order, American Railway Association, quoted in Henry S. Haines, *American Railway Management*, p. 75.
3. Haines, *American Railway Management*, pp. 62–75.
4. Ibid., pp. 38–61.
5. A detailed account of the adoption procedure and other problems is presented in Haines, *American Railway Management*, pp. 38–61.

4 | CHANGING TIMES, CHANGING NEEDS

During the nineteenth century the railroads adopted a structure which successfully met the competition of horse-drawn wagons and steamboats. In the face of modern competition it has not proven so successful. Passenger traffic which once moved largely by rail has been taken by the automobile, bus, and airplane. More importantly trucks, pipelines, and water carriers have inflicted severe losses on the railroads in the battle for freight traffic.

A simple indication of the shift away from the railroads is found in a comparison of rail and highway mileages (Figure 1). Throughout the last half of the 1800's the railroads dominated the national transportation scene. At the turn of the century, the automobile, truck, and surfaced highway were just coming into their own as a transport mode, but the change was rapid. By 1914 surfaced highway mileage surpassed railroad mileage: 257,000 highway miles versus 252,105 railroad miles. Railroad mileage peaked in 1916 at 254,251 miles and a steady decline followed. In contrast, highway mileage grew throughout the following years.

At first highways attracted only local traffic. With the automobile it was no longer necessary to have railroad stations located every ten miles along the line as it was with horses and wagons. Many branch lines which crossed and paralleled the main rail routes were made obsolete. Passengers and small shipments formerly handled by branch line trains moved more efficiently by automobile and truck.

The creation of state and federal highway networks extended the range and capacity of automobiles and trucks. Larger trucks and truck-trailer combinations competed successfully for less-than-carload (LCL) rail traffic and began taking carload rail shipments. Pipelines and water carriers provided cost-based competition for low-rated bulk shipments. In far too many cases, the attitudes of the previous monopolistic era prevented the railroads from meeting their new competition head-on with aggressive strategies in pricing, service, and marketing. Instead, they reacted defensively and sought the extension of railroad regulatory practices to the newer modes. Only in the

Figure 1. Railroad and Highway Mileage, 1875 to 1975

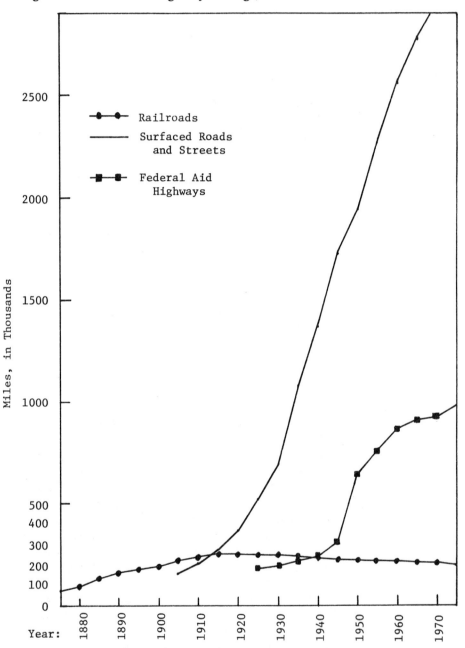

Source: Table 1.

postwar era did most railroads begin to utilize offensive strategies, and even then defensive attitudes remained commonplace.

SHIFTS IN VOLUME AND REVENUE

To analyze the aforementioned traffic changes, several statistics must be considered. The basic unit of transportation volume is the *ton-mile*: the movement of one ton over a distance of one mile. *Tonnage* carried represents volume without the distance factor *(average length of haul)*. *Revenue*, the payment for transportation services, is measured in dollars. In addition to these absolute figures, *market share analysis* compares the relative performance of one mode to the others in terms of each measure. Market share is expressed as a percentage of all modes' total.

Ton-Mile Volume

The total ton-miles produced by all modes expanded continually due to the United States' economic growth. Highway, water, pipeline, and air carriers all shared in the increases (Figure 2). Although the railroads carried enormous freight volumes during World War II, rail ton-miles declined afterward and continued to decline into the late 1950's. By that time the rising economy and improvements in rail service reversed the railroads' downward ton-mile trend. Nonetheless, rail ton-miles did not surpass World War II levels until 1973.

During the thirty years between 1947 and 1977 the total ton-miles of all modes more than doubled. To maintain a stable share of this ton-mile volume, a mode's ton-miles should have grown in equal proportion to total ton-miles. Waterway ton-miles increased by a factor of 2.5 while waterway ton-mile share remained nearly constant, hovering between 15 percent and 16 percent (Figure 3). The two winners in the volume share competition were the trucks and pipelines: each mode doubled its share in an expanding total market. Pipeline share grew steadily; truck share doubled by 1960 and remained stable thereafter. Air freight, despite its phenomenal growth, amounted to less than 1 percent of all ton miles in 1977.

In contrast with the other modes, the railroad share of ton-miles eroded steadily over the past three decades. Prior to World War II the railroads produced over 60 percent of all domestic ton-miles. By 1955 their share declined to 50 percent, and in 1974 it fell below 40 percent. A sizeable portion of the other modes' growth was evidently at the expense of the railroads. Even though rail ton-miles grew during the 1960's—a point often made by railroad executives—the fact remains that rail ton-miles declined as a percentage of the total in a period when all other modes were increasing or maintaining their volume shares. Railroads failed to participate as fully as the other modes in the overall growth of freight traffic.

Figure 2. Freight Volume, in Ton-Miles, by Mode

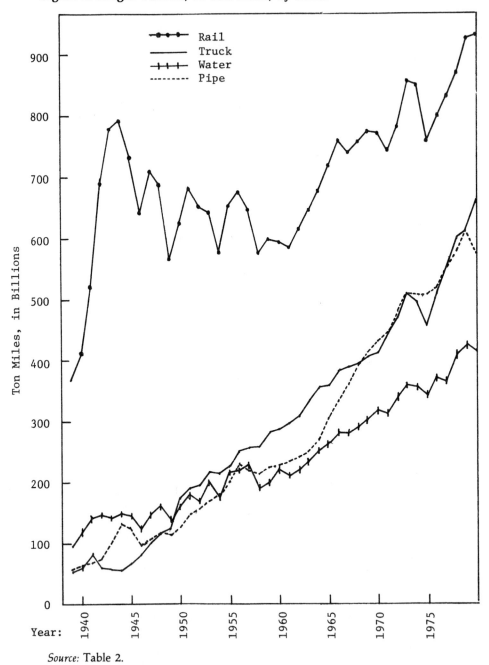

Figure 3. Freight Volume Share, Percentage of Ton-Miles, by Mode

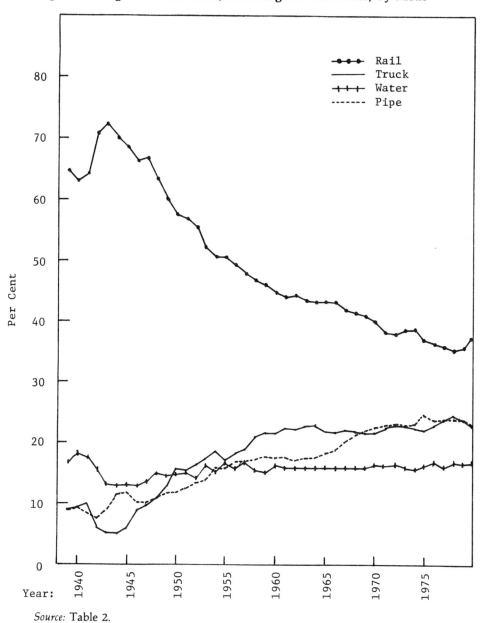

Tonnage Volume

Ton-mile data provide a valuable aggregate measure of traffic volume, but equally important are the component parts: tonnage and average haul (mileage). Tonnage statistics eliminate the effects of varying haul distances incorporated in the ton-mile data.

The total tonnage moved by all modes increased by 193 percent between 1947 and 1977 (Figure 4). The growth was felt by all modes except the railroads. Rail tonnage fluctuated in the 1.25 to 1.60 billion ton range but remained generally stable throughout the period. Waterway tonnage increased slowly until the late 1960's and remained level after that time. Pipeline tonnage grew at a more rapid pace during the same period. The greatest rise, however, was in truck tonnage. In 1961 truck tonnage surpassed rail tonnage, and the gap has widened in the following years.

With total tonnage of all modes nearly doubling and rail tonnage remaining almost level, rail share dropped from roughly 60 percent to 28 percent (Figure 5). Truck tonnage share rose from 16 percent in 1947 to 40 percent in 1964 and plateaued at that point. Pipeline tonnage share more than doubled. Waterway share held steady, with tonnage keeping pace with overall economic growth.

Comparing rail ton-miles, tonnage, and average haul it becomes apparent that the recent growth in rail ton-miles is due almost entirely to an increasing length of haul. Although definitive average haul data are difficult to obtain for the other modes because of different reporting methods, it is evident that their average hauls have held stable or increased by varying degrees. Coupled with increasing tonnage, trucks and pipelines have substantially improved their market positions, and water carriers have held their position in a growing market. The railroads, on the other hand, have relied on longer and longer hauls and roughly stable tonnage volumes to increase their ton-miles. Reliance on progressively longer hauls means the railroads have had to retreat into an ever-smaller segment of the transportation market, leaving the sizeable short- and medium-distance markets almost entirely to the trucks. Through the emphasis on longer hauls, larger minimum shipment sizes, and low-rated bulk traffic instead of high-value, service-oriented commodities, the railroads have largely abdicated those transportation market segments with the greatest growth and profit potential.

Revenue

As might be expected during the postwar inflationary era, the revenues of all five modes increased (Figure 6). Railroads experienced revenue growth during most of the 1939–1977 period despite their declining ton-mile traffic volume. Inflation also affected costs, so profits did not rise with greater

Figure 4. Freight Volume, in Tons, by Mode

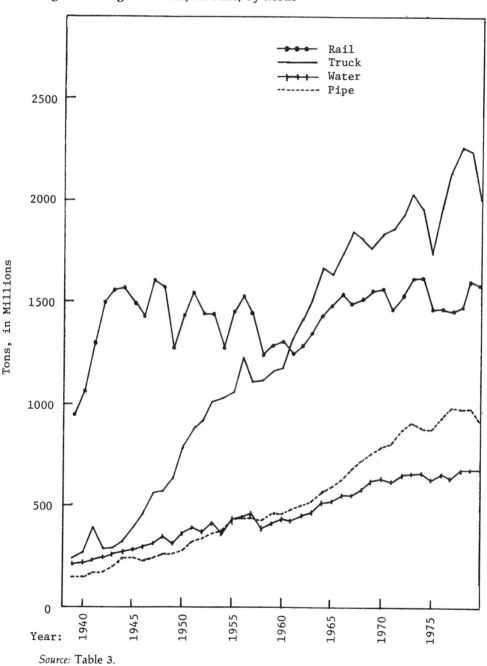

Source: Table 3.

Figure 5. Freight Volume Share, Percentage of Tons, by Mode

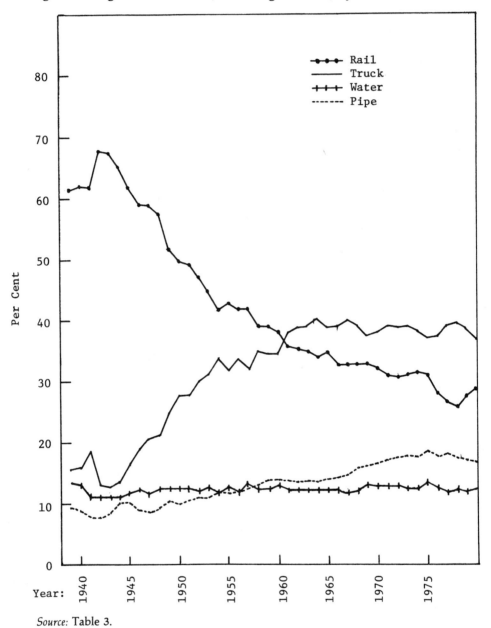

Source: Table 3.

Figure 6. Freight Operating Revenues, by Mode

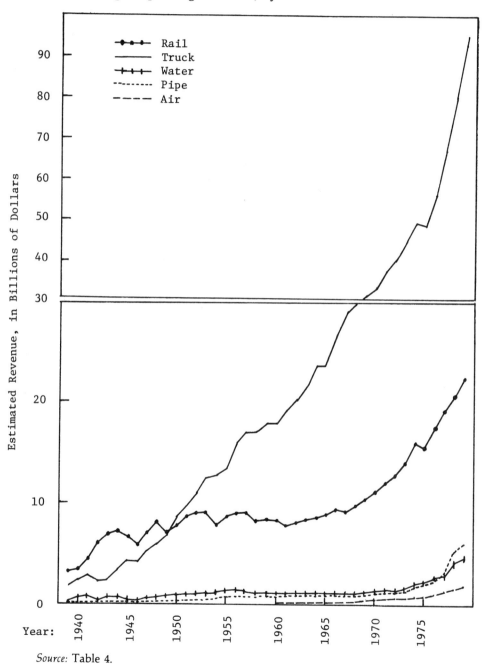

Source: Table 4.

27

ᵣₑᵥₑₙₗes. More significantly, higher rates reduced the railroads' ability to compete and drove substantial amounts of traffic to other modes.

Truck revenues grew dramatically and consistently from $2.3 billion in 1940 to $67.4 billion in 1977. In 1949, truck revenues exceeded rail revenues for the first time. Truck revenues continued their rapid growth, further outpacing rail revenues in the years that followed. Water carrier and pipe-line revenues increased by a factor of ten between 1939 and 1977. Air freight revenues grew from $21.0 million in 1939 to almost $1.5 billion in 1977 (see Table 4).

In terms of revenue share, the pipelines held their position while the water carriers' share declined slightly (Figure 7). Air cargo increased its share of transportation revenues. Highway carriers made large gains in revenue share, rising from 31 percent in 1939 to 71 percent in 1977. During the same period railroads lost over half of their 1939 revenue share, dropping from 58 percent to 22 percent.

Industry statistics such as volume and revenue figures are the net result of numerous changes in specific rates and types of traffic; consequently, only general conclusions can be drawn from such figures. Some facts are notice-able. The railroads lost traffic volume during 1945–1960 and did not exceed World War II ton-mile levels until 1973. During the same period the total volume for all modes rose steadily with only temporary interruptions. The railroad share of total volume decreased, with increases experienced by the trucks and pipelines. Railroad revenues increased in dollar terms, due in part to rising inflation, but rail revenue share dropped substantially. Losses in tonnage share, ton-mile share, and revenue share reveal the serious problems affecting the railroad industry.

ENERGY CRISIS

Given the railroads' fuel efficiency, it is generally expected that rising oil prices will encourage diversion of traffic from truck to rail and reverse the long-term trend. The question, however, is whether the fuel advantage can be translated into an economic advantage.

Properly operated, railroads are significantly more energy-efficient than trucks in intercity operations. So far, however, this theoretical advantage has not paid off for the railroads. In fact, since the energy situation became of concern in 1973, railroads have lost, not gained, market share. And truckers have made important engineering advances increasing the energy-effectiveness of their vehicles—entirely apart from their success in winning the right to operate even larger and heavier vehicles.[1]

It is unclear whether further increases in energy prices and possible energy shortages would improve the railroads' position in intermodal competition. In a report entitled *The Railroad Situation: A Perspective on the Present,*

Figure 7. Freight Operating Revenue Share, by Mode

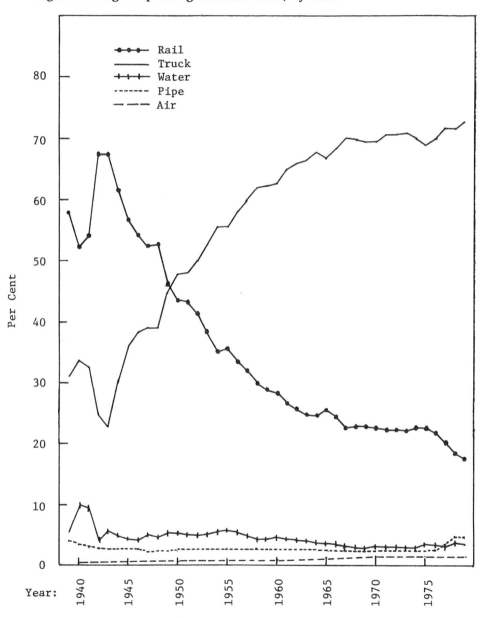

Source: Table 4.

Past and Future of the Railroad Industry, the Department of Transportation (DOT) examined this subject in detail.[2] The report noted that the Federal Energy Administration predicted little change in rail market share, with most shifts from truck to rail offset by shifts from rail to barge.[3]

Of all the options considered, the truck-rail freight shift produced the least results. It actually produced smaller results than having short auto trips replaced by walking or bicycling! Consequently, it is unlikely that the Federal government will take deliberate actions to force a shift in freight transport from truck to rail.[4]

Many difficulties face the railroads in their efforts to wring economic advantage from the energy crisis. Significant advances are possible in truck fuel efficiency, but only minor gains are expected in locomotive fuel efficiency.[5] To save fuel some railroads have reduced train service frequency, run longer trains, lengthened schedules, and loaded locomotives to maximum tonnage ratings. These practices usually have a negative effect on service and result in the diversion of service-sensitive traffic *from* rail *to* truck.

Cost trends have favored truck over rail during the past several years.[6] Railroad costs for labor, fuel, and fixed ways have grown faster than truck costs in the same categories. Capital costs have increased less for railroads than for trucking, but trucks have made greater gains in productivity. The DOT report concludes that total rail costs have been increasing faster than total truck costs. "The net result has been that rail freight rates have risen faster than those for truck in recent years, which has encouraged the diversion of traffic from rail to truck."[7]

In short, railroads cannot count on the energy crisis as a solution to the long-term loss of market share.

SUMMARY

Railroad industry statistics reveal several trends. Most evident is the decline of the railroads relative to the other modes of transportation. The railroads' market share, whether in volume or revenue, was halved over the past three decades. Railroad ton-miles only recently surpassed their 1944 level despite a two-fold increase in total ton-miles produced by all modes over the same period. Rail revenues were buoyed by inflation; yet over twenty years ago truck revenues exceeded rail revenues.

The railroads are doing what they do better and more efficiently, but the traffic shifts show that fewer and fewer customers want that service no matter how efficiently it is produced. The other modes have done better at offering what the shippers want, as evidenced by their gain in shares of ton-miles, tonnage, and revenue.

NOTES

1. Tom Shedd, "The Savior?" *Modern Railroads*, Volume 32, Number 7 (July 1977), p. 55. See also Tom Shedd, "Energy: What Role for the Rails?" *Modern Railroads*, Volume 34, Number 11 (November 1979), pp. 37–42.
2. U.S., Department of Transportation, *The Railroad Situation*, pp. 420–437.
3. Ibid., p. 421.
4. Ibid., p. 423.
5. Ibid., p. 428.
6. Ibid., pp. 425–427.
7. Ibid., p. 427. See also Robert Roberts, "Insight: Mr. Lang Sees Trucker Gains," *Modern Railroads*, Volume 36, Number 4 (April 1981), p. 25.

TABLES 1–4

Table 1 Railroad and Highway Mileage, 1875 to 1975

Year	Rail[1]	Highway Existing Surfaced[2]	Highway Federal Aid System[3]
1975	199,000	n.a.	985,000
1970	205,782	2,946,000	919,000
1965	211,384	2,776,000	908,722
1960	217,552	2,557,000	866,841
1955	220,670	2,273,000	749,166
1950	223,779	1,939,000	643,949
1945	226,696	1,721,000	308,741
1940	233,670	1,367,000	235,482
1935	241,822	1,080,000	219,869
1930	249,052	694,000	193,652
1925	249,398	521,000	179,501
1920	252,845	369,000	—
1915	253,789	276,000	—
1910	240,293	204,000	—
1905	218,101	161,000	—
1900	193,346	—	—
1895	180,657	—	—
1890	163,597	—	—
1885	127,689	—	—
1880	92,147	—	—
1875	74,096	—	—

SOURCES: U.S., Bureau of the Census, *Historical Statistics of the United States, Colonial Times to 1970*; U.S., Bureau of the Census, *Statistical Abstract of the United States*, annual editions.

[1] Railroad mileage, road owned: 1875–1890 data, *Historical Statistics*, Series Q322, p. 731; 1890–1970 data, *Historical Statistics*, Series Q287, pp. 727–728; 1975 data, *Statistical Abstract 1978*, Table 1114, p. 660.

[2] Mileage of rural roads and municipal streets, existing surfaced mileage, total, 1905–1970, *Historical Statistics*, Series Q56, p. 710.

[3] Miles of highway, total designated as part of Federal systems, 1925–1965, *Historical Statistics*, Series Q64, p. 711; 1970–1975 data, *Statistical Abstract 1978*, Table 1077, p. 643.

Table 2 Freight Volume in Ton-Miles, Domestic Intercity Traffic, by Mode, 1939 to 1980 (in billions, except percentages)

Year	Rail[1] Vol.	%	Truck Vol.	%	Water[2] Vol.	%	Pipe[3] Vol.	%	Air[4] Vol.	%	Total
1980	932	37.6	560	22.6	411	16.6	572	23.1	4.3	0.2	2,479
1979	927	36.0	608	23.6	425	16.5	608	23.6	4.4	0.2	2,572
1978	868	35.2	599	24.3	409	16.6	586	23.8	4.6	0.2	2,467
1977	834	36.2	555	24.1	368	16.0	546	23.7	4.2	0.2	2,307
1976	800	36.3	510	23.2	373	16.9	515	23.4	3.9	0.2	2,202
1975	759	36.7	454	22.0	342	16.6	507	24.5	3.7	0.2	2,066
1974	852	38.5	495	22.4	355	16.0	506	22.9	3.9	0.2	2,212
1973	858	38.4	505	22.6	358	16.0	507	22.7	3.9	0.2	2,232
1972	783	37.8	470	22.8	339	16.4	476	23.0	3.7	0.2	2,072
1971	746	38.2	445	22.3	315	16.1	444	22.7	3.5	0.2	1,954
1970	771	39.8	412	21.3	319	16.5	431	22.3	3.3	0.2	1,936
1969	774	40.8	404	21.3	303	16.0	411	21.7	3.2	0.2	1,895
1968	757	41.2	396	21.5	291	15.8	391	21.3	2.9	0.2	1,838
1967	742	41.8	389	21.9	281	15.8	361	20.3	2.6	0.1	1,776
1966	762	43.3	381	21.7	281	16.0	333	18.9	2.3	0.1	1,759
1965	721	43.7	359	21.8	262	15.9	306	18.5	1.9	0.1	1,650
1964	679	43.6	356	22.9	250	16.1	269	17.3	1.5	0.1	1,556
1963	644	43.9	336	22.9	234	15.9	253	17.2	1.3	0.1	1,468
1962	616	44.4	309	22.3	223	16.1	238	17.2	1.3	0.1	1,387
1961	586	44.2	296	22.3	210	15.8	233	17.6	0.9	0.1	1,326
1960	595	44.7	285	21.4	220	16.5	229	17.2	0.8	0.1	1,330
1959	599	46.0	279	21.4	197	15.1	227	17.4	0.7	0.1	1,303
1958	575	46.7	256	20.8	189	15.3	211	17.1	0.6	—	1,232

Year											
1957	645	47.6	254	18.8	232	17.1	223	16.5	0.6	—	1,355
1956	677	49.2	249	18.1	220	16.0	230	16.7	0.6	—	1,377
1955	655	50.4	223	17.2	217	16.7	203	15.6	0.6	—	1,299
1954	578	50.5	213	18.6	174	15.2	179	15.7	0.4	—	1,144
1953	643	52.2	217	17.6	202	16.4	170	13.8	0.4	—	1,232
1952	651	55.6	195	16.6	168	14.3	158	13.5	0.4	—	1,172
1951	686	56.8	188	15.6	182	15.1	152	12.6	0.4	—	1,208
1950	628	57.5	173	15.8	163	14.9	129	11.8	0.3	—	1,093
1949	567	59.9	125	13.2	139	14.7	115	12.2	0.2	—	946
1948	689	63.4	115	10.6	162	14.9	120	11.0	0.2	—	1,086
1947	707	66.6	102	9.6	147	13.9	105	9.9	0.2	—	1,060
1946	643	68.0	82	8.7	124	13.1	96	10.2	0.1	—	945
1945	736	68.6	67	6.2	143	13.3	127	11.8	0.1	—	1,073
1944	795	70.0	58	5.1	150	13.2	133	11.7	0.1	—	1,136
1943	780	72.4	57	5.3	142	13.2	98	9.1	0.1	—	1,077
1942	689	70.8	60	6.2	149	15.3	75	7.7	—	—	973
1941	521	64.3	81	10.0	140	17.3	68	8.4	—	—	810
1940	412	63.3	62	9.5	118	18.1	59	9.1	—	—	651
1939	370	64.3	53	9.2	96	16.7	56	9.7	—	—	575

SOURCES: 1939–1970 data: U.S., Bureau of the Census, *Historical Statistics of the United States, Colonial Times to 1970*, Series Q12–22, p. 707; 1971–1975 data: Transportation Association of America, *Transportation Facts and Trends*, 15th ed. (Washington, D.C., 1979), p. 8; 1976 1980 data: Transportation Association of America, unpublished data.

NOTE: Truck and air, prior to 1959, and other types of transportation, prior to 1960, exclude Alaska and Hawaii, except as noted below. A *ton-mile* is the movement of one ton of freight for the distance of one mile. Comprises public and private traffic, both revenue and nonrevenue. Percentages may not sum to 100 due to rounding.

[2]Railroads, including electric railways. Beginning 1970 excludes mail and express traffic.

[2]Inland waterways, including Great Lakes. Includes Alaska for all years and Hawaii beginning 1959. Part of increases in 1948, 1951, and 1953 are due to coverage of existing waterways not previously included.

[3]Oil pipelines.

[4]Airways, domestic revenue service only. Includes express, mail, and excess baggage.

35

Table 3 Freight Volume in Tons, Domestic Intercity Traffic, by Mode, 1939 to 1980 (in millions, except percentages)

Year	Rail[1] Vol.	%	Truck[2] Vol.	%	Water[3] Vol.	%	Pipe[4] Vol.	%	Air[5] Vol.	%	Total[6]
1980	1,589	30.6	2,007	38.6	679	13.1	919	17.7	4.0	0.1	5,198
1979	1,600	29.1	2,240	40.7	679	12.3	979	17.8	3.7	0.1	5,502
1978	1,481	27.4	2,260	41.8	678	12.5	982	18.2	3.9	0.1	5,405
1977	1,467	28.0	2,143	40.9	638	12.2	986	18.8	3.6	0.1	5,238
1976	1,477	29.3	1,974	39.1	656	13.0	934	18.5	3.4	0.1	5,044
1975	1,471	31.1	1,744	36.9	633	13.4	879	18.6	3.2	0.1	4,730
1974	1,619	31.6	1,955	38.2	657	12.8	885	17.3	3.5	0.1	5,120
1973	1,616	31.0	2,028	38.9	660	12.6	912	17.5	3.5	0.1	5,220
1972	1,531	30.6	1,934	38.7	652	13.1	876	17.5	3.3	0.1	4,996
1971	1,472	30.9	1,862	39.1	620	13.0	807	16.9	2.9	0.1	4,764
1970	1,572	32.6	1,828	37.9	629	13.0	790	16.4	2.9	0.1	4,822
1969	1,558	33.1	1,768	37.5	622	13.2	760	16.1	2.6	0.1	4,711
1968	1,515	32.7	1,811	39.1	581	12.5	726	15.7	2.4	0.1	4,635
1967	1,498	32.7	1,845	40.3	553	12.1	679	14.8	1.9	—	4,577
1966	1,543	34.5	1,744	39.0	554	12.4	630	14.1	1.7	—	4,473
1965	1,479	34.9	1,641	38.8	524	12.4	588	13.9	1.4	—	4,233
1964	1,420	34.1	1,670	40.2	509	12.2	559	13.4	1.2	—	4,159
1963	1,347	35.0	1,507	39.1	474	12.3	521	13.5	1.0	—	3,850
1962	1,294	35.3	1,421	38.7	452	12.3	502	13.7	0.9	—	3,670
1961	1,253	35.9	1,323	37.9	431	12.3	484	13.9	0.8	—	3,492
1960	1,301	38.3	1,181	34.8	446	13.1	468	13.8	0.6	—	3,397
1959	1,293	38.9	1,156	34.8	413	12.4	464	14.0	0.6	—	3,327
1958	1,247	39.0	1,122	35.1	393	12.3	433	13.6	0.5	—	3,196
1957	1,449	41.8	1,113	32.1	463	13.4	441	12.7	0.5	—	3,467
1956	1,521	41.9	1,223	33.7	444	12.2	441	12.1	0.5	—	3,630

36

1955	1,459	43.3	1,063	31.5	435	12.9	413	12.3	0.5	—	3,371
1954	1,279	42.0	1,033	33.9	362	11.9	373	12.2	0.4	—	3,047
1953	1,448	44.9	1,007	31.2	414	12.8	359	11.1	0.4	—	3,228
1952	1,447	47.2	913	29.8	371	12.1	338	11.0	0.4	—	3,069
1951	1,547	49.4	871	27.8	391	12.5	325	10.4	0.3	—	3,134
1950	1,421	49.7	794	27.8	361	12.6	284	9.9	0.4	—	2,860
1949	1,284	51.6	630	25.3	312	12.6	261	10.5	0.3	—	2,487
1948	1,580	57.3	572	20.8	342	12.4	262	9.5	0.2	—	2,756
1947	1,613	59.3	556	20.4	313	11.5	238	8.8	0.2	—	2,720
1946	1,432	59.2	466	19.3	297	12.3	222	9.2	0.2	—	2,417
1945	1,493	61.9	394	16.3	285	11.8	241	10.0	0.2	—	2,413
1944	1,565	65.1	323	13.4	272	11.3	244	10.1	0.2	—	2,404
1943	1,557	67.5	292	12.7	260	11.3	196	8.5	0.1	—	2,305
1942	1,498	67.8	287	13.0	248	11.2	175	7.9	0.1	—	2,208
1941	1,296	62.0	389	18.6	236	11.3	171	8.2	0.1	—	2,092
1940	1,069	62.2	272	15.8	223	13.0	154	9.0	0.1	—	1,718
1939	955	61.4	241	15.5	211	13.6	148	9.5	0.1	—	1,555

SOURCES: 1939–1975 data (except author's estimates): Transportation Association of America, *Transportation Facts and Trends*, 15th ed. (Washington, D.C., 1979), p. 10; 1976–1980 data: Transportation Association of America, unpublished data.

NOTE: Percentages may not sum to 100 due to rounding.

[1] Classes 1 and 2 railroads.

[2] ICC regulated and non-regulated motor carriers.

[3] Rivers, canals, and Great Lakes; excludes domestic deep sea tonnage. Data for 1939–1946 were not available, so estimates were made by the author by projecting tonnage amounts backward in time from the 1947 1977 period. The projection equation used was $y = 690.37 - (12.291 \times$ time period) with 1977 = time period 1 through 1947 = time period 31. Tonnage and ton-mile data (Table 2) for waterways are not entirely compatible since ton-mile data include waterway portion of domestic deep sea movements and tonnage amounts do not (refer to *Transportation Facts and Trends*, page A-7).

[4] Oil pipelines.

[5] Tonnage for air carriers during 1939–1946 was not available, so estimates were made by the author by projecting tonnage amounts backward in time from the 1947–1977 period. The projection equation used was $y = 5.2262 \times (-0.10415) ** $ (time period), a negative exponential function with 1977 = time period 1 through 1947 = time period 31.

[6] Total for 1939–1946 period includes water and air tonnage estimates as defined above.

37

Table 4 Estimated Freight Revenue, Domestic Intercity Traffic, by Mode, 1939 to 1979 (in millions of dollars, except percentages)

Year	Rail[1]		Truck[2]		Water[3]		Pipe[4]		Air[5]		Total[6]
	Rev.	%	Rev.	%	Rev.	%	Rev.	%	Rev.	%	
1979	22,300	17.4	93,163	72.8	4,613	3.6	6,011	4.7	1,947	1.5	128,034
1978	20,610	18.5	79,569	71.3	4,242	3.8	5,452	4.9	1,729	1.5	111,602
1977	19,232	20.4	67,356	71.5	2,922	3.1	3,209	3.4	1,484	1.6	94,203
1976	17,707	22.0	56,245	69.8	2,825	3.5	2,532	3.1	1,247	1.5	80,556
1975	15,623	22.8	47,272	68.9	2,434	3.5	2,220	3.2	1,073	1.6	68,622
1974	15,993	22.9	48,818	69.8	2,243	3.2	1,878	2.7	1,043	1.5	69,975
1973	14,003	22.2	44,648	70.7	1,831	2.9	1,711	2.7	969	1.5	63,162
1972	12,790	22.5	40,000	70.3	1,669	2.9	1,583	2.8	849	1.5	56,891
1971	11,996	22.5	37,549	70.3	1,594	3.0	1,492	2.8	759	1.4	53,390
1970	11,124	23.0	33,553	69.4	1,546	3.2	1,396	2.9	720	1.5	48,339
1969	10,538	23.2	31,397	69.3	1,342	3.0	1,309	2.9	748	1.6	45,334
1968	9,942	23.2	29,721	69.5	1,318	3.1	1,205	2.8	593	1.4	42,779
1967	9,329	22.6	28,930	70.2	1,273	3.1	1,157	2.8	543	1.3	41,232
1966	9,487	24.4	26,560	68.2	1,315	3.4	1,096	2.8	490	1.3	38,948
1965	9,037	25.5	23,628	66.7	1,286	3.6	1,051	3.0	428	1.2	35,430
1964	8,575	24.7	23,567	67.8	1,268	3.6	1,013	2.9	360	1.0	34,783
1963	8,271	25.5	21,588	66.6	1,239	3.8	980	3.0	320	1.0	32,398
1962	8,115	26.1	20,463	65.9	1,234	4.0	939	3.0	311	1.0	31,062
1961	7,859	26.8	19,127	65.1	1,219	4.2	914	3.1	253	0.9	29,372
1960	8,152	28.6	17,958	63.0	1,286	4.5	895	3.1	220	0.8	28,511
1959	8,442	29.3	17,957	62.4	1,268	4.4	890	3.1	210	0.7	28,767
1958	8,193	29.9	16,965	62.0	1,190	4.3	838	3.1	191	0.7	27,377
1957	9,064	31.9	16,926	59.6	1,376	4.8	844	3.0	184	0.6	28,394
1956	9,089	33.2	15,849	57.8	1,456	5.3	851	3.1	166	0.6	27,411
1955	8,665	35.4	13,475	55.1	1,382	5.7	781	3.2	141	0.6	24,444
1954	7,915	35.0	12,607	55.8	1,220	5.4	710	3.1	138	0.6	22,590
1953	9,078	38.5	12,476	52.9	1,196	5.1	679	2.9	134	0.6	23,563
1952	8,915	41.2	10,897	50.4	1,040	4.8	644	3.0	122	0.6	21,618
1951	8,758	43.3	9,729	48.1	1,031	5.1	600	3.0	111	0.5	20,229

1950	7,934	43.4	8,717	47.7	1,012	5.5	506	2.8	113	0.6	18,282
1949	7,151	46.3	6,911	44.8	844	5.5	430	2.8	96	0.6	15,432
1948	8,090	52.9	5,968	39.0	727	4.8	430	2.8	90	0.6	15,305
1947	7,141	52.5	5,354	39.3	690	5.1	370	2.7	56	0.4	13,611
1946	5,866	54.2	4,119	38.1	454	4.2	334	3.1	41	0.4	10,814
1945	6,617	56.5	4,170	35.6	531	4.5	345	2.9	48	0.4	11,711
1944	7,087	61.5	3,456	30.0	577	5.0	351	3.0	44	0.4	11,515
1943	6,866	67.4	2,367	23.2	601	5.9	314	3.1	35	0.3	10,183
1942	6,026	67.4	2,229	24.9	377	4.2	277	3.0	32	0.4	8,941
1941	4,510	54.0	2,745	32.8	791	9.5	284	3.4	28	0.3	8,358
1940	3,584	52.5	2,312	33.8	650	9.5	255	3.7	24	0.4	6,825
1939	3,297	58.0	1,786	31.4	340	6.0	239	4.2	21	0.4	5,683

SOURCES: Author's estimates as noted. Rail data: U.S., Interstate Commerce Commission, Transport Statistics in the United States, annual issues; also reported in U.S., Bureau of the Census, Historical Statistics of the United States, Colonial Times to 1970, Series Q343, p. 732; 1976–1978 data: U.S., Bureau of the Census, Statistical Abstract 1980, Table 1140, p. 660. Truck, water, and pipeline data: Transportation Association of America, Transportation Facts and Trends, annual issues; and TAA unpublished data. Air data: Transportation Association of America, Transportation Facts and Trends, annual issues; TAA unpublished data; and U.S., Federal Aviation Administration, FAA Statistical Handbook of Aviation, annual issues; also reported in U.S., Bureau of the Census, Historical Statistics of the United States, Colonial Times to 1970, Series Q593–596, pp. 770–771.

NOTE: Percentages may not sum to 100 due to rounding.

[1] Railroad freight revenue, all railroads (Class 1, 2, and 3). Estimated for 1979.

[2] Includes revenues of ICC regulated motor carriers and estimated revenues of non-regulated motor carriers. Non-regulated revenue for 1958–1979 estimated by Transportation Association of America (TAA). Non-regulated revenue for 1939–1957 estimated by the author using the same method as TAA, described as follows: ICC regulated revenue divided by ICC regulated ton miles to yield regulated revenue per ton mile. One cent subtracted from this rate as an estimated operating differential. Adjusted rate is applied to non-regulated ton miles to produce estimated revenue for non-regulated traffic. Non-regulated and regulated revenue added to produce total revenue for trucks.

[3] Includes revenues of ICC regulated water carriers and estimated revenues of non-regulated water carriers. Includes coastal (domestic), Great Lakes, and inland waterways. Non-regulated revenue for 1958–1979 estimated by TAA. Non-regulated revenue for 1939–1957 estimated by the author by projecting ICC revenue as a percentage of total revenue backward in time from 1958–1975 period. This percentage was then applied to ICC regulated revenue each year 1939–1957 to produce an estimated total revenue (regulated and non-regulated). The projection equation used was $y = 32.355 + (7.2427/\text{time period})$ with 1975 = time period 1 through 1958 = time period 18.

[4] Includes revenues of ICC regulated pipelines and estimated revenues of non-regulated pipelines. Non-regulated revenue 1961–1979 estimated by TAA. Non-regulated revenue 1939–1960 estimated by the author by projecting ICC revenue as a percentage of total revenue backward in time from 1961–1975 period. This percentage was then applied to ICC regulated revenue each year 1939–1960 to produce total estimated revenue (regulated and non-regulated). The projection equation used was $y = 84.084 + (0.12797 \times \text{time period})$ with 1975 = time period 1 through 1961 = time period 15.

[5] For 1958–1979, TAA estimates of domestic traffic are used. This includes freight, express, excess baggage, adjusted mail, and freight-charter revenues of Certificated Airlines as reported to the Civil Aeronautics Board. For 1939–1957, estimates consist of scheduled airlines' freight, express, excess baggage, mail (including subsidy), and other freight. Revenue for 1939–1957 is somewhat overstated by the inclusion of subsidy payments, but the amount is insignificant for the purposes of this appendix.

[6] Sum of individual modes, as defined in this table.

5 | FOR EVERYONE ELSE: THE TYPICAL TRANSPORTATION INDUSTRY STRUCTURE

The highway, water, and air transport modes have maintained or expanded market share in the growing economy of the last several decades. The railroads have lost market share. The advantage of the first three modes is their "typical" industry structure. The success of this structure stems from its encouragement of competition and diversity as constructive forces.

To understand the structural reasons for the success of the highway, water, and air modes of freight transportation and the relative decline of the railroads, the structures of each mode must be examined. This chapter explores the typical structure shared by the highway, water, and air modes. The following chapter describes the railroads' industry structure.

Industry structure encompasses the physical components of a transportation mode, the public and private entities which control the components, and the operating relationships between the entities.[1] The physical components can be categorized as fixed ways and carriers, the latter encompassing terminals. These categories serve as demarcations of the owning entities and as divisions within companies which own multiple components.

The typical transportation industry structure can be described as privately owned carriers operating over a publicly owned, jointly used fixed way. In contrast, the railroads operate as privately owned carriers over privately owned fixed ways, with each fixed way reserved for the exclusive use of its owner-carrier.

FIXED WAYS

The typical structure utilizes publicly owned, jointly used fixed ways. Highways, waterways, and airways are all built or improved with public funds.[2] Ownership and control of the fixed ways rests with government agencies at several levels. Fixed way physical components vary according to the mode under study, but all modes require maintenance and traffic control for their fixed ways.

Traffic control can be classified as indirect or direct. *Indirect control* relies on the operators of individual vehicles to control their craft according to established procedures, regulations, and/or instructions from traffic controllers. *Direct control* bypasses the vehicle operator, allowing vehicles to be controlled directly by traffic controllers, computers, or other devices.

Traffic control can be further defined as passive or active. *Passive control* does not require continuous monitoring or intervention. *Active control* requires constant monitoring by traffic controllers. Highway driving rules represent a passive form of traffic control; an airport control tower functions as an active control system.

Highways

Highways are owned by public entities: states, counties, and cities. Local roads and streets are the jurisdiction of counties and cities; state highway departments own the secondary, primary, and Interstate highway systems. Local governments usually support road work through general revenue funds which come primarily from property taxes. The federal and state governments use trust funds and some general-revenue funds to finance highway activities. Taxes on fuel, tires, and other items provide income for the trust funds; expenditures are related to the funds' income and balances. The states can receive federal aid for projects which meet standards set by the Federal Highway Administration (FHWA). Highways designated as part of the primary and secondary system (850,000 miles) are eligible for 70 percent federal funding. The federal government provides 90 percent of the cost of the 42,500-mile National System of Interstate and Defense Highways.[3]

In some states legislatures have created toll road authorities to operate turnpike systems set apart from the public highway system. Toll roads allow states to finance modern limited access highways through use of tolls and state-guaranteed bond issues instead of relying on inadequate trust fund revenues or general appropriations. Toll roads have declined in favor during recent years due largely to the advent of 90 percent federal funding for the Interstate network.

The physical components of highways are relatively simple, ranging from a dirt road to a multi-lane limited access Interstate. Unpaved dirt or gravel roads are almost entirely local; more important routes are paved with asphalt or concrete. In recent years wider pavement and shoulders have been used to increase traffic safety and accommodate larger trucks. Increased truck weights have necessitated the use of stronger bridges and pavement designs.

Highway traffic control consists largely of indirect controls: laws, regulations, and passive control devices such as stoplights. Experiments with direct vehicle control, such as vehicle guidance by electrical cables buried in the pavement, have not found practical application. The likelihood of direct control systems proving feasible appears slim due to the size of the highway network, its extensive usage, and the flexibility demanded of it by different users. Some types of indirect active controls have been implemented, like computerized control of city stoplights to expedite urban traffic flows. A few freeways have been equipped with electronic speed limit displays, allowing a dispatcher to vary traffic movement. Access ramps in a number of cities are governed by traffic lights, with some ramps closed during rush hours and others utilizing a metering system to limit the number of vehicles entering the freeway system.

Most traffic, however, is controlled only by each individual driver's observance of rules, signs, and automatic traffic signals. Basic to this effort are the driver licensing laws of each state. License testing helps assure that drivers are familiar with highway rules. State highway police usually supervise the state's licensing program as a part of their greater overall responsibility for traffic law enforcement. Local police provide enforcement of municipal ordinances and supplement the state police activities.

Signs and pavement markings play a most important role in highway traffic control. Signs regulate traffic, convey warnings, and convey information. Pavement markings assist in guidance and indicate traffic flow (number of lanes, direction, passing lanes).

The extensive use of signs, markings, and traffic lights accounts for a sizeable part of each highway department's maintenance budget. Maintenance of the roadway itself—pavement, shoulders, and the related drainage system—represents the greatest share of maintenance costs.

Waterways

In keeping with the typical transportation industry structure, the navigable waterways of the United States are reserved by law for public use and federal ownership. State, regional, and local governments play a small role in the waterway industry, generally limiting themselves to working through port authorities, river terminals, and riverside industrial development activities. The waterway itself is public property, and enforcement of navigation laws is a function of the United States Coast Guard (USCG). Since waterways are seldom suitable for modern navigation in their natural state, the U.S. Army's Corps of Engineers is responsible for their improvement and maintenance.

Financing for waterway activities comes largely from federal general revenues, reflecting the dominant roles of the Coast Guard and the Corps of Engineers. The budgets of the various port authorities are almost insignificant in comparison and are more properly a terminal function rather than a fixed way function. Waterway carriers have historically paid no user fees, but as of October 1, 1980, a 4 cents-per-gallon tax on diesel fuel was imposed. This user fee is scheduled to increase to 10 cents per gallon by 1985. The legislation which established the user fees also created the Waterway Trust Fund, though waterway expenditures are not limited to fund proceeds.

The primary physical component of a waterway is, simply, water—but there must be enough to form a channel of sufficient width and depth.

Of the 17,047 miles of U.S. river and intracoastal waterway routes in commercial service in 1960, only 668 miles had required no improvement. In fact, some have required so much work and change that the only "free and natural" thing left in or about them *is* the water! The same is true of our natural harbors.[4]

The Corps of Engineers improves waterways as part of its Civil Works Program. The Corps builds and maintains "dams, reservoirs, levees, harbors, waterways, locks, and many other types of structures."[5] Although many improvements facilitate water transportation, some are not transport-related or serve multiple purposes such as flood control, irrigation, water supply, electric-power generation, wildlife conservation, water pollution abatement, and recreation. Transport-related improvements include dredging, channel stabilization, construction and operation of locks, and bank stabilization. Dredging by hydraulic or mechanical means enlarges the channel and must be repeated at periodic intervals to remove silt and other debris. Construction of revetments and dikes, paving of banks, and installation of underwater concrete mattresses are methods for maintaining the desired channel location and dimensions. Dams are one means for maintaining channel pool depths, but they also require locks to lift or lower boats past the dam. The size of lock chambers is often a factor limiting the size of tows on a waterway.

Certain functions of the U.S. Coast Guard relate to the waterway and its carriers:

. . . administering the alteration of obstructive bridges; approving the location, clearance, and lighting of bridges over navigable waters of the United States; and regulating drawbridge operations.[6]

Most of the Coast Guard's activities involve water-carrier safety and traffic control. The growth of river traffic has prompted the installation of indirect, active traffic control systems in a few areas. Vessel Traffic Service (VTS) systems are operating at San Francisco, Houston-Galveston, Morgan City (Louisiana), and Valdez (Alaska).[7] Under VTS all towboats and ships report their locations periodically to a control center which monitors and directs traffic movements. Check points are established along the VTS waterway segment, and each craft using the segment reports by radio when passing each check point. VTS control center personnel can prevent waterway traffic jams and other dangerous situations from occurring.

Outside of the few VTS areas—on most of the nation's waterways—traffic control consists only of Coast Guard rules and navigation aids. Light structures, buoys, daybeacons, radiobeacons, long-range electronic aids (LORAN), and fog signals are some of the aids to inland and ocean shipping provided by the Coast Guard. On-board equipment found on most tow-boats includes multi-channel radio for communications, radar, electronic depth finders, air horns, searchlights, and market lights.

Coast Guard regulations govern normal operating procedures and special situations such as radar-assisted operation during inclement weather and lighting of tows for night operation. An important part of the Coast Guard's efforts is its licensing of river mates, masters, pilots, operators, engineers, and tankermen. The Corps of Engineers assists navigation by compiling charts of each waterway and offering them to interested parties. The charts give information about the waterway, navigation channel, shore facilities, navigation aids, and waterway obstructions (such as bridges, underground pipelines, etc.). Waterway traffic control depends largely on trained towboat personnel and Coast Guard navigation aids, supported by USCG licensing procedures, enforcement efforts, and Corps of Engineers improvement projects.

Airways

The nation's navigable airspace is regarded as a public asset in much the same manner as its navigable waters. The Federal Aviation Administration (FAA), part of the Department of Transportation, is given the authority to control use of the airspace. The FAA serves both civilian and military needs.

The safe and efficient utilization of the navigable airspace is a primary objective of the Federal Aviation Administration. To meet this objective, the agency operates a network of airport traffic control towers, air route traffic control centers, and flight service stations. It develops air traffic rules and regulations and allocates the use of the airspace. It also provides for the security control of air traffic to meet national defense requirements.[8]

Financing of the federal airway system comes from user taxes paid into the Airport and Airway Trust Fund, created by the Airport and Airway Development Act of 1970.[9] Some facilities at airports are considered to be part of the airway system and are financed jointly by federal and local funds: runways, taxiways, and runway lighting systems. Other airport facilities such as passenger and cargo terminals, hangars, and servicing facilities are considered part of the terminal and not part of the airway. Terminal facilities are locally owned and funded, with few exceptions. Landing fees provide a source of income for airports, as do rental fees for building space and appropriations from local governments. Portions of the airport budget are used to construct and maintain airway facilities (runways, taxiways, runway lighting) but are not usually restricted by income source.

Landing fields are an important part of the airway system, as are the numerous navigation and traffic control activities of the FAA. FAA flight service stations provide pilots with weather information and flight planning assistance. Airport traffic control towers supervise all air traffic within three to thirty miles of their respective airports. Major airports have instrument landing systems which allow properly equipped aircraft to land under conditions of minimal visibility. The FAA also sets standards for rotating light beacons, runway design, runway lighting, runway marking, and other airport navigation aids.

Between airports aircraft can use specified routes (airways) or point-to-point navigation, depending on flight altitude and type of operation. Altitude layers are reserved as follows:

    18,000 feet or less—short and intermediate operations
    18,000–45,000 feet—jet routes
    45,000 feet and up—random route point-to-point flights.[10]

In 1961 the FAA required all aircraft using airports with active control towers to have a two-way radio communication system.[11] The FAA's predecessor agency in 1958 designated a system of airways subject to continuous "positive" air traffic control. Positive control was later expanded to cover 110,000 square miles of high-altitude airspace.

Within the positive control area all aircraft not only had to operate under instrument flight rules regardless of weather, but also had to be equipped with two-way radios for pilot-controller communications and a coded radar beacon transmitter for identification.[12]

Under positive control each flight is tracked by a series of FAA air route traffic control centers (ARTCC's).

The United States is divided into 21 of these centers that jointly coordinate the flow of IFR [instrument flight rules] traffic between their assigned areas. The centers throughout the country each have direct communications with adjacent centers. Each center is geographically divided into sectors with individual controllers directing IFR traffic in those sectors. As a flight leaves one sector for another, the controller's responsibility is passed to controllers working in the adjacent sectors.

Today, almost all control by ARTCC of aircraft flying at sufficiently high altitude is exercised by the use of radar.[13]

Federal Aviation Regulations (FAR's) are established by the FAA and serve as the basis for all air traffic control. To assist in enforcing its regulations the FAA licenses pilots and is empowered to discipline violators. Much material of an informative nature is provided by the FAA, the most basic being the sectional chart, a topographical map of part of the nation with air navigation information. Specialized charts are available to cover major terminals, long-distance flights, flight planning, and radio facilities.

Automation or direct control of aircraft is not used in commercial service; about its only use is by the military for target aircraft. The flexibilities and economies of indirect traffic control and piloted aircraft are preferred to automated operation. Indirect passive controls (FAR's) and extensive indirect active controls (control towers, ARTCC's) are the major means of airway traffic control.

CARRIERS

The typical transportation industry structure consists of privately owned carriers operating over publicly owned, jointly used fixed ways. As private sector companies, carriers perform the usual business functions in addition to those unique to transportation: dispatching and equipment maintenance.

Dispatching activities include: (1) the assessment of immediate demands for transportation service; and (2) the coordination of personnel and equipment to meet those demands. Carrier company dispatchers determine when, where, and how transportation will be provided, subject to certain restraints in the carrier-fixed way system. Fixed way traffic controllers, in situations where active control is imposed, direct the actual vehicle movements once the carriers' dispatchers decide to originate them. Although traffic controllers are occasionally referred to as "dispatchers," traffic control is a fixed way function and dispatching—as defined above—is a carrier function.

Equipment maintenance is supportive of the dispatch function but is considered a separate activity because of its importance, mechanical orientation, and size relative to the other business functions. Trucks, boats, or aircraft taken out of service for maintenance represent non-productive assets; both the quality and quantity of transportation service offered by the carrier are affected.

Carrier physical components include equipment (vehicles), equipment maintenance facilities, and terminal facilities. Individual components can be owned by a carrier, several carriers together, a shipper, or an independent company. A vehicle or facility can be used only by its owner (i.e., private use) or made available commercially to other carriers.

Transport vehicles are usually provided by the carrier, either by ownership or some form of lease-rental. In some instances carriers interchange equipment: one carrier uses another carrier's equipment, usually to transport a shipment moving over portions of both carriers' routes. Interchange practice varies with each mode and with different carriers in the same mode. Carrier companies, equipment manufacturers, and independent firms all provide equipment repair services.

Terminals serve a variety of purposes. Shipments must be loaded and unloaded from carrier vehicles; they might require sorting or storage. Terminals are logical locations for vehicle maintenance and servicing facilities. The specific needs of each mode vary, but the basic functions remain the same for all modes.

Highway Carriers

Most highway carriers own fleets of tractors, trailers, and local delivery trucks. Carriers can supplement their fleets with leased or rented units.

Truck size and weight limits are set by individual states. Most states allow trucks to weigh up to 80,000 pounds gross. Single trailers up to 45 feet and twin trailers up to 65 feet are allowed in most states. A few western states allow triple trailers. Several states permit trucks to operate on specific highways (usually turnpikes) with twin trailers of 40 feet length each, or a total length with tractor of over 100 feet.

The variety of trailer designs reflects the broad array of commodities shipped by truck. Trailers can be classified as vans, refrigerated vans, open-top vans, livestock vans, tanks, dry bulk hoppers, flatbeds, dumps, auto transports, and other types.

When trailers are interchanged, it is usually between common carriers of less-than-truckload (LTL) freight. Since most LTL shipments are unloaded, sorted, and reloaded at a connecting city, interchange of trailers is somewhat unusual even in the LTL business. The growth of rail piggyback service has encouraged interchange of trailers, since motor carriers can use railroads as connecting carriers or as substitutes for over-the-road movement. In most segments of the trucking industry, trailer interchange is uncommon, because the same carrier handles the shipment from origin to destination.

Truck terminals vary, depending on the carrier, its traffic, and volume handled. In major cities a large common carrier might provide all terminal services itself, performing shipment classification, storage, and vehicle maintenance. Contract and private carriers typically use shipper facilities for loading and unloading, so they need only facilities for equipment maintenance. Servicing and repair work can be done by garages, service stations, and truck stops which are independently owned (that is, not affiliated with any carrier). Equipment dealers and leasing firms also offer maintenance services.

Water Carriers

Water carriers, like highway carriers, usually own the towboats and barges they use. A few companies exist which own only barges and contract their towing to other firms; they are primarily industries in other fields which operate as private carriers (grain companies, chemical manufacturers). Many small operators own one or a few towboats, moving barges for private industries and other carriers.

The predominance of contract and private towing accounts for the lack of widespread interchange of barges among carriers. Shipments are usually moved from origin to destination by the same carrier. Common carrier barge lines interchange barges on occasion, but again most shipments can be handled by a single carrier.

Water carrier terminals provide four categories of services: (1) docks, where cargoes are loaded and unloaded; (2) fleeting and harbor services; (3) shipyards and repair facilities; and (4) midstream supply services.

The *1977 Inland River Guide* listed over 200 dock facilities open to public use and nearly 1600 private docks.[14] Public docks may be owned by public agencies or by private enterprises which serve all customers. Private docks include grain elevators, coal docks, oil tank farms, and so forth. Docks can be classified by type of cargo handled: general cargo, dry bulk, and liquid bulk.

Fleeting and harbor services assist towboats in working their tows, providing switchboats (or tugs). The switchboats aid towboats in picking up barges, setting out barges, and rearranging their tows. Barge storage is offered as a service of many harbor services.

Supply services are the waterway's counterpart of highway truck stops and make dockside or midstream delivery of fuel, lubricating oil, drinking water, foodstuffs, and other supplies. By using a small switchboat to maneuver a supply barge alongside the moving towboat, stops and delays to the moving tow are minimized.

Air Carriers

Most air carriers are passenger carriers, transporting baggage, mail, and express (freight) as an adjunct to passenger operations. Some use aircraft convertible to freight-only service for late-night freight flights; some have sufficient freight volume to justify cargo aircraft on certain routes. There are also cargo-only air carriers which operate solely on air freight business.

Cargo handling facilities consist of loading-unloading machinery (conveyors, lift trucks, ramps) and trucks or carts to move shipments to the terminal building. With few exceptions—military airlifts, for example—air cargo traffic is comprised of small shipments and terminals reflect this fact. Shipments are collected and delivered locally by truck. The terminal dock acts as a clearinghouse, sorting inbound shipments and consolidating outbound shipments. The terminal facilities are usually leased by carriers from the local public authority which operates the airport. Air carriers and independent firms offer aircraft fueling, supply, and repair services.

ECONOMIC REGULATION

Carriers can be classified as common, contract, or private depending on the clientele they serve. Common carriers are found in all modes; they offer their services to all shippers who desire to use them. Contract carriers serve a limited number of customers, usually with a special type of transportation service. Contract carriers give service to a shipper for a specified period and price as set forth in a contract. Private carriers are shipper-owned. Any person or company can operate a transportation service if it is for his own use and not for hire to others. The private carrier is an integral part of the production-distribution system of its parent firm.

Carriers are subject to economic regulation in some situations and in others they are exempt. Exemptions vary by mode, the result of compromises and concessions granted to various interests when the regulatory legislation was passed. As an indication of the scope of regulation, consider the percentage of total ton-miles in each mode which were federally regulated in 1976.[15]

Rail	100.0%
Truck	44.1
Water—Rivers and Canals	16.3
Water—Great Lakes	0.2
Oil Pipeline	84.4
Air	100.0

Since 1976, air cargo has been completely deregulated. Rail, truck, and water carrier regulations have been relaxed and in some cases eliminated. In general, common carriers are the focus of most regulation, but even they are exempt in some situations. Contract carriers are usually subject to minimal regulation, principally to protect common carriers, if they are regulated at all. Private carriage is typically exempt from economic regulation.

Highway common and contract carriers are subject to regulation by the Interstate Commerce Commission (ICC), with exemptions as specified in the Interstate Commerce Act:

... property carriers using motor vehicles controlled and operated by farmers engaged in the transportation of agricultural commodities or farm supplies; vehicles controlled and operated by co-operative associations, as defined in the Agricultural Marketing Act; vehicles used in carrying livestock, fish, or agricultural commodities; vehicles used exclusively in the distribution of newspapers; vehicles used in the transportation of property incidental to transportation by aircraft; vehicles used in transportation of property wholly within a municipality or zone adjacent to or commercially part of such a municipality; and vehicles used in casual, occasional, or reciprocal transportation of property in interstate or foreign commerce by a person not engaged in transportation by motor carriers as a regular business.[16]

The exemption covering intercity transportation of agricultural commodities accounts for the greatest portion of exempt highway traffic. Common, contract, and private carriers may transport exempt commodities if they "are not moved in the same vehicle at the same time with a nonexempt commodity."[17] Although common and contract trucking is still regulated, the ICC has moved to relax regulation recently and, in so doing, has greatly increased competition among highway carriers.[18]

Most water transportation is exempt, though there is some traffic subject to ICC regulation. In general, exemptions apply to (1) transportation of bulk commodities; (2) contract carriers moving commodities found not to be competitive with other common carriers; (3) private carriers; and (4) water transportation incidental to that of a "railroad, motor carrier, or express company that is in the nature of transfer, collection, or delivery services in terminal areas or has to do with the performance of floatage, car ferry, lighterage, or towage."[19] The operation of ferries, certain small craft, and harbor operations has also been exempted by the ICC.

Air cargo transportation is exempt from economic regulation.[20] The Civil Aeronautics Board's (CAB's) successful elimination of air cargo regulation prompted passage of the Airline Deregulation Act of 1978 and served as a model for passenger airline deregulation. The Act provided for (1) termination of CAB authority over route assignments in 1982; (2) elimination of CAB rate authority in 1983; (3) transfer of merger authority to the Justice Department in 1985; and (4) a report by the CAB, due in 1984, stating if the agency should be eliminated or not.[21]

The movement toward deregulation in the highway, air, and water modes indicates a growing appreciation of competitive market forces and recognition of the artificial nature of entry/exit restrictions when applied to fixed ways open to the public.

SAFETY REGULATION

Safety regulation for transportation is provided by the Department of Transportation and by state and other government bodies. In all modes the National Transportation Safety Board (NTSB) is authorized to investigate transportation accidents, report on causes, and make recommendations regarding safety regulations. The NTSB works closely with the Department of Transportation (DOT) but is an autonomous federal agency. In minor accidents the NTSB delegates its investigatory duties to the appropriate DOT administration: Federal Highway Administration (FHWA); Federal Aviation Administration (FAA); Federal Railroad Administration (FRA); United States Coast Guard (USCG); or Office of Pipeline Safety (OPS).

The Federal Highway Administration sets safety standards for federally funded highway projects and "exercises jurisdiction over the safety performance of commercial motor carriers engaged in interstate or foreign commerce, including those whose operations are specifically exempt from economic regulation."[22] FHWA checks driver qualifications, inspects vehicles and terminals, investigates accidents, and enforces safety regulations in general. The National Highway Traffic Safety Administration assists the FHWA in setting highway and vehicle safety standards and also aids the Environmental Protection Agency in establishing pollution standards. State governments set length, width, and weight limits for highway vehicles and also administer driver licensing requirements.

Air carrier safety regulation is conducted by the Federal Aviation Administration which

issues and enforces rules, regulations, and minimum standards relating to the manufacture, operation, and maintenance of aircraft as well as the rating and certification (including medical) of airmen and the certification of airports serving air carriers certified by the Civil Aeronautics Board. The agency performs flight inspection of air navigation facilities in the United States, and, as required, abroad.[23]

The Coast Guard is charged with the enforcement of all federal laws on the seas and on domestic navigable waters. In terms of water transportation safety, its primary responsibility is the enforcement of navigation and vessel inspection laws. Specific Coast Guard safety functions include:

inspection and regulation of vessels and related equipment to provide physical protection for crews, passengers, and cargo; licensing, regulation, and protection of the rights of merchant marine personnel; approval of plans for construction, alteration, and repair of vessels; approval of vessel equipment and appliances; investigation and review of marine casualties and acts of incompetency or misconduct; liaison with the maritime industry and international bodies; admeasurement and documentation of vessels; and publication of vessel registers.[24]

USCG regulations also govern safety devices and procedures such as radar equipment and the lighting of tows for night operation.

Safety regulation of pipelines is performed by the Office of Pipeline Safety which is responsible for "special statutorily assigned responsibilities for the safety of natural gas and liquid pipelines."[25] State agencies often enforce their own safety regulations, particularly for intrastate pipelines. Liquid pipelines under OPS jurisdiction include not only oil and petroleum pipelines but also anhydrous ammonia pipelines.

SUMMARY

Highway, air, and water transportation all share a common industry structure—a structure typical of transportation in the United States. This typical industry structure consists of privately owned carriers operating over a publicly owned, jointly used fixed way. Carriers are classified as common, contract, or private, depending on the clientele served. Authorities responsible for each mode's fixed ways establish operating rules, provide traffic control, and can require carriers to use specific navigation and communication devices.

The typical transportation industry structure must be understood so that a comparison can be made with the railroad industry's unusual structure. The use of a common fixed way available to all carriers and the coexistence of different types of carriers are characteristic of the typical structure. The railroad industry, by contrast, maintains separate fixed ways for each carrier and has only common carriers.[26]

NOTES

1. For an excellent study of each mode's structure see Donald V. Harper, *Transportation in America: Users, Carriers, Government.*
2. Pipelines do not share the typical structure because of their technology. Motive power is part of the fixed way, as is the pipe (the carrying vehicle). Pipelines, furthermore, cannot compete for general freight and must transport only a narrow range of fluid commodities.
3. Harper, pp. 367–374.
4. *Waterways of the United States*, p. 85.
5. U.S., General Services Administration, *United States Government Manual 1974-1975*, p. 177.
6. Ibid., p. 369.
7. Jeff L. Yates, "Delayed VTS Popular Topic at Annual Maritime Seminar," *Waterways Journal*, Volume 91, Number 26 (September 24, 1977), p. 4.
8. *U.S. Government Manual*, pp. 371–372.
9. Harper, pp. 396–399.
10. Robert Burkhardt, *Federal Aviation Administration*, p. 75.
11. Ibid.
12. Ibid.
13. *Aviation Fundamentals*, rev. ed. (Denver, 1974), p. 3-25 to p. 3-26. For discussions of future air traffic control systems, see Henry Lefer, "Air Traffic Control System for the 1990's and Beyond Is Gestating at FAA," *Air Transport World*, Volume 17, Number 4 (April 1980), pp. 30–33; and Gilbert F. Quinby, "Anticipating Avionics Evolution," *Air Transport World*, Volume 17, Number 4 (April 1980), pp. 36–41.
14. *Inland River Guide, 1977 Edition*, pp. 171–365, 403–429. For detailed descriptions of waterway port operations see Eugene H. Lederer, *Port Terminal Operations.*
15. Transportation Association of America, *Transportation Facts & Trends*, 15th ed. (Washington, D.C.), p. 9. For a detailed account of economic regulation see Marvin L. Fair and John Guandolo, *Transportation Regulation*, 7th ed. (Dubuque, Iowa, 1972).
16. Charles A. Taff, *Commercial Motor Transportation*, p. 115.
17. Ibid., p. 120.
18. Charles G. Burck, "Truckers Roll Toward Deregulation," *Fortune*, Volume 98, Number 12 (December 18, 1978), pp. 74–85; "ICC Evaluating Chairman's Scheme for Wide-Spread Truck Deregulation," *Traffic World*, Number 7, Vol-

ume 176, Whole Number 3734 (November 13, 1978), pp. 13–14; Albert R. Karr, "Major Cuts in ICC Control over Truckers Are Proposed by Commission's Chairman," *Wall Street Journal*, Volume LIX, Number 17 (November 7, 1978), p. 3.

19. Harper, p. 508; D. Philip Locklin, *Economics of Transportation*, pp. 755–757.

20. "Air Freight Leader Says Deregulation Producing Gains for Shipping Public," *Traffic World*, Number 10, Volume 175, Whole Number 3724 (September 4, 1978), pp. 37–38; Albert R. Karr, "The Deregulator: CAB Chairman Kahn Leads Agency Activists Spurring Competition," *Wall Street Journal*, Volume LVIII, Number 182 (July 3, 1978), p. 1; and Morten S. Beyer, "Elephants on Thin Ice: The Coming Crisis in Airline Yields," *Air Transport World*, Volume 15, Number 11 (November 1978), pp. 22–25.

21. "Deregulation Begins as Kahn Resigns," *Air Transport World*, Volume 15, Number 11 (November 1978), p. 7; "House, Senate Conference Agrees on Terms of Airline Deregulation Bill," *Traffic World*, Number 3, Volume 176, Whole Number 3730 (October 16, 1978), p. 37.

22. *U.S. Government Manual*, p. 374.

23. Ibid., p. 371.

24. Ibid., p. 369.

25. Ibid., p. 367.

26. It is accepted practice to consider the railroad industry as composed entirely of common carrier railroad companies. Private industrial railroads do exist but are a minor part of the rail transport mode. The ICC also allows common carrier railroads to offer contract rates to customers under certain conditions. "ICC Acts to Permit Contract Rates Between Railroads and Shippers," *Traffic World*, Number 8, Volume 176, Whole Number 3735 (November 20, 1978), pp. 44–46.

6 | RAILROAD INDUSTRY STRUCTURE

Railroads have a unique industry structure. Formed during the mid-1800's, it survives with little change to this date. Privately owned common carriers, each operating over its own fixed way, are characteristic of the railroad industry. In contrast, the other modes' structures consist of several types of carriers sharing use of publicly owned fixed ways.

Industry structure can be defined as (1) the physical components required for producing the transportation service; (2) the public and private entities which own the various components; and (3) the operating relationships between the different entities and their components, including the regulatory environment. Physical components can be classified according to their function as part of fixed way, carrier, or terminal activities—three functions found in all transportation.[1] Under the railroad industry's present structure, all three functions are performed by each railroad company.

FIXED WAY FUNCTIONS

Physical Components

The railroad *fixed way* includes the right of way, track, supporting structures, and traffic control system. The right of way, track, and supporting structures form the roadway; the traffic control system provides orderly traffic movement over the roadway.

Right of way is the land on which the track and its supporting structures are built. The track itself is made of several parts. Ballast is placed on the subgrade, forming the roadbed and providing an elastic, well-drained surface for the track. Wooden or concrete crossties are laid in the ballast. Steel rails are then spiked or bolted to the ties, resting on steel tie plates to reduce tie wear.

Supporting structures are necessary to maintain a grade which is level enough for efficient train operation. To take full advantage of the economies inherent in steel-wheel-on-steel-rail technology, grades and curves must be kept as gentle as possible. Large and expensive supporting structures are often needed to keep the track within acceptable grade and curvature limits. These structures include tunnels, bridges, trestles, culverts, cuts, and fills.

Traffic control systems vary in sophistication and can be classified as indirect passive, indirect active, direct passive, and direct active. *Indirect systems* rely on train crews to operate trains, and *direct systems* use automation or remote control methods to actually control the trains' operation. *Active control systems* depend on a dispatcher to control traffic actively. *Passive systems* operate without active intervention and include rules, timetables, computer control programs, or other devices.

The foundation of all railroad traffic control systems is the *Standard Code of Operating Rules,* drafted in 1886 by the General Time Convention (predecessor of the Association of American Railroads).[2] Over time individual railroads have modified the *Code* to suit conditions on their particular systems. The rules are printed in book form and given to all operating department employees. The employees are tested over the rules and given rule cards, the railroad equivalent of a licensing procedure. Employee timetables contain information about each track segment and train schedules where such schedules are in use. Operating rules and timetables are occasionally supplemented or superceded by general orders posted in general order books at all of a railroad's crew terminals. Rulebooks, timetables, and general orders are printed materials which reflect the railroad company's reliance on its corporate organization for disseminating information. Trackside signs are used to convey information, but are often regarded as supplements to printed information. Speed restrictions, for example, can be imposed by timetable, general order, or train order without having trackside signs at the restricted location. Other signs warn of railroad junctions, stations, street crossings, and other situations requiring the train crew's attention.

The simplest and one of the oldest traffic control systems is the staff system. In its original British form, a wooden staff is kept at a station and is taken by a train crew when they use a particular section of track. Other trains cannot use the section until the first returns. On American lines a register book or register ticket is kept at the station, and a train's crew signs in while using the track. Other trains cannot enter unless they contact the first train crew and obtain permission to also use the track. Crews register out when leaving. The staff system is an indirect passive system used mostly on low-traffic branch lines.

Operating rules and a timetable schedule form a relatively simple but inflexible type of indirect passive traffic control. With a means of communication linking the stations and trains, a dispatcher can issue train orders to change or cancel timetable schedules and run extra trains. Employees at each station copy the dispatcher's train orders in writing and give copies to the affected train crews. Train orders allow flexibility but depend on each crew's strict observance of the rules, schedules, and train orders to prevent collisions. Train order traffic control is indirect active: "indirect" since it requires the train crew to implement the dispatcher's orders, and "active" because the dispatcher must constantly monitor and direct train movements.

Automatic block signal (ABS) systems provide an added measure of safety by protecting a train to its front and rear through the use of trackside signals.[3] The track is divided into blocks which range from several thousand feet to several miles in length. Within each block a low-voltage circuit is maintained in the rails. A train entering the block shunts the circuit and, through a system of electrical relays, sets red signals behind to protect against following trains and ahead to protect opposing trains. ABS provides safety protection for trains but is not a means of active traffic control since it is automatic. Schedules and/or train orders are used to control train movements on ABS routes.

Centralized traffic control (CTC) combines the safety features of ABS with dispatcher control of signals and track switches.[4] With CTC the dispatcher changes signal indications to direct train movements, conveying information directly to the train crew instead of relaying it via written orders. Safety interlocks and built-in electronic safeguards prevent the creation of dangerous traffic situations.

CTC is an indirect active system, using active dispatcher control of traffic but relying on indirect (train crew) implementation of dispatcher orders. CTC is more efficient and much safer than train order traffic control. A single track CTC line can handle almost as much traffic as a double track non-CTC line.

Direct traffic control systems (which do not rely on train crews to operate trains) are rarely found in the railroad industry; however, industrial use of remote control locomotives is common. Using a portable radio pack, a crewman on the ground can operate an unmanned switching locomotive. Radio remote control provides direct active control: the traffic controller, from a remote location, actually directs the train's movements.

Direct passive control is found in automated train operations. Cost and labor opposition have generally confined automated freight operations to private industrial railroads. The greatest advances in automation have been made by urban mass transit railways where safety is paramount and conventional indirect traffic control systems are too cumbersome to handle efficiently the high volume of traffic movements.

Ownership

Railroad companies perform both fixed way and carrier functions. With rare exception, railroad companies are private enterprises and their fixed ways are under private ownership. The tracks of a railroad company are generally available only for the use of its own trains because the tracks are private property.

There are some situations in which rail fixed ways are publicly owned. Common carrier railroads owned by government agencies perform both carrier and fixed way functions. Like their private sector counterparts, the government-owned railroads perform all train service over their own tracks. The Long Island Rail Road, the Alaska Railroad, and various port railroads serve as examples of publicly owned railroads.

In a few instances public ownership of rail fixed ways departs from normal industry practice and separates ownership of the fixed way from the carrier. The State of Vermont bought portions of the Rutland Railway prior to its abandonment.[5] Separate segments are leased to two privately owned railroad companies, the Vermont Railway and the Green Mountain Railroad. Each company has exclusive use of its leased trackage.

When Conrail planned to abandon several routes in Michigan, the state government purchased the trackage and contracted with two private companies to operate the railroads. The Hillsdale County Railway and the Michigan Northern Railway each have exclusive use of separate segments of the state-owned fixed ways.[6] Similar situations exist in Maryland, Delaware, and other states where Conrail gave up unprofitable branch lines.[7] Under recent federal legislation, state and local governments can subsidize, acquire, and otherwise preserve rail fixed ways threatened with abandonment.

Regulation

Rail fixed ways are almost entirely privately owned and are subject to government regulation. Economic regulation is related to carrier functions and affects the fixed way indirectly through the carrier's exclusive use of its fixed way. Abandonments, extensions of trackage, trackage rights, and joint use are the primary areas of economic regulation.

Safety regulation of rail fixed ways is under the jurisdiction of the Federal Railroad Administration. FRA standards govern track materials, track defects, allowable speed limits, signaling, and operating procedures. The National Transportation Safety Board, through its accident-investigation duties, acts as an advisor to the FRA for various safety standards.

CARRIER FUNCTIONS

Railroad companies, like carriers in the other modes, perform the business functions common to private enterprises and some peculiar to transportation companies. Unlike the other modes' carriers, railroads perform their own fixed way functions and rarely engage in joint use of fixed ways.

As a business, a railroad company performs activities related to finance, accounting, treasury, labor relations, personnel, purchasing, law, and data processing.[8] Most of a railroad company's activities relate to operations and marketing (Figure 8).

The Operating Department operates the company's trains, tracks, and yards. It consists of three sub-areas: Maintenance of Equipment, Maintenance of Way, and Transportation.

The Maintenance of Equipment (or Mechanical) Department maintains the railroad company's cars and locomotives. This is a carrier function, similar to the equipment maintenance functions of carriers in the other modes.

The Maintenance of Way Department maintains the fixed way (track, roadbed, bridges). Its functions are similar to those of a highway department or the Corps of Engineers.

The Transportation Department provides the personnel and supervision necessary to operate the trains and yards. The railroad is divided into geographic regions, divisions, and subdivisions which form the basis for operations. Managers are assigned to each area: regional general managers, division superintendents, terminal superintendents, and trainmasters. Specialized managers supervise station accounting, railroad police, and damage claims and prevention. Staff groups support the line managers in the field with specialized services such as industrial engineering, operations planning, and service quality control. Computerized information systems, once a minor part of the Accounting Department, have become a key element in transportation management's control of operations.

In terms of carrier and fixed way functions, the role of the Transportation Department is most complex. Carload shipments are assembled into trains and moved over the railroad—carrier functions—subject to traffic control procedures, a fixed way function. Traffic control, conducted by personnel of the Transportation Department, is the area where the two functions are integrated. Even in this organizational area, the different jobs and duties can be separated as fixed way and carrier functions.

A principal distinction occurs in the dispatchers' office: the chief dispatcher moves the tonnage and the train dispatcher moves the trains. The chief dispatcher performs the carriers' dispatch function, analyzing the immediate demands for transportation service and determining in conjunction with other personnel how best to meet those demands. Assisted by yardmasters and other supervisory personnel, the chief dispatcher determines when sufficient tonnage (number of cars) is available to run or not run trains. The chief dispatcher generally decides which trains will pick up and deliver cars to specific points. Standard procedures for train service are established by staff and supervisory personnel, but the execution of the procedures and their exceptions are the responsibility of the chief dispatcher.

Train dispatchers, also known as trick or shift dispatchers, report to the chief dispatcher and perform a traffic control function. Once the chief dis-

Figure 8. Typical Railroad Company Organization Structure

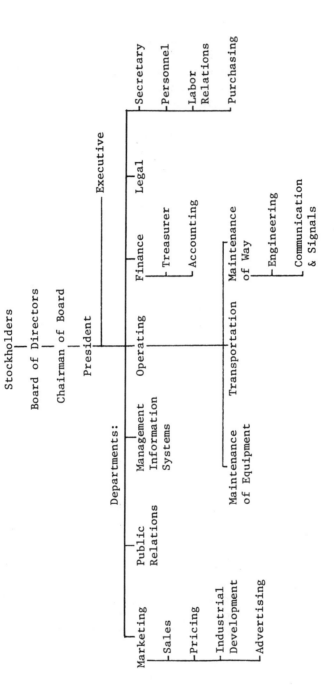

patcher decides which trains will be run and the work they will perform, the train dispatchers direct the train movements. Timetable schedules, train orders, and CTC signal indications are the train dispatcher's means for controlling train movements. Since the train dispatcher performs the fixed way's traffic control activities, he is the logical point for interface with maintenance of way functions. Track repair gangs, inspectors, and other personnel report track conditions and similar factors affecting the safety of train operations to the train dispatcher. In turn, he relays this information to train crews through slow orders (train orders describing speed limitations and track conditions).

Physical Components

The physical components necessary for the performance of carrier functions are cars, locomotives, and terminal facilities. Terminals are discussed separately in a later section of this chapter.

Routine maintenance and minor repairs to freight cars are made by the railroad company which has the car at the time the repairs are needed. The car's owner is billed for the repairs at rates set by the Association of American Railroads (AAR), if a party to the AAR agreements. Industrial companies with private car fleets often perform their own maintenance, though some contract this work to railroad companies or independent firms. Heavy repairs are made by the car owner, private line car shops, independent repair facilities, or another railroad's car shops.

Railroads perform maintenance and servicing for their locomotives. The timing and scope of periodic inspections are specified by the Federal Railroad Administration. Major repairs are made in the railroad's shops, although some might be made in the shops of a locomotive manufacturer or an independent repair firm. The repair process is sometimes expanded into a general overhaul or a complete rebuilding of the unit, with the emerging locomotive barely resembling the original.

Ownership

Each railroad company provides its own fleet of locomotives for use on its system. A railroad which runs short of motive power (say, during a season of peak traffic) can lease units from another railroad or from a locomotive leasing company. Rental fees are based on kilohorsepower-hours or kilohorsepower-miles.[9] Some railroads routinely interchange locomotives in runthrough trains' power pools. In several cases shippers have provided cars and locomotives for unit trains, with the railroad company operating the trains over its tracks.[10] Shippers frequently use their own locomotives for in-plant switching, but the use of shipper-owned locomotives in road service is a recent development.

The operation of the car fleet is similar in many respects to that of the locomotive fleet, except that freight cars are interchanged among railroads much more extensively than locomotives and the use of shipper-owned freight cars is a common practice. Cars having other than railroad company ownership are known as private cars and total about 20 percent of the freight car fleet nationally, with the percentage increasing in recent years. Private cars include fleets of specialized cars owned by railroad subsidiaries, such as refrigerator car companies, and the Trailer Train Corporation, which operates a large flatcar fleet and is owned by a group of railroads. Most private cars are owned by shippers (industrial companies) or by private car line companies which rent and lease cars to shippers.

The interchange of cars between railroads is guided by the AAR's Car Service and Car Hire Agreement. The rental rate is set for each car based on the type of car, its age, and its original cost. When a railroad-owned freight car is on the tracks of the railroad which owns it—its home road—there is no rental charge. The railroad pays rental for all cars it uses which are owned by other railroads or private car lines. Rentals are based on time and/or mileage.

When shippers use cars provided by the railroad they are given a specified period to load each car. Beyond this time they are assessed demurrage charges for delaying use of the car. Similar arrangements pertain to unloading. Private cars are exempt from demurrage when on the tracks of their owner or lessee and have no per diem.

Regulation

The greatest number of railroad companies are common carriers, though a few private carrier industrial railroads exist in the form of logging, mining, or in-plant railroads.[11] Common carrier railroads are regulated by the Interstate Commerce Commission.

> In the transportation economics area, the Commission settles controversies over rates and charges among competing and like modes of transportation, shippers, and receivers of freight, passengers, and others. It rules upon applications for mergers, consolidations, acquisitions of control, and the sale of carriers and issuance of their securities. It prescribes accounting rules, awards reparations, and administers laws relating to railroad bankruptcy. It acts to prevent unlawful discrimination, destructive competition and rebating. It also has jurisdiction over the use, control, supply, movement, distribution, exchange, interchange, and return of railroad equipment. Under certain conditions, it is authorized to direct the handling and movement of traffic over a railroad and its distribution over other lines of railroads.[12]

Private carriers are not subject to economic regulation; they function as part of their owner's production process. Common and private carrier railroads seldom share trackage. There have been cases in history when this was done, as when a logging company's private railroad created a common carrier subsidiary to offer freight and passenger service to other customers.

Private carrier railroads range from a few thousand feet to several miles, though most are even smaller than common carrier short lines.

Some industrial firms own common carrier railroads. These railroads, as common carriers, serve any shipper and are subject to ICC regulation. A private carrier serves only its owner. One advantage of common carrier status is that it allows the industrial company's railroad subsidiary to negotiate divisions (i.e., share in shipment revenues) with other railroad companies. A disadvantage is the assumption of common carrier obligations and responsibilities. Among the industrial firms which own railroads are United States Steel, Weyerhaeuser, Alcoa, and Georgia Pacific.

Safety regulation is primarily the responsibility of the Federal Railroad Administration. Areas of regulation include:

Rolling stock equipment standards
Locomotive inspections and standards
Hours of service laws for employees
Hazardous commodity regulations
Accident investigation

Accident investigation is also the jurisdiction of the National Transportation Safety Board. The Occupational Safety and Health Administration (OSHA) sets workplace safety standards in situations not covered by FRA standards.[13] Environmental regulations are set by the Environmental Protection Agency and state agencies. Private mining railroads must meet safety standards set by the Department of Interior's Mining Enforcement and Safety Administration (MESA).

TERMINAL FUNCTIONS

In railroading the word *terminal* has many meanings. The simplest definition is the origin or destination of any shipment, but this is too simple to be of much use. The basic terminal in a railroad company is the station, also known as an agency. Each station is responsible for serving all customers on a specific portion of the railroad's system. A terminal can also be the trackage, yards, and other facilities of a railroad company in a large city. The entire urban area, including the facilities of all railroads in the area, is a terminal in the broadest sense of the word.[14]

To distinguish each type of terminal better, the different kinds of train service must be understood. Rail customers outside urban areas are usually served by local freight trains. Local freights travel over an assigned section of track, picking up and setting out cars for customers along the route. Locals take the cars they pick up to the station at the end of their run—

usually a point on a main line—and block the cars for pick up by through freight trains.

In urban terminal areas, local service is provided by switch jobs which work only within the terminal area. A railroad might have one or two large yards and several smaller yards, each serving a given area. Cars are picked up by the switcher and brought to the yard where the switcher is based. Outbound cars from the small yards are brought to the main yard where they are classified by destination and made into outbound through freights. Inbound cars follow the reverse process.

Physical Components

Rail shipments originate and terminate at a variety of facilities. Most common is the private spur track serving one or more customers. Warehouses, factories, grain elevators, tank farms, and mines often have their own spur tracks connecting with the track of a nearby railroad. For those customers who do not have private spurs, loading-unloading facilities for public use are provided by the railroad. Team tracks are simple spurs adjacent to streets or open areas where shipments can be transferred between rail cars and trucks. At many stations, railroads have ramp or crane facilities for loading and unloading highway trailers from rail flatcars (piggyback service).

Rail yards vary in purpose, capacity, and size.[15] The purpose of most yards is classification, or the sorting of cars by destination. Yards are also used to store loaded cars awaiting movement and empty cars held for distribution as needed. Small and medium-size yards are flat yards where cars are sorted by switch engines moving back and forth among the yard tracks. In the largest classification yards incoming cuts of cars are pushed to the top of an incline (hump), uncoupled, and allowed to roll forward into the proper yard track under the force of gravity. While moving down the hump, track switches are aligned by remote control to direct the cars into the desired track. A large yard is often a group of yards—inbound receiving yard, classification yard, outbound departure yard, storage yard for empty cars, shop yard for cars awaiting repairs, and a train yard for holding through trains while changing crews and picking up or setting out blocks of cars. A scale track is frequently part of the yard, since the shipper's freight bill is usually based on shipment weight.

In some cities, two railroads share the use of a yard and its related facilities, either by joint ownership or rental arrangements. As a rule, however, each railroad has its own yard, team track, and piggyback ramp for competitive and convenience reasons. This is true even when a railroad enters a city via joint track or trackage rights over another railroad.

Interchange of cars between railroads is another function associated with terminals. Direct interchange is possible when two railroads have a connection track: the railroads exchange cars bound for destinations on each other's systems. Where no track directly links the two railroads, cars must be handled by one or more intermediate railroads which form a connection.

In several large cities terminal railroads provide interchange among railroads and service to local industries. The terminal railroad can be an independent entity or owned by other railroad companies. In a few cases, a terminal railroad is owned by state or local agencies.[16]

SUMMARY

The railroad industry structure is essentially the same today as it was during the 1840's when the toll railroad concept gave way to steam locomotives, iron rails, and a monopoly of service over each company's tracks. As the nation and its railroad industry grew and matured, the concept of each railroad having its own fixed way resulted in a paradox of monopoly and competition, of independence and interdependence. The problems symptomatic of the traditional industry structure became known as the "Railroad Problem." During the past half century the railroads have come to a state of crisis because their structure has been unable to deal effectively with rising intermodal competition and the expanding free market environment of transportation as a whole.

NOTES

1. Pipelines have terminals and fixed ways; the commodity serves as its own carrier "vehicle." Motive power is provided by fixed pumping stations.
2. Henry S. Haines, *American Railway Management*, p. 2.
3. Edmund J. Phillips, Jr., *Railroad Operation and Railway Signaling*, pp. 38–96.
4. Ibid., pp. 193–203.
5. Bruce P. Curry, "Rutland Revival—Part 1: The Vermont Railway," *Railfan*, Volume 1, Number 3 (Summer 1975), pp. 18–27; Bruce P. Curry and Donald Valentine, Jr., "Rutland Revival—Part 2: Green Mountain Railroad," *Railfan*, Volume 1, Number 4 (Fall 1975), pp. 23–29; and E. H. Blabey II, "Rutland Revival—Part 3: Ogdensburg Bridge & Port Authority," *Railfan*, Volume 1, Number 4 (Fall 1975), pp. 30–32.
6. Kevin P. Keefe, "How Michigan Got into the Railroad Business," *Trains*, Volume 36, Number 12 (October 1976), pp. 46–49; Rush Loving, Jr., "Michigan's Wacky Ride on the Little Railroad That Couldn't," *Fortune*, Volume 98, Number 8 (October 23, 1978), pp. 48–57.
7. A number of "designated operator" companies have contracted to operate former Conrail routes under state-federal subsidy programs. David M. Beers, "Short Line, Bridge Carrier, Marine Operator, Terminal Road," *Trains*, Volume 38, Number 12 (October 1978), pp. 48–57.
8. The following contain detailed descriptions of railroad corporate organization structures: Merle Armitage, *Operations Santa Fe*; Illinois Central Railroad Company, Research and Development Bureau, *Organization and Traffic of the Illinois*

Central System; D. Daryl Wyckoff, Railroad Management; John H. Armstrong, The Railroad—What It Is, What It Does.

9. Jim Panza, "Union Pacific into Chicago," Railfan, Volume 2, Number 3 (April 1978), pp. 18–24; J. David Ingles, "We Are Now Able to Compare Conrail with Conrail," Trains, Volume 37, Number 12 (October 1977), pp. 42–50.

10. Detroit Edison, Amax Coal, and Southeastern Coal are shippers which provide locomotives for use by common carrier railroads. J. David Ingles, "For a Diesel Medley," Trains, Volume 34, Number 12 (October 1974), p. 53; "Coal Operator Solves L&N Problem," Modern Railroads, Volume 33, Number 12 (December 1978), p. 13.

11. For examples of private carrier railroads, see Joseph L. Oates, "The Creatures of Bone Valley," Railfan, Volume 2, Number 7 (November 1978), pp. 46–55; and Louis Saillard, "Last of the Cane Haulers," Rail Classics, Volume 3, Number 2 (May 1974), pp. 18–27.

12. U.S., General Services Administration, United States Government Manual 1974-75, p. 513.

13. Robert D. Bartley, "OSHA: What It's All About, How Railroads Are Complying," Railway Age, Volume 174, Number 24 (December 31, 1973), pp. 31–33; "Arrivals and Departures," Trains, Volume 35, Number 5 (March 1975), p. 13.

14. Descriptions of rail terminals include the following: John A. Droege, Freight Terminals and Trains; H. M. Mayer, The Railway Pattern of Metropolitan Chicago; Railway Systems and Management Association, Terminal Operations; Railway Systems and Management Association, Railroad Terminal Strategy; Ken Kraemer and Devan Lawton, "Buffalo Terminal," Trains, Volume 36, Number 4 (February 1976), pp. 29–43; Herbert H. Harwood, Jr., "Horse-Era Railroading at the Harborside," Railfan, Volume 2, Number 2 (February 1978), pp. 50–58; Jay H. Miller, "Houston's Belt," Railfan, Volume 2, Number 8 (January 1979), pp. 20–26; Daniel L. Overbey and Patrick D. Hiatte, "SY 03-08-80," Trains, Volume 41, Number 3 (January 1981), pp. 22–31.

15. Railway Systems and Management Association, "The Design and Management of Railroad Yards," Railway Management Review, Volume 72, Number 2 (1972), pp. A1–A119.

16. Edward A. Lewis, American Short Line Railway Guide.

7 | ASPECTS OF JOINT USE

Under the traditional structure, each railroad company functions as an independent entity, providing its own fixed way and its own carrier services. Unlike the other modes' carriers which routinely share fixed ways, railroad companies do not usually engage in joint use of fixed ways. The categories of joint use which are found in the railroad industry play an important role as examples showing the feasibility of joint use and the limitations imposed on it by the traditional structure.

Railroad companies enter into certain types of joint operations in which two or more railroads coordinate train service, with each railroad retaining exclusive use of its own tracks. These operations allow railroad companies to integrate independent carrier services to a limited extent. Even though corporate boundaries are respected, coordinated operations indicate the degree of standardization achieved in the railroad industry. In recent years, the Federal Railroad Administration has implemented standards and policies which further encourage standardization and joint use.

JOINT USE

Unlike the other modes which routinely share fixed ways, joint use of trackage plays a minor role in the railroad industry. Joint ownership and trackage rights are two means for sharing track.

Joint Ownership

During previous eras of railroad construction, two competing railroads occasionally compromised and built a jointly owned railroad. In other cases, two or more railroads purchased another railroad to guarantee themselves a "friendly" connection. Owner railroads might share the joint line's trackage, as was often done with terminal railroads serving large cities. In many instances, however, the jointly owned railroad company maintained exclusive use of its own tracks, and even its owners had to interchange cars moving over the joint line.

Trackage Rights

By far the more common means of providing joint use was—and is—trackage rights.[1] Under a trackage rights agreement, the owner railroad grants a tenant railroad the right to operate trains over the owner's tracks. In return, the tenant railroad agrees to pay rental fees. Both railroads share maintenance and operating (traffic control) expenses of the jointly used track, usually on the basis of car-miles or train-miles. A flat fee is often included, based on a percentage of the investment (original cost) in the jointly used line. Ownership of the track remains with the owner railroad.

Several points should be stressed regarding trackage rights. First, the Interstate Commerce Commission must approve most trackage right agreements; however, *it cannot order railroads to enter into trackage right agreements.* In several cases the Commission knowingly permitted the building of parallel, redundant lines, because it lacked the power to compel the joint use of existing tracks. The Commission noted its lack of authority to require joint use, even in cases where substantial benefits would result. The railroad owning a certain segment of track grants trackage rights only if it desires to do so. The owner road can refuse to share its track when doing so is not in its own best interests, regardless of whether the public's best interests are served or not.[2]

Second, the owner road can (and almost always does) prohibit the tenant road from providing local service on the joint segment. Railroads compete fiercely to get industries to locate on their lines. Once a firm builds its plant next to a railroad company's track it becomes a permanent customer—a captive industry, at least as far as rail service is concerned. It can ship by truck, but that is often uneconomic. If it shorthauls the railroad company by routing traffic to another railroad at the nearest junction point, the railroad serving the industry can retaliate by giving bad service between the shipper's plant and that junction point. The shipper is wedded to that railroad company, for better service or worse.

Because of the highly competitive nature of industrial development activity and the security of traffic from captive industries, railroads are extremely reluctant to allow another railroad to directly serve "their" customers. Trackage right agreements specify which tracks may be used by the tenant road, providing control for the owner road.

Further control is given the owner railroad, since it provides dispatching (traffic control) services for all trains using its track. Typical agreements call for equal treatment of each railroad's trains, and experience has shown this to be the rule in most cases. When discrimination occurs it usually happens because of differences in train length, type of train, and other physical factors. Perhaps more disconcerting to railroad managers is the fact that tenant railroad employees come under the jurisdiction of owner road management while on joint track. Owner road managers sometimes resent having to supervise employees of a tenant railroad and tenant road managers dislike losing control of both train crews and train dispatching. Where different codes of operating rules or different signal systems are used by tenant and owner roads, the tenant road's employees must be qualified (examined) on both.

Despite the disadvantages, railroads often find trackage rights useful. In earlier years trackage rights allowed a railroad to enter a new market when building a separate line would have been too costly. The Atchinson, Topeka, & Santa Fe Railway entered southern California over the rails of rival Southern Pacific Railroad. The Santa Fe was prepared to build its own tracks, but both railroads found joint use more economical. Shippers in the region were given competitive rail service without excessive duplication of trackage (Santa Fe did build its own branches to serve shippers). Similarly, the Cotton Belt Route (St. Louis Southwestern Railway) entered East St. Louis by running over the Missouri Pacific Railroad's tracks for 120 miles from southern Illinois. At the time when joint Cotton Belt-Missouri Pacific use began, both railroads were affiliated by ownership. Since that time they have separated but continue joint use of the line, which is one of the most heavily trafficked routes on the Missouri Pacific system. These are but a couple of the numerous examples.

In recent years trackage rights have been used to allow the abandonment of little-used or redundant trackage. A branch line could be abandoned, keeping intact only those segments necessary to connect important shippers with another railroad's track at a nearby junction. The abandoning railroad could continue to provide service by using trackage rights over other railroads to reach the isolated segment(s). The new route would usually be more circuitous but would also be more economic than maintaining many miles of branch line railroad for a small amount of traffic. A number of these isolated branches exist in Oklahoma, where good highways made criss-crossing rail lines uneconomic.

There has also been a revival of sorts in the use of trackage rights to enter new markets, this time under government direction. It was feared by many that the government-sponsored creation of Conrail would stifle competition in the northeastern states. Merged from the bankrupt remains of the Penn Central and several other railroads, Conrail (Consolidated Rail Corporation) would have been a true monopoly of rail service in the Northeast. Conrail's planners therefore offered trackage rights to the Delaware and Hudson (D&H) Railway, a small railroad in upstate New York. D&H service was extended via trackage rights over Conrail lines into Buffalo, Harrisburg, and Newark, all connecting points with non-Conrail lines serving other parts of the nation. This dramatic move nearly doubled the size of the D&H, from 747 miles to 1400-plus. It also provided other railroads with competitive connecting service to major cities in Conrail territory.[3]

Amtrak

The National Rail Passenger Corporation, or Amtrak, was created by Congress to take over intercity rail passenger operations. Amtrak purchased cars and locomotives and bought or leased passenger stations and service facilities. Its trains are operated by railroad companies under contract for Amtrak. Railroad crews operate the Amtrak trains over tracks owned by the railroad company, and the contracts specify performance and service criteria.

Commuter operations in many cities are performed by railroads for government agencies under service contracts. They vary widely from simple subsidies to more stringent contracts with agency-owned equipment. In some cities urban trackage not needed for freight operations has been bought or leased from railroads by local or regional governments for exclusive commuter use.

Amtrak and commuter operations constitute a third form of joint use, since each involves use of railroad company trackage by trains of another entity.

JOINT OPERATIONS

Railroad companies cooperate with each other in a number of ways to offer improved connecting service. Two important examples of interrailroad cooperation are runthrough trains and pre-blocking.

Runthrough trains have flourished during the past decade.[4] Runthroughs operate over two or more railroads using the same locomotive, frequently bypassing intermediate terminals and pausing only to change crews. The direct service afforded by runthrough trains can save several days' transit time on shipments.

Pre-blocking provides expedited handling in cases where there is an insufficient volume of traffic to justify a separate runthrough train. By performing extra switching (sorting) of cars at the train's origin, the train can be split easily at its destination into blocks (groups of cars) for delivery to connecting railroads. This reduces the amount of handling required for all railroads concerned. Cars leapfrog intermediate terminals and move directly to their destination terminal.

Runthrough trains and similar operations where motive power is interchanged as part of a train require that the railroads' locomotives be compatible. Both railroads usually designate a number of locomotives and cabooses for use in the pool service. As motive power requirements vary, locomotives of participating railroads are often mixed in service. Trains may be seen with locomotives from several railroads on a single train. Mixing is possible because locomotives are highly standardized. General Motors' Electromotive Division (EMD) promoted this practice in the 1930's by offering standard diesel locomotives with optional equipment, much as automobiles and trucks were sold. No longer did each railroad's mechanical staff draw complete plans and request bids from builders, as was done with steam locomotives. Instead, models and options were selected from the builder's catalog. General Electric, which entered the domestic locomotive market in 1960, followed suit and offered units compatible with EMD's. Multiple-unit (m.u.) control allowed several locomotive units to be controlled from one unit's cab. The number of units could then be varied with the size of the train, adding or subtracting units to achieve the proper power-tonnage balance.

Although standardization of diesel locomotives has encouraged the creation of runthrough trains and far-ranging power pools, not all problems have been solved. Amtrak passenger diesels, which operate over many railroads, must have three types of fuel tank filler openings to fit the various fuel spouts now in use. Different radio frequencies are used on different railroads. Multiple-unit control cable fittings can be of several types, some compatible and some not. These problems, though, are relatively minor. The greatest hindrances to standardization—standard gauge and standard couplers—were removed nearly a century ago.

INFLUENCE OF THE FEDERAL RAILROAD ADMINISTRATION

The Federal Railroad Administration has taken the initiative in recent years for the development of national rail transportation policy. The most concrete aspect of this has been the creation of track, equipment, and operating procedure standards. Less definite but more influential have been the various stipulations and incentives found in FRA regulations and research which were designed to encourage joint use.

FRA Standards

Prompted by reports of widespread deferred maintenance on several railroads, Congress passed the Federal Rail Safety Act of 1970 and authorized the FRA to set safety standards for various aspects of railroad operation. The first area subject to regulation was track maintenance. Track, the basic component of rail transportation, had not been subject to federal regulation prior to the FRA standards. Standards did exist, promoted by several industry organizations, but compliance was voluntary, and each railroad set its own internal standards. Railroad opposition to the strict new FRA track standards was stiff, and revisions were made.[5] By 1973 FRA track standards were in effect. Tracks were classified on the basis of the number of defects allowed in ties, rails, and other track components. Track class in turn set the maximum speed and other limits. If a section of track contained a sufficient number of defects it could be reduced in class or closed to operations if necessary. FRA inspectors shut down several sections of the Penn Central as unsafe until repairs were made.

FRA Freight Equipment Inspection Standards faced less resistance, as ICC and FRA jurisdiction already existed. The newer standards related to initial and subsequent periodic inspections of rolling stock components.[6] Freight Equipment Inspection Standards were implemented in 1974–75.

The most recent effort of FRA regulation has been the standardization of operating rules and procedures. Although the *Standard Code of Train Rules* was adopted by the American Railroad Association (ARA) in 1886, individual railroads have modified and revised the original *Code* so that substantial differences have developed. Furthermore, as FRA noted,

at present there are no Federally prescribed operating rules and, as a result, the quality, comprehensiveness, and enforcement of each carrier's rules vary considerably from railroad to railroad.[7]

In essence, the FRA was trying to re-accomplish what the ARA had done nearly a century earlier: bring about the common use of a well-designed set of standardized operating rules. Several reasons prompted this effort. First, standardized rules would insure safety and allow federal enforcement on individual railroads. Second, standard rules would remove a major impediment to joint operations.

FRA Policies

Encouragement of joint use has also come from policy activities. The Railroad Revitalization and Regulatory Reform Act of 1975 (the 4-R Act) established a fund administered by FRA for rehabilitation and improvement projects on the nation's railroads. Eligibility for loans was determined by a FRA study entitled "Classification and Designation of Rail Lines" and from railroad-supplied information on capital needs.[8] The study designated Class A Main Lines, Class B Main Lines, and Branch Lines. More importantly, the study identified corridors of consolidation potential (CCP's)—routes served by three or more railroads with total capacity exceeding actual traffic levels by 50 percent or more. The intent was to spotlight those areas where trackage was redundant and where it greatly exceeded the amount needed for adequate service levels. By identification of excess capacity corridors and through its approval and denial of rehabilitation loan applications FRA sought to promote joint use.

The Federal Railroad Administration, unhampered by corporate allegiances, was free to consider railroad problems on an industrywide basis. The FRA recognized that competition need not preclude cooperation and efficiency. By sharing use of trackage, railroads could lower expenses while customers gained the benefits of competitive rail service. Various FRA efforts encouraged joint use, but they were often met with reluctance and resistance on the part of the railroad companies. As preceding chapters have shown, the technological barriers to joint use have been removed; only economic and legal barriers remain.

NOTES

1. Daniel L. Overbey, "Trackage Rights: Advantages and Disadvantages," Transportation Research Forum, *Proceedings—Sixteenth Annual Meeting* (Oxford, Indiana, 1975), pp. 339–347; Jerry A. Pinkepank, "When (and Where and Why) Railroads Share Track," *Trains*, Volume 39, Number 3 (January 1979), pp. 20–29.

2. Among the cases which illustrate the ICC's lack of legal authority to compel the granting of trackage rights are *Alabama, Tennessee, and Northern* (124 ICC 114), *Oregon, California, and Eastern* (124 ICC 529), and *Western Pacific* (162 ICC 5).

3. "Possibility of a Profitable D&H Line Held Out in Study Made for FRA," *Traffic World*, Number 11, Volume 182, Whole Number 3817 (July 16, 1980), pp. 25–27; K. R. Zimmerman, "Big Little D&H," *Trains*, Volume 37, Number 2 (December 1976), p. 12.

4. "Runthrough Trains: The Proof Is in the Bottom Line," *Railway Age*, Volume 175, Number 4 (February 25, 1974), pp. 28–29.

5. "FRA Publishes Proposed Track Standards," *Railway Age*, Volume 170, Number 12 (June 28, 1971), p. 12; "FRA Revises Track Standards," *Railway Age*, Volume 173, Number 5 (September 11, 1972), p. 20.

6. "FRA Proposes Equipment Inspection Standards," *Railway Age*, Volume 173, Number 6 (September 25, 1972), p. 40.

7. "FRA Will Draft Operating Rules," *Railway Age*, Volume 175, Number 21 (November 11, 1974), p. 12.

8. "Congress, Coleman Clash on Rail Bill," *Railway Age*, Volume 177, Number 2 (January 12, 1976), p. 10; "An Advance to 1880?" *Trains*, Volume 37, Number 1 (November 1976), pp. 7–9.

   The FRA classifications are as follows: Class A Main Line, 20 million or more gross ton-miles per mile per year; Class B Main Line, 5 to 20 million gross ton-miles per mile per year; and Branch Lines, less than 5 million gross ton-miles per mile per year. Other designations and subcategories exist, but these are the major ones.

   Corridors of consolidation potential include: Chicago-St. Paul, Chicago-Pittsburgh, Chicago-Buffalo, Chicago-Ohio River, Chicago-Kansas City, Kansas City-Ft. Worth, Ft. Worth-Houston, Chicago-Omaha, Kansas City and Omaha to Colorado, Chicago-St. Louis, and Chicago-Detroit.

8 | ASPECTS OF INNOVATION

The traditional structure of the railroad industry limits and often discourages innovation. Any new idea must pass a number of hurdles prior to implementation, and many never start the course. To consider an idea, a railroad company must decide that it is technically acceptable (meets engineering standards, for example). Then the idea must meet the commercial standards and policies peculiar to that railroad company. The process must be repeated by a number of railroad companies if "the industry" is to accept the idea. Since each railroad company can serve only as far as its own tracks extend, an innovation is frequently of little value unless most railroads adopt it.

In spite of the structure, several important operational and technological innovations have appeared in recent decades. Some have been far-reaching, and others have significance only as precedents and pioneering efforts. These innovations are primarily related to rail service, though labor productivity and technological developments are also involved. Improvements in technology alone can help make railroads more efficient, but they cannot win the traffic war—at best they provide only a rear-guard holding action. In the other modes, a broad array of carrier services and prices are available. To compete effectively rail carriers must offer a similar diversity. Instead, the present railroad structure discourages diversity and promotes service at the least common denominator level.

The following examples indicate the potential for rail transportation if a wider range of services were made available. They also show the resistance to change found in the traditional railroad structure.

OPERATIONAL CHANGES

The Fireman Dispute

In 1937 the railroads and their unions signed the Diesel Agreement. Diesels were being used as yard switchers and on a few passenger trains, but steam locomotives ruled the rails. Diesels amounted to less than 1 percent of all locomotives.[1] Most people in the industry felt electrification would be the next big change, following the example of the Pennsylvania Railroad's electrified Harrisburg-New York main line. Diesels would serve branch lines.

The committee representing railroad management had achieved a good agreement with the unions, or so it seemed. Firemen were a necessity on steam locomotives, shoveling coal or operating other fuel feed devices. On diesels and electrics they served no purpose. In their contract, the railroads agreed to use firemen on all diesels over 90,000 pounds (45 tons). Small diesels, such as those which would be used on branch lines, would not have a fireman and—most important—firemen would not be required on any electric locomotive.

Problems developed after World War II when the railroads did not electrify. Significant advances in diesel technology turned the economics in the diesel's favor. By 1959, diesels moved over 97 percent of all rail freight tonnage.[2] The unions requested that a fireman be placed on each unit of a multiple-unit diesel; railroads asked to drop firemen from freight trains and switchers. The final settlement, reached after nearly a decade of disagreement, allowed the elimination of firemen on all except 10 percent of freight runs. Passenger trains would still have firemen. One account states that 20,000 of the 45,000 firemen "elected other railroad positions or accepted severance pay and left the industry."[3]

Both sides lost money and public prestige during the long battle, which began during the mid-1950's. The unions lost jobs and members. The railroads "won" the right to eliminate a non-essential crew member which had been on the payroll for years. Perhaps the most important result was that the dispute had been resolved. In any case, efficiency had finally triumphed.

Florida East Coast Strike

Another long battle with a significant resolution was the Florida East Coast (FEC) Railway's strike, which began in 1962.[4] To this day many railroad men consider "Florida East Coast" to be fighting words. FEC emerged from bankruptcy only to face demands for large wage increases in 1962. FEC decided to reject the national settlement of a 4.5 percent increase given to non-operating employees. A strike quickly followed, with operating employees honoring the pickets. Calculations indicated FEC could survive longer on strike than it could by paying the wage increases from its meager cash flow. Management made plans to resume operation despite the strike.

FEC's management learned a lot about training and productivity during the following years. Under the union's "100-mile day" each crew was paid a full day's wages for the few hours it took to run 100 miles. Three different five-man crews were needed to take a train from Jacksonville to Miami. After the strike a single two-man crew (conductor and engineer) regularly made the entire run in ten or eleven hours, drawing two or three hours' overtime. Total labor cost for such a run at that time was approximately $120, much less than the $690 under union rules. FEC could afford to run four of its sixteen daily trains just to move empty cars off its line, avoiding per diem (rental) charges. FEC trains operated by timetable, rather than waiting for enough cars to accumulate in the yard to justify running a full-tonnage train (common practice on many railroads). With the non-union rules customers received better service which allowed FEC to carry more traffic with a smaller capital investment, since there was no need to store large numbers of cars waiting for trains.

Yard and road work divisions, found in union rules, were abolished. Road crews helped switch their trains both at terminals and along their route. The Jacksonville yard used an unmanned switching locomotive, radio-controlled by a switch foreman on the ground.

Labor savings led to increased profits which were consistently reinvested in FEC's fixed plant. Block-signaled double track was taken up and replaced by single track with centralized traffic control. Traffic capacity was increased; maintenance costs decreased.

Today, three-mile sidings with high-speed turnouts allow trains to pass without slowing down. The rail is 132 pound, continuous welded, bolted to concrete ties on crushed granite ballast. In many respects the Florida East Coast is one of the best maintained and most efficiently operated railroads in the world, due in large measure to its elimination of obsolete work rules and outmoded operating practices.

Illinois Central Minitrain

In 1969 the Illinois Central Railroad conducted experiments with a new train service designed to be competitive with truck highway service. Shippers, railroad employees, and railroad officials all felt the service was a success—except in one regard:

> The only way the train proved unsuccessful was in generating a profit for the Illinois Central. And that is the most important way in determining whether or not the Mini-Train will run again.
>
> —Sheldon Landy, Manager
> Marketing Services, IC[5]

For the experiments IC rented a locomotive, five covered hoppers, and a caboose to Swift & Company. IC operated the train to local rural grain elevators, moving soybeans to Swift's processing plant in Champaign, Illinois. The train left empty hopper cars at the elevators and brought in loaded ones. IC charged Swift a $400.00 per day flat rate plus $3.50 per train-mile based on the most distant point served.[6] Soybeans were shipped from 27 points on five different union-seniority districts, with a round-trip distance of 70 miles average. The train moved over the main lines and branches without interfering with other traffic.

Illinois Central had hoped to experiment with crew sizes and crew jurisdiction, but an agreement could not be reached in time. *Railway Age* reported:

> As a result, IC is using "standard" crews. And in at least one case, this involves payment for 32 man-days for a mini-train movement between Champaign and the Rantoul, Illinois, area.[7]

Crews were changed when the train moved into a different seniority district. In some cases a road crew waited while a yard crew switched the cars. A conductor, engineer, two brakemen, and (at times) a fireman made up the full-size crews. Labor rules made the Minitrain unprofitable. There was hope IC could subsequently negotiate more favorable agreements after proving the concept feasible, but the revised agreements did not materialize.

According to IC President Alan S. Boyd, the test proved railroads could compete with trucks in the short-haul market "under certain conditions for which we need the cooperation of the unions."[8] The tests were conducted in the 50- to 75-mile market which, under standard railway thinking, was "all but conceded to the trucks." The tests proved Minitrain could be truck competitive at line hauls of less than *two* miles.

For the railroads, efficiency was often equated with long trains operated only when a sufficiently large number of carloads was available. Boyd, previously Secretary of Transportation, had hoped that the concept of short trains could be used to compete for highly profitable short-haul traffic being moved by trucks. "One is tempted to wonder," said Boyd, "if the railroads might not be a little more successful if they could bring themselves to be a little less efficient."[9] He continued, "about 80 percent of all dollars spent by our economy for transportation is spent for carriage less than 300 miles long. *And that is exactly the market that railroads, increasingly, are abandoning to the trucks*" (Boyd's italics). Minitrain sought to meet truck competition head-on, by operating trains like trucks. Lack of agreement over work rules necessitated the use of standard rules, rules never meant for such innovative situations. The Minitrain project failed to meet the economic test of profitability because of outmoded work rules.

Commoditrain

Thirty years ago railroads carried over a third of all sand and gravel shipped in the United States. Today, they carry only about 7 percent and wish they had less, for in most cases it is not profitable.[10] Moving this short-haul traffic in conventional local train service means up to several days transit time, requiring the customer to maintain in-transit inventories. Much of the transit time finds the cars sitting in yards along the way. Even more important, the time involved necessitates that a large number of cars be assigned to the service. As railroad analyst John Kneiling observes, "Conventional railroading is a lost cause in this business."[11]

The Chicago and Northwestern Railroad negotiated an experimental agreement with the United Transportation Union (UTU) and the Brotherhood of Locomotive Engineers covering a 60-day period during the summer of 1971. Three-man crews took the 20- to 25-car trains over five seniority districts without changing crews. The crews performed both road and yard work, handling switching at both ends of the run as well as over-the-road movement. Three round trips a week were made between South Beloit, Illinois, and Chicago. Empties were moved to Beloit one day and returned to three Chicago locations with loads the next day. *Commoditrain* crews were paid on a time, not distance, basis.[12] Each man received $13 per day plus the amount paid for a regular freight run.

The experiment proved successful for C&NW, the unions, and the shippers involved.[13] What had previously been at best marginal traffic was made profitable under the new operation and also provided more jobs for C&NW employees. Car utilization greatly increased, allowing the railroad to handle greater traffic volumes with the existing car fleet. Shippers got faster, more dependable service at rail rates lower than truck rates.

Commoditrain service was expanded the following summer. One train handled aggregates in South Dakota; another moved cement between two plants in Mason City, Iowa, and distributors in Burnsville, Minnesota.[14]

A. T. Kearney and Company, transportation consultants, termed *Commoditrain* the "most significant new aggregate-train concept to date."[15] Their report to the Constructive Aggregate Shippers Conference (CARS) recommended that railroads seek agreements giving flexibility to preserve existing traffic and attract new business. "Rails should ultimately operate like trucks," concluded the Kearney study.[16] The train would move between supplier and consignee—like a giant truck.

The Chicago, Rock Island, and Pacific Railroad (Rock Island) began operating "mini-unit trains" in 1973.[17] Manned by three-man crews, the trains ran 93 miles in Oklahoma from a quarry to a concrete batch plant. The train used 15 air-activated side-dump cars taken from track-maintenance service. Under previous procedures, this traffic "got four separate rail moves and two yardings, and rock cars commonly required two weeks for a roundtrip."[18] On the minitrain, the roundtrip was cut to 10 hours since two runs could be made in a single day. The unions agreed that the service could only be successful with a streamlined operation, including price reductions made possible by smaller crews. The new service made jobs for rail employees while adding much-needed profits for the Rock.

Commoditrains and similar operations have proven successful not only on the C&NW and Rock Island but also on the Milwaukee Road and other lines where they have since been instituted. The service efficiency and cost of these minitrains have enabled them to make a profit from what was previously unprofitable traffic, securing it from truck competition. They have proven that rail efficiency, given the proper operational structure, can be more than just textbook theory.

Short Line Practice

Short lines are small railroads, usually only a few miles long and serving at best a handful of industries. Many are marginal in economic terms and survive only on the tightest of budgets. Their localized nature allows them profitably to perform services a major railroad could not.

"Everyone has to carry his own weight on a shortline," states Craig Burroughs, President of Trans-Action Associates, a railroad consulting firm specializing in short lines.[19] The major railroads have many labor-protective practices which result in "pay for work not done and unnecessary jobs."[20] Most short lines are not unionized, even though employees may have worked for larger lines and still retain union membership. On the few short lines that are unionized, labor tends to be more flexible and cooperative than on major railroads. Short lines use fewer workers and pay them less than a large railroad would for the same tasks.[21]

Employees accept these conditions, because they have regular hours and are never far from home. The short line's financial status has a much closer effect on its employees than would that of a large railroad. Unions usually recognize that it is better to have a job at local wage rates than no job at all. Officials of the unions seldom find it worthwhile to organize the few workers on a short line. In any case they will not do so unless the workers request unionization.[22]

A short line which might serve as a precedent for larger railroads is the Providence and Worcester Railroad (P&W). The P&W, under lease to larger railroads since 1892, resumed independent operation in 1973. An agreement signed with the United Transportation Union (UTU) in 1974 had repercussions throughout the industry. "The tiny Providence and Worcester Railroad has rolled to a precedent-shattering agreement," wrote the *Wall Street Journal*.[23] It noted, "the United Transportation Union gave the Providence and Worcester major work-rule concessions, that, three days later, it struck the giant Penn Central railroad to avoid giving."[24]

The agreement removes most craft distinctions. One classification covers all employees except clerical and maintenance personnel. Three-man crews operate the trains, which carry cabooses only because of Massachusetts law.[25] Since the 100-mile rule was abolished, crews can cover more than 100 miles in a day without receiving extra pay. "Arbitraries" were eliminated, allowing crews to cross certain craft lines, carry radio handsets (walkie-talkies), and perform other duties without receiving extra pay. Overtime was eliminated. Employees work approximately the same number of hours each month regardless of seniority.

R. H. Eder, P&W President, called the agreement "a very progressive contract" which could serve as a model for other railroads.[26] Archaic work rules were eliminated by offering employees money in return. The UTU, which had threatened to strike Penn Central over proposed three-man crews, did not consider the P&W agreement as a precedent. "You can't even talk about them in the same context," answered UTU President Al Chesser.[27] The size difference—Penn Central's 20,000 miles versus P&W's 50 miles—removed any similarity, according to Chesser. However, the agreement was given wide coverage in the press, and, although it did not serve as a model for later national agreements, it has served as an example of innovation in railroad work rules and operations.

Slingshot, Sprint

In 1975 the Illinois Central Gulf inaugurated the *Slingshot*, a new train service designed to meet the special needs of piggyback traffic between Chicago and St. Louis.[28] That corridor, a relatively short 280 miles, has long been characterized by intense highway competition and the presence of several other railroad companies. For piggyback shippers, the *Slingshot* offers speed, frequency, dependability, and rate reductions ranging from 23 percent to 43 percent. Train frequency and scheduling are aimed at customer convenience, with three trains daily in each direction.

The *Slingshots* achieve efficiency through high productivity of capital and labor. Each train has a maximum of 15 cars and operates with a single-unit locomotive. The trains run without cabooses, and—most importantly—crews consist of only a conductor and an engineer. *Slingshots* make no intermediate stops, perform no switching, have a 65 mph maximum speed, and use an eight-hour schedule.

The *Slingshot* service began with an experiment during one week in February 1975, after which the ICG negotiated a special agreement with the union. *Slingshot* began regular service with one train daily each way on August 18, 1975. Service expanded to three trains daily by the end of the year. The service incurred a loss during its first year, but in 1977, 31,000 trailers were carried, gross revenues were $3.9 million, and profits were reportedly over 5 percent. The *Slingshot* was successful with the shippers, the unions, and the railroad.

The Milwaukee Road started its *Sprint* trains between Chicago and St. Paul on June 4, 1978.[29] The Federal Railroad Administration sponsored the service as demonstration of the potential for fast, frequent piggyback service. *Sprint* trains had a maximum of 25 cars and a maximum speed of 60 mph. Instead of the six four-man crews usually needed for a round trip on their route, a special agreement allowed the *Sprints* to use three three-man crews. Trains ran on a ten-hour schedule over the 400-mile corridor and made one round trip daily. In late 1978, *Sprint* offered customers 42 trains a week, with no departures over six hours apart.[30] *Sprint* trains did not earn a profit until early 1979, but they later became profitable enough to warrant continued operation after assistance through the FRA program ceased.

The Milwaukee's *Sprint* trains provided valuable information as an FRA demonstration, but they served largely to confirm what ICG's *Slingshots* had been proving daily for two and a half years previously. Of course, both services are roughly patterned after the fast, frequent trains which Florida East Coast (FEC) Railway began during its strike in the early 1960's. In late 1978, FEC was running seven piggyback trains daily between Jacksonville and southern Florida.

Slingshot, Sprint, and FEC have proven that the railroads can compete with trucks for traffic in short-haul (under 300-mile) markets if the train service is designed properly. Speed, frequency, and reliability are essential to successful competition in these markets. This kind of service can be offered profitably only if the productivity of labor and capital are maximized through the use of reduced crew consists and high utilization of equipment. Significantly, these trains have attracted mostly traffic from nearby highways, which is new traffic for the railroads.[31]

Three-Man Crew Agreements

In early 1978 the Milwaukee Road reached an agreement with the United Transportation Union (UTU) which provided for the operation of trains with a three-man crew consisting of an engineer, conductor, and brakeman.[32] Before, crews were required to have two brakemen for a total of four men. A few previous local agreements allowed three-man crews for special operations such as *Commoditrains.* The Chicago and North Western (C&NW) had signed an agreement providing for three-man crews in regular operations, but it was generally regarded as an exception in the rail industry. The Milwaukee Road agreement set a precedent followed subsequently by the Consolidated Rail Corporation (Conrail), the Richmond, Fredericksburg, and Potomac Railroad, and the Missouri Pacific Railroad agreements.[33]

The UTU-Milwaukee Road agreement permits three-man crews to operate trains of up to 70 cars (not exceeding 3955 feet). Trains over 120 cars (6780 feet) must have a four-man crew. Use of three-man crews on trains of 70 to 120 cars is possible if agreement is reached with UTU representatives on a local basis.

For each duty tour (train or yard job) worked with a three-man crew the initial agreement called for the railroad company to pay $48.25 into an Employee Productivity Fund. This amount is not subject to wage increases or cost-of-living adjustments; it represents the wages which would have been paid to the fourth crewman. The railroad's savings come from the reduction in fringe benefits and other expenses. Periodically the fund's proceeds are divided among "protected" conductors and brakemen on the basis of the number of duty tours worked during the period. Protected employees are those on the roster as of the agreement's initial date. The amount received from the fund is limited to one-third of the crewman's total compensation.

In addition to the Employee Productivity Fund payments, all conductors and brakemen (protected or not) receive extra pay of $4.00 for each duty tour worked on a three-man crew. Nicknamed "lonesome pay" since the conductor usually rides alone on the caboose, the extra pay is recognition of the "additional services and responsibilities" assumed by crewmen in a reduced crew. The lonesome pay is subject to wage and cost-of-living increases.

The Milwaukee Road's agreement provides that any reduction in the brakeman positions available to protected employees would come only through attrition. A provision in the new contract does allow for early retirement in certain cases to encourage attrition.

Two Canadian railroads, the Canadian National and the Canadian Pacific, both reached crew consist agreements with UTU on more favorable terms.[34] The Canadian agreements have no train length limits, have no lonesome pay provisions, limit employees' share of savings to 25 percent, and put a time limit of ten years on the sharing of savings. The Canadian union leaders expressed the belief that the railroads' financial condition was of prime concern to the employees and that, in the long run, profitability contributed more toward job security than specific work rules. In the United States, UTU leaders held to the terms set initially by the Milwaukee Road contract. If financially troubled railroads like Milwaukee and Conrail could afford the agreement, it was felt the profitable railroads could also. Although a national agreement had not been reached—crew consist was to be decided on an individual railroad basis—a precedent had been established and other railroads were trying to reach agreements along the same lines.

Further Work Rule Developments

As the railroad industry entered the 1980's, the Florida East Coast approached twenty years of safe, efficient, and economically successful operation with two-man crews and no cabooses on its trains. The ICG *Slingshots* had over five years of operation with two-man crews. During a long strike with the Clerks' union, the Norfolk and Western Railway showed that normal-length trains could be run successfully with two-man crews.[35] Yet, although a handful of railroads had signed three-man crew agreements, the four-man crew remained the norm throughout the railroad industry.

If anything is obvious, it is how slowly change comes to the rail labor scene.[36] The fireman dispute lasted from around 1939 to 1959; it took nearly twenty years to change from a five-man to a four-man crew. The three-man crew issue had its roots in the fireman dispute and reached its present state of resolution during the late 1970's—again, about twenty years. Since the feasibility of two-man crews has been proven several times over, the question arises: Will the railroads and rail unions wait until the year 2000 to accept the two-man crew? Moreover, can they afford to wait that long?

TECHNOLOGICAL ADVANCEMENTS

Two general areas of technological advancement have the potential to affect train operations significantly. Control of a locomotive by radio from a remote location allows the engineer's functions to be assumed by another person, like a yardmaster or switch foreman. Automation provides for operation without any crewmen on board the train.

Remote Control

The earliest example of remote control of a locomotive was an experiment conducted in 1914 by the Union Pacific Railroad.[37] A small steam locomotive was successfully controlled via radio by an operator located over a mile away. It was not until the 1960's, however, that remote control left the experimental stage and achieved widespread practical use.

The first unmanned switch locomotive to enter regular service in the United States did so in 1962, about the time of America's first manned space flight. Transportation Services, Incorporated, operated it at their Florence, Alabama, rail-to-barge coal transfer terminal.[38] From a central tower, one man controlled both the locomotive and the conveyor system used to load barges. Radio was used to control the locomotive as it pulled loaded cars over the conveyor dump and returned them to the nearby yard. A failsafe system retarded the locomotive's throttle and applied the brakes if the radio signal failed.

Another unmanned switcher entered service at a plant owned by the DuPont Company. A five-pound remote control pack was carried by an operator on the ground who also acted as brakeman. As *Modern Railroads* reported:

> With this portable radio equipment, the operator becomes a one-man crew. Besides remotely controlling the movements of the locomotive, he throws switches, flags at crossings, spots and couples cars, and rides the locomotive into long storage tracks.[39]

Since the early 1960's, remote control locomotives have flourished at mines, factories, and other industrial applications.[40] Acceptance has been rapid and widespread, because such locomotives are highly efficient. Another factor promoting industrial use of remote control locomotives is the greater tolerance of technological innovation exhibited by industrial unions as compared to railroad unions.

Use of remote control locomotives by common carrier railroads has been rare. The New York Central Railroad had a remote control switching unit ready for use at its Elkhart, Indiana, yard when that facility opened in 1957.[41] The unit was used only for demonstration purposes due to threatened labor retaliation and was soon retired. During the late 1960's the Florida East Coast Railway began using a remote control switcher at its Jacksonville, Florida, yard. It was essentially the same control device used in numerous industrial applications, except this time a common carrier was using it.

One form of specialized remote control locomotive which is used by major railroads is the slave unit. Controlled by radio from the usual locomotive at the front end of the train, slave units are placed in the middle of the train. This offers several advantages over the addition of more power at the head end of the train. When all of the locomotive units are located at the front of the train, tremendous forces are exerted on the train's couplers and drawbars. By locating some of the units back in the train, motive power forces are spread more evenly. The lead units pull some of the cars; some are pushed by the slave units, and the rear portion is pulled by the slaves. This type of operation has been particularly successful in mountain railroading where the mid-train units can also utilize their dynamic braking to assist in train control.

Specialized types of remote control such as slave units are significant, but the greatest potential for productivity improvement on common carrier railroads has yet to be addressed. Switching services—both yard switching and road switching—could be performed by one-man (or at most, two-man) crews. This is fact, not supposition, since industrial firms do so every day. The technology is proven and readily available, waiting only to be applied.

Automation

Beyond remote control lies automation. Remote control allows the locomotive operator to be located someplace other than the locomotive's cab; automation replaces the operator with machine control. Simpler forms of automation utilize trackside markers and are applicable to rigid operations such as shuttle trains between a mine and a power plant on a private track. More complex forms of automation would link computerized traffic control systems to locomotives via radio. There are some types of train operations, industrial switching for example, that are so complex that automation would be difficult and uneconomic. There are operations, however, which could be automated with relative ease.

Automated rail operations began to appear during the early 1960's. Automated subways came into use in both New York and Moscow at that time.[42] The New York train operated between Times Square and Grand Central Station at 30 miles per hour, controlled by coded electric-current signals in the rails. The motorman had no duties to perform, but his job was required by the union.[43] Rapid transit systems have since turned to automated control in great numbers. Philadelphia's Lindenwold Line and San Francisco's Bay Area Rapid Transit (BART) are two examples.

Automation technology has been applied to freight operations as well as passenger operations. In September 1962 *Railway Age* reported the successful operation of the first crewless freight train.[44] Owned by the Iron Ore Company (IOCO) of Canada, four 18-car trains shuttled six miles between loader and dumper at IOCO's western Labrador plant. The locomotives were modified General Motors GP-9's, general purpose locomotives used on almost every major American railroad.

In the United States, only one automated freight railroad is currently in operation.[45] The Muskingum Electric Railroad began operation in February 1969 and has served as a prototype in several respects. It is owned by American Electric Power Company, not a railroad company.[46] It was the first electrified railroad to use 25,000-volt commercial alternating current for propulsion in the United States, and it is fully automated. Two crewless 15-car trains shuttle between the coal mine's loading tipple and a transfer dumper. The locomotives have radio remote control, but in automated service they are controlled by trackside markers which actuate controls for speed, direction, and other functions. For over a decade, the Muskingum's automated trains have delivered 18,000 tons of coal daily.

Five years after the Muskingum Electric Railroad began service, another automated railroad was started in Arizona. The Black Mesa and Lake Powell (BM&LP) Railroad was built to haul coal from the Black Mesa mine 80 miles to the Navajo Power Plant at Page, Arizona.[47] The BM&LP was designed to carry 17,000 tons of coal daily in trains of 77 120-ton cars. The mine, railroad, and generating plant are owned by the Salt River Project, a joint venture utility.

The BM&LP was designed to run automatically with an operator riding the locomotive to monitor the train. However, the automated control system had problems and was eventually retired in favor of manual operation. The BM&LP's experience with automation, while less than successful, advanced the state of the art and indicated technical problems which required further attention.

OBSTACLES TO IMPLEMENTATION

The use of modern work rules and advanced technology has been frustrated by labor opposition, lack of capital, and general resistance to innovation. Rail unions have fought changes in order to protect jobs and wages. Although such an attitude may be shortsighted, it can be politically successful for union leadership. The railroads' financial problems are well known and are felt throughout the interdependent rail industry, even by the strong railroads. With some railroad companies struggling to maintain their track, investment in advanced technology is often out of the question.

More pervasive, however, is the reluctance of railroad management and labor to accept change. Due to their size and early rise to success, the railroads have tended to become conservative and remain so. They have long been the "establishment" in transportation. Daryl Wyckoff, an expert on railroad organization, has devoted an entire chapter of his book *Railroad Management* to the resistance to change.[48]

These obstacles to implementation have created a gap between the common carrier freight railroads—the railroad industry—and other forms of rail transport. For years, private industrial railroads have used one-man crews for switching with radio remote control locomotives. The Muskingum Electric Railroad and several rapid transit systems have proven the feasibility of automation, though the BM&LP has shown that further refinements are needed for large-scale applications. It is symptomatic of the railroads' problems that most research and innovation in the vital area of labor productivity and use of advanced technology have occurred outside the railroad industry.

Given the pace of previous productivity improvements in the crew consist issue, will it be fifty years before today's technology is accepted? As President of the Illinois Central Gulf Railroad, Alan S. Boyd said in 1975 that work rules inhibit productivity and prevent the application of available technology. "We should get rid of cabooses in most through train operations," he noted, "and we must have flexibility in crew sizes and operations. We've got to get some basis where we can be flexible; and it seems to me that if the requirement is a guaranteed annual wage or a lifetime contract—well OK!"[49]

Obstacles to the implementation of work rule changes and advanced technology are real. They are also surmountable if those responsible desire to address the problems at hand. There has been little inclination to face these issues squarely, however, because the existing railroad industry structure encourages the status quo, insulating both railroad companies and rail unions from many of the competitive free market forces found in the other modes. Change must come if the rail industry is to survive in the private sector.

NOTES

1. Derek C. Bok and John T. Dunlop, *Labor and the American Community* (New York, 1970), p. 272.
2. Raymond L. Cook, *The Railroad Work Rules Dispute 1959-1966: The Background, Issues, Settlement, and Implications,* unpublished M.B.A. Professional Report (The University of Texas at Austin, Austin, Texas, 1966).
3. Bok and Dunlop, p. 272.
4. Accounts of the Florida East Coast Railway include: "Fast On-and-Off at the FEC," *Progressive Railroading,* Volume 21, Number 11 (November 1978),

p. 43; "The FEC Story: Survival Without Unions?" *Railway Age*, Volume 157, Number 4 (July 27, 1964), p. 34; "Florida East Coast Strike: Beginning of the End," *Railway Age*, Volume 172, Number 1 (January 10, 1972), p. 11; Nancy Ford, "Can FEC Go It Alone?" *Modern Railroads*, Volume 18, Number 5 (May 1964), p. 61; Nancy Ford, "Florida East Coast: Still Struck, Still Operating, Still Militant," *Modern Railroads*, Volume 20, Number 3 (March 1965), p. 67; Rush Loving, Jr., "Ed Ball's Marvelous, Old-Style Money Machine," *Fortune*, Volume XC, Number 6 (December 1974), p. 170–185; Luther Miller, "Florida East Coast: We Dared to Be Different," *Railway Age*, Volume 180, Number 22 (November 26, 1979), pp. 26–30; David P. Morgan, "FEC: The Metamorphosis Road," *Trains*, Volume 30, Number 8 (June 1970), p. 3; David P. Morgan, "Where Did the Railroad Go That Once Went to Sea?" *Trains*, Volume 35, Number 4 (February 1975), pp. 22–28; "Now, This Is the Way to Run a Railroad," *Business Week* (September 7, 1974), p. 66.

5. "Mini-Train an Operating Success," *Illinois Central Magazine*, Volume 61, Number 2 (July 1969), p. 2.

6. "Mini-Train Lives," *Railway Age*, Volume 166, Number 23 (June 30, 1969), p. 11.

7. Ibid. The distance is approximately 14 miles.

8. Luther Miller, "As the Editor Sees It," *Railway Age*, Volume 167, Number 18 (November 10, 1969), p. 32.

9. "Meet a Heretic," *Trains*, Volume 30, Number 3 (January 1970), p. 8.

10. Frank E. Shaffer, "Profits in Aggregates by Rail Depicted in A. T. Kearney Study," *Modern Railroads*, Volume 27, Number 6 (June 1972), p. 56.

11. John G. Kneiling, "A Tale of Three Trains—1: How to Make Money Hauling Gravel," *Trains*, Volume 35, Number 3 (January 1975), p. 36.

12. "Commoditrain Gets Union Go Ahead," *Railway Age*, Volume 171, Number 5 (September 13, 1971), p. 16.

13. "C&NW/UTU Agreement," *Railway Age*, Volume 171, Number 9 (November 8, 1971), p. 24.

14. "C&NW Adds Commoditrains," *Railway Age*, Volume 172, Number 11 (June 12, 1972), p. 12.

15. "Can Rails Win a Bigger Share of Aggregates Traffic?" *Railway Age*, Volume 172, Number 8 (April 24, 1972), p. 30.

16. Ibid., p. 39.

17. "Marketing Effort Aims at Aggregates," *Railway Age*, Volume 174, Number 20 (October 29, 1973), p. 17.

18. Ibid.

19. "The Big Push into Shortline Railroads," *Business Week*, Number 2302 (October 20, 1973), p. 104.

20. Ibid.

21. Charles P. Zlatkovich and E. H. Enochs, "Short-Line Railroads of Texas," *Texas Business Review*, Volume XLIII, Number 9 (September 1969), reprint.

22. "Shippers Form Groups to Buy Lines the Big Railroads Are Seeking to Unload," *Wall Street Journal*, Volume CLXXXII, Number 126 (December 28, 1973), p. 11.

23. "Union Pact with Small Providence Road Grants Concessions Denied Penn Central," *Wall Street Journal*, Volume CLXXXI, Number 34 (February 16, 1973), p. 8.

24. Ibid.
25. Edwin Strauss, "The P&W Rolls Again," *Rail Classics*, Volume 3, Number 1 (February 1974), p. 40.
26. "P&W: New England's Newest," *Railway Age*, Volume 174, Number 4 (February 26, 1973), p. 14.
27. "Union Pact with Small Providence Road . . . ," p. 8.
28. Descriptions of the ICG *Slingshot* include: David P. Morgan, "The Cabooseless Trains," *Trains*, Volume 36, Number 3 (January 1976), pp. 3–4; Peter P. Novas, "Profitability in Intermodalism," *Progressive Railroading*, Volume 21, Number 11 (November 1978), pp. 29–31; Robert Roberts, "Service Is Golden," *Modern Railroads*, Volume 33, Number 6 (June 1978), pp. 44–47; Gus Welty, "Lines on Labor," *Railway Age*, Volume 176, Number 23 (December 8, 1975), p. 14.
29. "Will 'Sprint' Finish in the Money?" *Railway Age*, Volume 180, Number 20 (October 29, 1979), pp. 26–27.
30. Robert Roberts, "Hustling for Traffic," *Modern Railroads*, Volume 33, Number 12 (December 1978), p. 69.
31. "Innovative and Inventive," *Modern Railroads*, Volume 34, Number 6 (June 1979), p. 56.
32. The Milwaukee Road's formal name is the Chicago, Milwaukee, St. Paul, and Pacific Railroad Company. It should be explained that some articles make a distinction between train crew and engine crew. The engine crew is the engineer and, when used, a fireman. The train crew is the conductor and two brakemen. Even though a brakeman often rides the locomotive, he is part of the train crew, not the engine crew. Thus, some magazines speak of two-man crews and refer only to the train crew, excluding the engineer.

    Engine crews are usually represented by the Brotherhood of Locomotive Engineers (BLE), and train crews are typically represented by the United Transportation Union (UTU). This distinction frequently poses problems in crew consist issues: since the fireman dispute has been resolved, reduction has minimal effects on the BLE and significant effects on the UTU.

    For purposes of this chapter, the *train crew* is defined as all persons on the train including the engine crew. The three-man crew consists of an engineer, a conductor, and a brakeman. Although the terms are masculine, women are holding these jobs in increasing numbers and the job titles are defined as neutral with regard to sex.
33. Articles describing three-man crew agreements include: Terry Breen, "Labor Pains," *Modern Railroads*, Volume 33, Number 12 (December 1978), pp. 63–64; "Conrail, UTU Sign Crew Consist Pact," *Railway Age*, Volume 179, Number 8 (September 25, 1978), p. 14; "Milwaukee: A Breakthrough on Crew Consist?" *Railway Age*, Volume 179, Number 7 (April 10, 1978), pp. 10–12; Gus Welty, "Crew Consist: The New Pacts Are Paying Off," *Railway Age*, Volume 181, Number 6 (March 31, 1980), pp. 48–50; Gus Welty, "Lines on Labor," *Railway Age*, Volume 176, Number 23 (December 8, 1975), p. 14.
34. Welty, "Crew Consist," p. 48.
35. Robert E. Bedingfield, *The Norfolk and Western Strike of 1978* (Roanoke, Virginia, 1979); David P. Morgan, "The FEC of Appalachia," *Trains*, Volume 39, Number 3 (January 1979), p. 3.

36. Studies and commentaries advocating changed work rules and operations include: "The Comeback Is Getting Up Steam," *Forbes* (January 15, 1967), reprint; Robert H. Leilech, *The Economics of Short Trains*, p. 28; Reed C. Richardson, *The Locomotive Engineer 1863-1963* (Ann Arbor, Michigan, 1973), p. 433 (findings of the Presidential Commission on work rules); Tom Shedd, "Understanding and Trust," *Modern Railroads*, Volume 30, Number 1 (January 1975), p. 58; U.S., Department of Labor, Bureau of Labor Statistics, *Railroad Technology and Manpower of the 1970's*, Bulletin 1717 (Washington, D.C., 1972), p. 63.

37. "Remote Control," *Trains*, Volume 19, Number 3 (January 1959), p. 21.

38. "Remote Control Aids Fast Coal Transfer," *Railway Age*, Volume 152, Number 10 (March 12, 1962), p. 12.

39. "Radio Controls Plant Switcher," *Modern Railroads*, Volume 17, Number 3 (March 1962), p. 97.

40. John H. Armstrong, "Industrial Car Movers: New Power in an Old Package," *Railway Age*, Volume 181, Number 5 (March 10, 1980), pp. 25–26.

41. Frank E. Shaffer, "The Elusive Goal," *Modern Railroads*, Volume 34, Number 11 (October 1979), p. 69.

42. "First Crewless Freight Train," *Railway Age*, Volume 153, Number 10 (September 3, 1962), p. 12.

43. "Radio Controls Plant Switcher," p. 97.

44. "First Crewless Freight Train," p. 12.

45. John B. Corns, "Ohio's Robot Railroad," *Trains*, Volume 39, Number 5 (March 1979), pp. 22–28; Frank E. Shaffer, "The Elusive Goal," p. 68.

46. Tom Shedd, "Mine Railroad Previews Future Electrification," *Modern Railroads*, Volume 24, Number 9 (September 1969), p. 75.

47. Articles on the Black Mesa and Lake Powell Railroad include: "BM&LP: First 50 Kv Electrification," *Railway Age*, Volume 175, Number 5 (March 11, 1974), p. 9; M. H. Dick, "What Really Happened on the Black Mesa & Lake Powell," *Railway Age*, Volume 172, Number 1 (January 12, 1976), pp. 26–29; Frank E. Shaffer, "The Elusive Goal," pp. 68–69; "The Story Behind Arizona's New Railroad," *Railway Age*, Volume 170, Number 12 (June 28, 1971), p. 14.

48. Chapter 5: "The Loss of Adaptiveness," pp. 87–101.

49. Tom Shedd, "Understanding and Trust," p. 60.

9 ECONOMICS AND STRUCTURE

The Railroad Problem is an economic problem. It is only by the application of economic principles that a final solution will be found. Any attempt to resolve railroad difficulties is doomed to failure if it ignores economic fundamentals, regardless of the intentions of its proponents and the amount of public or private funds spent in its behalf.

The concepts of competition and monopoly have special significance in the railroad industry, since economic regulation depends to a large extent on their interpretation. Despite nearly a century of regulatory efforts by the Interstate Commerce Commission, debate continues about whether the railroad industry is predominantly competitive or monopolistic, and how regulatory policy should be addressed.

A BRIEF REVIEW

To understand the railroad industry's problems, the problems must be analyzed in terms of economic fundamentals. The concepts of competition, monopoly, fixed and variable costs, economies of scale, and natural monopoly are essential to this analysis.

Competition

Competition is fundamental to the free market system and is generally regarded as beneficial. The classic competitive market is characterized by numerous independent firms selling a highly standardized product. Each seller (producer) is so small that it has no influence over the market. Price is determined by the market's supply and demand, not by individual buyers or sellers. Firms enter and leave the market freely. The most efficient firms earn the highest profits. Less efficient firms have lower profits, operate at a loss, or shut down and leave the market. Agriculture, with many farmers selling the same products on open markets, is often cited as an example of a classic competitive market.

Competition is beneficial for several reasons. The consumer, through his purchases, determines what will be produced and at what price. The market matches demand, supply, and price. The customer is given alternatives under competition. High cost and inefficient producers are weeded out. Over the long run prices are lowered, efficiency is increased, and the standard of living is raised. Nonetheless, competitive markets may require a minimal amount of regulatory supervision.

Competition is thus held to be a stern disciplinarian. It has long been recognized, however, that there still is need, in a competitive economy, for public controls. The existence of competition is not always assured. Many firms may agree among themselves that they will not compete. Two or more firms may combine to make a single unit. One or a few firms may come to dominate an industry, through the employment of unfair methods or through the enjoyment of special advantages. If the consumer is to reap the benefits of competition, government must make sure that competition is maintained.[1]

Under competition, the only role played by the government is to see that competitors compete and do so fairly.

Monopoly

Monopoly is the opposite of competition: a single firm is the only seller in a monopolistic market. Pure monopoly is not common, but the theoretical case is useful in understanding oligopolistic markets (which have only a few sellers). For monopoly to exist there must be some barrier to stop other firms from entering the market—a means of preventing competition. Barriers to entry include (1) raw material ownership; (2) possession of patents or exclusive rights; (3) use of fair or unfair anticompetitive methods; and (4) existence of economies of scale.[2]

Compared to competitive markets, monopolistic markets are usually less efficient.

The monopolist may persist in offering inferior quality at a high price, since the purchasers of his product lack the alternative of turning to other sources of supply. He may obtain his profit, not by serving the community, but by refusing to serve it. Monopoly inflicts no penalty on inefficiency. The monopolist may eliminate wastes and cut costs, but he is under no compulsion to do so. Through inertia, he may cling to accustomed techniques. His hold upon the market is assured. Monopoly, as such, is not conducive to progress. . . . Because it does not compel the enhancement of quality or the reduction of price, because it fails to penalize inefficiency, because it is not conducive to progress, it makes the total output of goods and services smaller than it would otherwise be.[3]

A monopoly can be efficient and sell its product at a low price, but experience shows that monopolies tend toward inefficiency and high prices.

Fixed and Variable Costs

Whether an industry tends toward competition or monopoly is frequently determined by its cost structure, particularly the relative importance of fixed and variable costs.

Fixed costs, as their name implies, remain constant in total over a wide range of production volumes. A factory's fixed costs would include office expenses, executive salaries, property taxes, insurance, capital investment costs, and other overhead expenses. The total amount of these costs stays the same whether production is 70 percent of capacity or 99 percent. Of course, with higher production volumes the fixed costs can be spread over more units, and the amount of fixed cost per unit declines.

Variable costs change in total with the changes in production volume. Raw materials, hourly labor, machine repair, and shipping expense depend on the number of units produced. While the cost per unit is constant, the total amount of variable costs changes with production volume.

Some costs vary but not in direct proportion to production volume. For example, a factory might need to rent additional warehouse space on a temporary basis as production nears capacity. Understanding of simple fixed and variable costs allows recognition of more complex step-wise variable and semi-variable costs. For the present analysis, costs will be classified only as fixed or variable.

Economies of Scale

In certain industries the production process becomes more efficient once volume reaches a given level. Labor, management, and equipment can be specialized. When these economies of scale are present, the variable cost per unit actually declines as production volumes pass the minimum level. Any competitor must reach that level—the optimum size plant—or risk the consequences of being too small and inefficient. A local garage could assemble automobiles from parts, but the cost would be so high that it could not compete with an assembly plant. This illustrates the economies of scale in automobile production.

Economies of scale involve a trade-off between fixed costs and variable costs. In the previous example, the local garage has few fixed costs and high variable costs (parts and labor). The auto assembly plant incurs considerable fixed costs: a large factory, specialized machinery, capital investment, and other production overhead expenses. In return, for normal production volumes its variable costs per automobile are much less than those of the local garage. To build three cars a year the local garage method would be less expensive; to build thousands of cars annually the assembly plant would be more efficient.

When economies of scale are related to the size of the market, the effects of cost on competition are evident. With low fixed costs a producer can enter and leave a market with little risk, encouraging widespread competition. In an industry with high fixed costs, each producer needs a given minimum volume of sales to support its plant. The size of the market determines how many producers can compete. In markets with only a few competitors, the government must guard against the competitors' tendency toward monopolistic practices.

In some industries both economies and diseconomies of scale are present. Diseconomies result when an upper limit is passed and cost per unit rises. This can result from a plant operating over its capacity or from a company getting too large for effective managerial control. There are industries with no economies or diseconomies of scale, in which case a producer's size has no bearing on its costs.

Natural Monopoly

Economies of scale can be so great relative to the size of the market that only a single firm can efficiently supply the market. These natural monopolies include utilities (electric, gas, water, sewer) and telephone companies.[4] The monopoly can be held by a public agency or can be granted to a private enterprise with the government acting as regulator.

Natural monopolies are characterized by a high proportion of fixed costs and great economies of scale. Having two or more competitors would result in duplication of fixed costs which, in the long run, would be borne by consumers. Having two electric power companies in a community—dual generating plants, dual distribution systems, and dual outlets in each building—would only serve to increase costs. Since a single firm could supply the entire market at less cost than two competing firms, it would be logical to grant a monopoly to one company and then regulate it so that the lower costs were passed on to its customers. Regulation cannot be as effective as a competitive market in setting prices and encouraging efficiency; but, given the cost advantages inherent in a natural monopoly, regulation is often the optimal solution.

THE CASE FOR COMPETITION

Railroads have both monopolistic and competitive characteristics. This has been true since the nineteenth century, when railroads used profits from monopoly markets to wage price warfare in competitive markets. During this century new modes of transportation have emerged and further complicated the railroads' monopolistic-competitive dichotomy. The debate continues over which characteristic—monopoly or competition—dominates the railroad industry and, therefore, how regulatory policy should be directed.

The Nature of Competition

To understand the multidimensional nature of railroad competition, it can be divided into price and service factors. Price competition needs no explanation. Service factors include reliability, speed, car supply, loss and damage, switching, and industrial development.

Railroads usually do not offer service reliability and speed comparable to that of highway trucks, so railroads offer a lower price. Even at a lower price, shippers still demand a certain level of service. Shippers and consignees maintain bigger inventories if rail service is unreliable. If transit time fluctuations become too great, the cost of larger inventories can make a more reliable form of transportation attractive. Many rail shippers have converted to truck service for this reason.

Speed is important to some types of traffic, particularly for piggyback (trailer on flatcar), perishables, and high-value items such as automobiles. Speed applies to total transit time, which includes both train speed and the handling of cars through switching yards.

The ability of a railroad to supply empty cars for loading is another competitive factor. This involves (1) the number of cars available versus the demand; (2) the availability of specialized cars; and (3) the ability to place empty cars rapidly at the shipper's facility once a request is received.

Competition occurs in the amount of loss and damage which shipments incur. If the use of one railroad results in greater loss and damage, the shipper will likely change routings or change to another mode. Likewise, the switching service received by a shipper can be a competitive factor if the shipper's plant is served by two or more railroads. If the shipper is served by one railroad only, poor switching can encourage diversion to another mode.

Industrial development activities are an element of competition, but apply over a longer time frame. Because a railroad company has the exclusive right to perform train service over its tracks, location of a new customer along those tracks means a relatively certain increase in railroad revenues. Furthermore, construction of a factory, warehouse, or other facility represents a commitment by that shipper for many years to come. It is not surprising that industrial development is the scene of the fiercest competition among railroads.

The Effectiveness of Competition

Having examined the elements of competition, the question arises as to whether there is too much or too little competition in the railroad industry and, moreover, whether the competition is beneficial or destructive.

Traditionally railroads have given too much attention to competition with other railroads (intramodal competition). This fact is easily explained by (1) the availability of comprehensive information on individual railroads from regulatory agencies, trade groups, and inter-railroad activities; and (2) the relative ease of influencing shippers to change routings of existing rail shipments as opposed to converting shipments from other modes to rail. Information on the other modes' traffic, in contrast, is usually incomplete and difficult to obtain in useful form. Simply put, the railroads have taken the path of least resistance and concentrated most sales efforts on available rail traffic.

Despite its over-emphasis, intramodal competition does benefit the railroads. Competition for bridge traffic—traffic which does not originate or terminate on a railroad, but only moves over it between connecting railroads—encourages precision, speed, and reliability on the part of each competitor, with a positive impact on other rail traffic. Competition in developing specialized equipment, services, and rates has improved rail service and often has resulted in diversion of traffic from other modes as well. Competition allows shippers to select and reward innovative railroads with their traffic. It provides strong incentives for conservative carriers to accept new ideas more quickly.

Critics of intramodal competition favor its elimination by agreement, coordination, merger into a few large railroads, or even nationalization. It is argued that removal of intramodal rail competition would allow railroads to concentrate their efforts on the other modes. This approach fails to recognize the contributions made by intramodal competition within the rail industry. Intramodal competition promotes efficiency, innovation, flexibility, and attention to customer needs. This is evidenced by the intramodal competition among numerous carriers in the highway, water, and air modes. The lower proportion of fixed to variable costs, greater freedom of entry and exit, and smaller size of firms in the non-rail modes promote intramodal competition and its benefits. Despite its structure, the rail industry also benefits from its own intramodal competition.

The flaws of intramodal competition as found in the rail industry are not due to intramodal competition *per se*. Rather, the problems arise from the railroads' unusual industry structure—a structure which exhibits both monopolistic and competitive characteristics. Given the proper structure, intramodal competition can serve as a successful replacement for government economic regulation, providing the efficiency found only in free markets.

Intermodal competition—the other factor in the railroad competitive equation—assumes greater importance as rail market share declines. Competition from the other modes has pitted the railroads collectively and individually against competitors which have different industry structures, different costs, and different services. The broad range of transportation alternatives available to many shippers has forced the railroads to reexamine traditional services and attitudes.

When the railroads had a collective monopoly over all transportation, competitive traffic was simply identified as that moving between common junctions or terminal areas. During the last five decades the advent of intermodal competition—especially truck competition—has brought a degree of competition to the entire length of each railroad line, not just junction points. Cities served by a single railroad are no longer under a transport monopoly: a rail service monopoly, yes, but with truck service competing as an alternative.

Intermodal competition cannot substitute completely for intramodal competition, because the cost structure of each mode is different. Two or more modes might compete for certain types of traffic, perhaps even offering similar combinations of price and service. For other types of traffic, the competition is limited, because the modes involved cannot or do not offer similar price/service combinations. The degree of intermodal substitutability varies considerably for different types of traffic (commodities, routes, shippers, vehicles, and so forth). The characteristics of some types of traffic allow only one mode to handle it economically. When intermodal competition is limited or absent—a common situation for some types of rail traffic—intramodal competition is essential if an unregulated free market is to be maintained.

THE CASE FOR MONOPOLY

Proponents of monopoly contend that railroads are more monopolistic than competitive, and that the monopoly should be recognized and even encouraged to promote maximum efficiency. Operated as a monopoly, total fixed costs and overhead costs could be reduced and traffic could be concentrated. This would allow lower rates and better service. The railroad industry would then be in a better position to compete with the other transportation modes.

The monopoly need not be absolute; it can be a matter of degree. Increased cooperation among railroads is one method for achieving some of the benefits of monopoly. During the 1930's, when competition was blamed mistakenly for many of the Great Depression's problems, federally sponsored railroad coordination was favored. In the mid-1800's prior to federal regulation, railroads sought monopoly through the operation of pools and other price-fixing agreements. In recent years, merger into larger and fewer railroads has been pursued to gain the advantages of monopoly: cost reduction, traffic concentration, and service improvement. Some proponents argue for nationalization, the ultimate merger, as the means for achieving a true monopoly. In any case, most economists agree that a monopoly must be regulated to assure that its benefits are passed on to its customers through lower rates and are not retained as excessive profits (or excessive inefficiencies, should the monopoly elect to apply less than maximum efficiency).

Three aspects of monopoly are found in the railroad industry. First is the monopoly of service each railroad company has over its own tracks (the track-train monopoly). Second, there is the natural monopoly inherent in the railroads' industry structure. Third, the railroad companies which form the railroad industry often act in a monopolistic or cartel-like manner. The three are highly interrelated; they are only different views of the same phenomenon.

Track-Train Monopoly

Each railroad company provides exclusive service over its own tracks. No other carrier can run trains over those tracks without the approval of the company which owns the tracks, and approval is rarely given so as to protect the owner's monopoly. This means a monopoly of rail service exists for most shippers since the shipper is located on one railroad's track and only that railroad company provides rail service. Unlike the highway, waterway, or airway which offers access for any number of carriers—including the shipper's private carrier—the rail fixed way is available only to one railroad company.

Natural Monopoly

The track-train monopoly was initiated during the early 1800's to cope with the advent of steam locomotives and iron rails when then-existing management and communications capabilities proved inadequate. The present railroad industry structure, based on the track-train monopoly, allows competition between railroad companies only if each has its own fixed way. The number of competing railroads which a route can support is limited since each must cover the high fixed costs of fixed way ownership, operation, and maintenance. Many routes can support only one railroad and its fixed way, thereby precluding any rail competition. Even on routes which can support two or more competitors' fixed ways, economies of scale promote monopoly and encourage destructive competition.

High fixed costs relative to market size, economies of scale, and a tendency toward destructive competition and eventual monopoly are characteristics of natural monopoly.

> Because firms are eager to spread their fixed costs and thereby achieve lower unit costs, cutthroat price competition tends to break out when a number of firms exist. . . . The result may be losses, the bankruptcy of weaker rivals, and the eventual merger of the survivors. The evolving pure monopoly may be anxious to recoup past losses and to profit fully from its new position of market dominance by charging exorbitant prices for its good or service.[5]

This textbook description of competition among firms in a natural monopoly industry applies exactly to the railroad industry before it was regulated in the late 1800's. Today, as then, natural monopolies require government regulation (1) to protect the firms themselves by preventing destructive competition; and (2) to protect consumers from abuses of the firms' monopoly power when and where such power exists.[6]

Cartel Behavior

The monopoly of service each railroad has over its own tracks requires a degree of cartel behavior in the railroad industry. Most shipments move over two or more railroads between origin and destination. It is common for two railroads to have roughly parallel lines throughout a region, to be each other's primary competitor, and yet to be each other's most important source of interchange traffic due to geographic proximity. Under this structure cooperation is essential, even among competitors. Over time this has evolved as a cartel-like "competition among gentlemen," in which the rules are agreed upon and followed by all. It is no wonder that the other modes, which do not abide by the railroads' rules, pose such a problem for the rail industry.[7]

Michael Conant, in his book *Railroad Mergers and Abandonments*, finds competition ineffective as an "operative social control."[8] He cites four dimensions of railroad cartel behavior: (1) lack of innovation; (2) lack of service competition; (3) barriers to entry; and (4) cartel pricing.

Lack of innovation applies only in a relative sense. Railroads have been innovative, primarily in technical (as opposed to commercial) areas. It is equally true that innovation has been hindered, because the present industry structure requires several (if not all) railroads to accept an innovation if it is to succeed.

The railroads' structure has minimized service competition. In a few markets, such as trailer on flatcar (TOFC) service between major cities, service competition is keen. In most cases, however, only one level of rail service exists. A shipper's facility is served by only one railroad, so that railroad has little incentive to offer anything other than a minimum level of service. When two or more railroads participate in a movement, it is difficult to place responsibility for service deficiencies (unreliability, slowness, and loss and damage, for example). This reinforces the tendency for all competitors to offer service at the least common denominator level.

Entry barriers are both economic and legal. The cost of building a new rail fixed way is prohibitive in most cases. Legally, the ICC must approve new rail fixed ways as being in the interest of public convenience and necessity. It has had little opportunity to exercise this authority, since total rail mileage has been declining since 1916. Most expansions have been spur tracks or branch lines to serve specific industries.

Until the Staggers Act and deregulation efforts restricted rate bureau activities, cartel pricing was a fact of life for railroads. The Reed-Bulwinkle Act of 1948 exempted rail rate bureaus from antitrust laws and subjected them to ICC regulation. Through the rate bureau, member railroads set prices jointly. This was done to protect the rate structure: that is, to maintain rates at established levels and prevent destructive competition. If rejected by the bureau, a railroad could implement a proposed rate—but only on its own tracks. Rate bureau actions could be appealed to the ICC and then to the courts. Figure 9 describes railroad rate making under rate bureau procedures.

The Staggers Act (described in the next section) greatly reduced the role of rate bureaus. It forced each railroad to determine its own prices without collaborating with other railroads. If two or more railroads formed a through route, they could set joint rates for that route. Competitors could not discuss rates, and much of the railroads' antitrust immunity was removed.

Deregulation and Natural Monopoly

As deregulation progressed in the other modes, particularly with the airlines, it became apparent that the railroads could achieve some long-sought reforms as part of the deregulation movement. No one seriously considered eliminating the ICC, but deregulation was more popular than regulatory reform.

Southern Pacific Transportation Company, a railroad, suggested that agricultural traffic by rail be exempted from economic regulation as it was in the other modes. Eventually, fresh fruit and vegetable traffic was exempted, though most agricultural traffic remained regulated. The main impetus for rail deregulation came not from industry leaders but from Conrail, the federally funded successor to the bankrupt Penn Central. Only a brief involvement convinced most politicians and government agencies that there was too much regulation—especially if Conrail was ever to move off the public dole and into the private sector. The Conrail plan called for greater freedom to (1) abandon tracks and operations; (2) raise or lower rates; and (3) substitute truck service for rail service.[9] These reforms necessitated a reduction in the power of the ICC. Seldom before had the outlook for reforms in these areas been so good, and the rail industry soon came to support Conrail's call for deregulation.

The deregulation efforts culminated in the Staggers Rail Act of 1980. The intent was to apply regulation only to those markets where competition did not provide effective control. A market was presumed to be competitive if the revenue to variable cost ratio was below the jurisdictional threshold (originally 160 percent using the ICC's Rail Form A costing method), and no rate regulation was needed for such markets. If the ratio was above the threshold, rates were regulated only if it were shown that the railroads involved had market dominance. Some entire markets were exempted, notably trailer on flatcar (TOFC) and fresh fruits and vegetables.

The Staggers Act offered railroads the prospect of financial improvement through quarterly rate increases based on a cost index. The ability to raise rates on traffic below the jurisdictional threshold also presented opportunities to increase revenue, though this option was constrained by the degree of competition in those markets. A negative factor was the ICC's difficulty in finding an acceptable method for determining maximum rate levels in regulated markets (such as those encompassed by several coal rate cases and some of the rate complaints filed under the provisions of the Staggers Act).

Deregulation set in motion a number of changes in the railroad industry. With the role of rate bureaus reduced, railroads were encouraged to act with greater independence. This created difficulties in an industry whose structure required a high degree of interdependence. By eliminating routes from joint rate tariffs or closing interchanges, a railroad company could unilaterally close a through route or relegate it to minor importance. Using this leverage a railroad could increase its revenue by seeking its longest possible haul on traffic. Although railroads always sought long hauls, regulation maintained a variety of routes and interchanges. Deregulation allowed a railroad to restrict the available routes and thereby improve its revenue. Concentrating traffic via major routes and gateways also offered better service for some shippers, though a few of the long-haul routes offered poorer service than did short hauls to closer interchange points. The reduction of alternative routes meant a reduction in competition, particularly when intermediate railroads were bypassed. Proponents argued that the changes would improve competition by producing fewer but financially healthier competitors.

The same logic prompted an acceleration of the merger movement, also intended to result in fewer but healthier competitors. Since cooperation was no longer required to the extent it was under full regulation, railroads sought to expand their market power through mergers. This allowed the merged company to control more shipments over a greater portion of their hauls, reducing the need to negotiate with connecting railroads. When negotiation was necessary, a railroad company with a bigger traffic base could bargain more effectively. It was commonly anticipated that joint rates on through routes might be replaced eventually by combinations of single-line rates (instead of a joint rate from A to C, the rate from A to B would be added to the rate from B to C). Ultimately, the railroad industry might be reduced to a handful of giant companies, maybe even only two as in Canada.

It first appears incongruous that deregulation, which was undertaken to increase railroad competition, should begin a trend toward eventual monopoly under two or three companies.[10] However, the application of basic economics—specifically, natural monopoly concepts—reveals the real logic. When regulation is removed, competing firms in a natural monopoly will move, as if pulled by gravity, towards monopoly. Destructive competition might play a temporary role, as might mergers or price-fixing schemes, but monopoly will be the end result.

Figure 9. Rate-Making Procedure Under Rate Bureaus

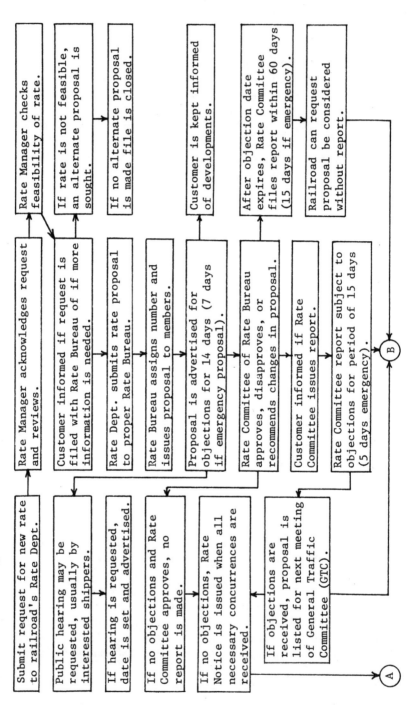

102

Figure 9 *—Continued*

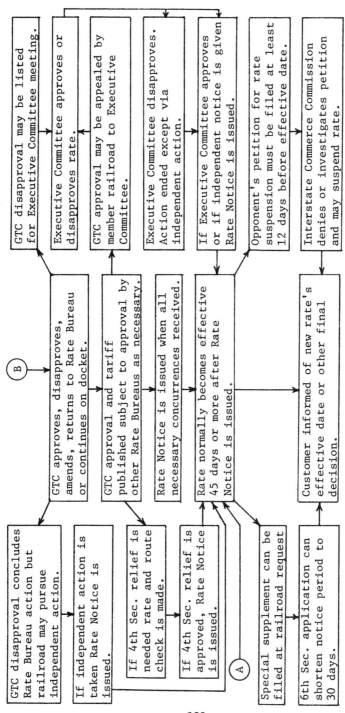

GTC disapproval concludes Rate Bureau action but railroad may pursue independent action.

If independent action is taken Rate Notice is issued.

If 4th Sec. relief is needed rate and route check is made.

If 4th Sec. relief is approved, Rate Notice is issued.

(A)

Special supplement can be filed at railroad request

6th Sec. application can shorten notice period to 30 days.

(B)

GTC approves, disapproves, amends, returns to Rate Bureau or continues on docket.

GTC approval and tariff published subject to approval by other Rate Bureaus as necessary.

Rate Notice is issued when all necessary concurrences received.

Rate normally becomes effective 45 days or more after Rate Notice is issued.

Customer informed of new rate's effective date or other final decision.

GTC disapproval may be listed for Executive Committee meeting.

Executive Committee approves or disapproves rate.

GTC approval may be appealed by member railroad to Executive Committee.

Executive Committee disapproves. Action ended except via independent action.

If Executive Committee approves or if independent notice is given Rate Notice is issued.

Opponent's petition for rate suspension must be filed at least 12 days before effective date.

Interstate Commerce Commission denies or investigates petition and may suspend rate.

103

Under the traditional railroad industry structure, national transportation policy has been given two choices. The railroad industry can be completely regulated, though history has shown that this necessitates accepting a degree of inefficiency, mediocre financial performance, and an impaired ability to compete with the other less regulated modes. The railroads can be deregulated, in which case reasonable actions of individual railroads propel the industry toward monopoly and its undesirable consequences. The railroads' industry structure does not allow unregulated competition to function effectively as a long-term substitute for economic regulation.

THE NATURAL MONOPOLY MYTH

The railroad industry as presently structured is a natural monopoly, whether or not regulated. In either case the consequences are not palatable.

The natural monopoly lies in the fixed way. Carrier functions are monopolistic only because a single carrier has exclusive use of each fixed way. The track-train monopoly thus magnifies the natural monopoly of the fixed way into a natural monopoly of the entire railroad industry. If the track-train monopoly did not exist, if exclusive service on each fixed way were not the norm, the railroad industry would not be a natural monopoly. It is the fixed way, not carrier functions, which creates the natural monopoly.

Exclusive use of each fixed way requires railroad companies to carry the competitive burden of high fixed costs. For the railroad industry, this structure perverts competition into a destructive force—one to be discouraged and avoided. The aversion to competition places railroads at a disadvantage in intermodal competition. Regulation is a problem, for although the railroad industry exhibits monopoly characteristics, it is comprised of numerous companies which compete yet are highly interdependent. The present industry structure is a compromise, with inherent tradeoffs and suboptimizations.

In the other modes carriers share public fixed ways and pay for them through user fees. This structure promotes competition as a constructive force. Carriers offer shippers a wide variety of price/service combinations. These carriers, lean and strong from their own intramodal competition, have taken full competitive advantage of the weaknesses of the railroad industry structure. The railroad industry, trapped within its century-old structure, has been like a spider caught within its own web, unable to defend itself against its predators.

NOTES

1. Clair Wilcox, *Public Policies Toward Business*, rev. ed. (Homewood, IL, Richard D. Irwin, Inc. 1960), p. 12. Copyright Richard D. Irwin, Inc. 1960.
2. Campbell R. McConnell, *Economics: Principles, Problems, and Policies*, pp. 487–490.
3. Clair Wilcox, *Public Policies Toward Business*, rev. ed. (Homewood, IL, Richard D. Irwin, Inc. 1960), pp. 12–13. Copyright Richard D. Irwin, Inc. 1960.

4. Proposals to restructure natural monopolies are described in Bro Uttal, "How to Deregulate AT&T," *Fortune*, Volume 104, Number 11 (November 30, 1981), pp. 70–75; and Tom Alexander, "The Surge to Deregulate Electricity," *Fortune*, Volume 104, Number 1 (July 13, 1981), pp. 98–105.

5. McConnell, p. 489.

6. Detailed descriptions of natural monopoly include: John Walker Barriger, *Super-Railroads for a Dynamic American Economy*; Richard H. Leftwich, *An Introduction to Economic Thinking*, pp. 217–218; H. H. Liebhafsky, *American Government and Business*, pp. 438–439; McConnell, pp. 488–489; Wilcox, pp. 644–665.

7. D. Daryl Wyckoff and David H. Maister, *The Owner-Operator: Independent Trucker*, pp. 107–145.

8. (Los Angeles, 1964), pp. 40–41.

9. Albert R. Karr, "Changing Signals: To End Conrail Losses, Federal Officials Study a Regulatory Cutback," *Wall Street Journal*, Volume LVIII, Number 249 (October 6, 1978), p. 1.

10. Related articles include: "BN's Bid to Scrap Merger Conditions Meets Opposition from Competitors," *Traffic World*, Number 11, Volume 187, Whole Number 3882 (September 14, 1981), p. 58; "BN to Fight ICC Grant to C&NW for New Coal Line in Wyoming," *Modern Railroads*, Volume 36, Number 9 (September 1981), p. 15; "East-West Rail Merger Predicted," *Modern Railroads*, Volume 36, Number 11 (November 1981), p. 27; F. Stewart Mitchell, "Loosening the Grip," *Modern Railroads*, Volume 36, Number 4 (April 1981), pp. 34–35; "More Regulation?" *Modern Railroads*, Volume 36, Number 11 (November 1981), p. 16; Harold E. Spencer, "Deregulation of Railroads: The Road to Nationalization," *Traffic World*, Number 6, Volume 189, Whole Number 3903 (February 8, 1982), pp. 89–93; Gus Welty, "Wallflowers at the Merger Ball," *Railway Age*, Volume 176, Number 23 (December 8, 1975), pp. 35–37.

APPENDIX TO
CHAPTER 9

MERGERS

Mergers have been widely heralded as a solution for many railroad problems, though in recent years their effectiveness has been questioned. Advocates cite cost savings and service improvements as benefits of mergers.

Mergers of companies whose systems are essentially parallel offer possibilities for reduction of capital requirements through reduction or downgrading of mainlines, yards, and terminals, and improved equipment utilization. Parallel mergers, also, are expected to reduce operating costs through the elimination of duplicate services and through increases in labor productivity. End-to-end mergers, on the other hand, are presumed to facilitate better service to customers through faster and more reliable point-to-point service in markets formerly served by interchange service. Both types of mergers have potential for reduction of corporate overhead (e.g., marketing, accounting, and executive departments); improvement in car availability; and elimination of unnecessary interchange facilities.[1]

Obstacles to merger effectiveness include labor agreements which reduce savings, regulatory restrictions which preclude abandonment of duplicate routes, and the need for capital expenditures to coordinate the merged properties. Parallel mergers have declined in popularity, because these obstacles often minimize cost savings, and because such mergers threaten to eliminate competitive rail service in many areas.

End-to-end mergers have come into favor since deregulation has encouraged railroads to act independently. Compared to its predecessors, the single merged company would control more shipments from origin to destination. As observed earlier, the impetus for end-to-end mergers stems from the railroads' natural monopoly structure, which explains the need to control ever-larger shares of rail traffic.

In two case studies, the Department of Transportation found service improvements resulted from merger. However, the improvements were of greater benefit in reducing railroad costs than they were in providing noticeable improvements for shippers. In other areas, the studies questioned the success of the mergers.

The two mergers did not significantly improve the market penetration or profitability of the merging companies. While the resulting organizations are financially successfully by rail industry standards, the act of merger did not improve the intermodal competitive capability of either firm. There was no evidence in the case studies that identifiable blocks of traffic shifted from another mode to rail. One of the mergers, however, did result in a shift of traffic from competing railroads to the newly formed organization.[2]

The difficulties encountered in achieving merger objectives led to a questioning of their value.

> The DOT has concluded that mergers are a less promising technique to improve the railroad industry than other approaches to restructuring. . . . The elements of rationalization contained in the concepts of line transfers, joint use agreements, and abandonments are what actually save costs—not corporate integration per se. The elements that reduce plant and save costs in a good merger are these same factors—service consolidation, optimization of an existing plant shared by two previously independent entities, and abandonment of unneeded facilities. All these elements can occur short of merger.[3]

Richard Saunders, author of *The Railroad Mergers and the Coming of Conrail*, described the late 1960's and early 1970's as "a decade wasted on the false panacea of consolidation."[4] A similar point was made by W. J. McDonald, Senior Vice President of Law, Union Pacific Corporation:

> Rail mergers, however consistent with the public interest, cannot in and of themselves solve the basic economic, financial, and regulatory problems which presently affect the industry. In the ordering of overall industry priorities, several fundamental needs rank ahead of the need for rail mergers.[5]

Historical trends reveal railroads have been merging into fewer and fewer companies with little effect on industry problems. Between 1900 and 1935 the number of railroad companies was halved, from 1,224 to 661. During the next thirty years it was halved again (see Table 5). Of the 300-plus companies remaining, most are shortline railroads of local importance only. A few large systems—corporate groups comprised of one or more major railroads and their smaller subsidiaries—control most rail mileage. As shown in Table 6, the nine largest systems in 1981 controlled 86 percent of U.S. rail mileage (including proposed and pending mergers). The sixteen largest systems controlled 97 percent of U.S. rail mileage. These large systems provide an even greater proportion of total rail traffic and revenue (see Table 7).

Arguments for merging the large rail systems into fewer entities—ten, five, or two—pale before the evidence of experience. Although the merger process has continued over the past seventy years, railroad problems remain serious.

Great Britain serves as a classic example of the fallacies of merger as a solution to railroad problems. During the 1930's merger was promoted as the only alternative to outright nationalization of Britain's railroads. Several hundred railroad companies were merged into four large regional systems. Instead of deterring nationalization, the problems were magnified to the point where nationalization was inevitable. The four remaining companies were nationalized much more readily than the earlier hundred-plus could have been.[6]

Mergers are not a solution to railroad problems; in fact, they are a symptom of deeper structural problems. Mergers are a manifestation of the natural monopoly forces inherent in the present railroad industry structure. To resolve the difficulties which have plagued the railroads for so long, fundamental structural issues must be resolved.

NOTES

1. U.S., Department of Transportation, *A Prospectus for Change in the Freight Railroad Industry*, p. 91.
2. Ibid., p. 92.
3. Ibid., pp. 92–93.
4. Richard Saunders, *The Railroad Mergers and the Coming of Conrail*, p. 335.
5. William J. McDonald, "Railview: UP's McDonald: Are We Expecting Too Much from Mergers?" *Railway Age*, Volume 179, Number 19 (October 19, 1978), p. 48.
6. Stewart Joy, *The Train That Ran Away—A Business History of British Railways 1948-1968*.

Table 5 Number of Operating Railroads

Year	Number
1977	320
1975	340
1970	351
1965	372
1960	407
1955	441
1950	471
1945	517
1940	574
1935	661
1930	775
1925	947
1920	1,085
1915	1,260
1910	1,306
1905	1,380
1900	1,224
1895	1,104
1890	1,013

SOURCES: 1890–1970 data: U.S., Bureau of the Census, *Historical Statistics of the United States, Colonial Times to 1970*, Series Q284, pp. 727–728; 1975–1977 data: U.S., Bureau of the Census, *Statistical Abstract of the United States: 1980*, Table 1140, p. 660.

NOTE: Operating companies, including unofficial companies and, through 1960, circular companies. As of December 31, 1920–1977; as of June 30, 1890–1915.

Table 6 Mileage Controlled by Major Systems, 1981

Railroad System		Miles Operated
Atchison Topeka & Santa Fe Ry		12,179* 7
Burlington Northern (BN, C&S, FW&D, SLSF)		29,996* 1
CSX (B&O, C&O, CRR, L&N, SCL, WM)		26,562* 2
Chicago & North Western Transportation		9,561* 4
Chicago Milwaukee St. Paul & Pacific		5,080
Consolidated Rail Corporation		18,987* 4
Denver & Rio Grande Western RR		1,848
Grand Trunk Western (DT&I, GTW)		1,474
Illinois Central Gulf RR		8,522* 5
Kansas City Southern Lines		1,664
Mellon (B&M, D&H, MEC proposed)		3,823
Missouri Kansas Texas RR		2,167
Norfolk Southern (N&W, SOU proposed)		17,661* 8
Pacific Rail (MP, UP, WP proposed)		22,269* 3
Soo Line RR		4,495
Southern Pacific (SSW, SP)		12,728* 6
Total, 16 Largest Systems	97%	179,016
Total, 9 Largest Systems	86%	158,465
U.S. Miles of Road Owned (approximate)	100%	185,000

SOURCES: Miles of Road Operated, Freight Service, Association of American Railroads, *Operating & Traffic Statistics, Year 1980* (Washington, D.C.), p. 1. Miles of Road Owned, estimated from Association of American Railroads, *Yearbook of Railroad Facts,* 1980 ed., p. 46; and data in *Trains,* Volume 42, Number 4 (February 1982), p. 3.

NOTE: Asterisks indicate nine largest systems. Miles Operated includes routes operated via trackage rights, joint use, and so on, but not owned. Total miles operated by all railroads therefore exceeds total miles owned, but the difference is relatively insignificant.

Table 7 Railroad Industry Rate of Return on Net Investment

Year	Rate
1980	4.25
1979	2.87
1978	1.52
1977	1.24
1976	1.60
1975	1.20
1974	2.70
1973	2.33
1972	2.34
1971	2.12
1970	1.73
1969	2.36
1968	2.44
1967	2.46
1966	3.90
1961–65 average	2.94
1956–60 average	2.98
1951–55 average	3.92
1946–50 average	3.54
1941–45 average	4.97
1936–40 average	2.51
1931–35 average	1.94

SOURCE: Association of American Railroads, *Yearbook of Railroad Facts,* annual editions.

10 | IN THEORY, IN CONGRESS

In the earliest days of railroading the concept of separating carrier and roadway functions was more than just an idea—it was a daily fact of life. Railroads, like turnpikes and canals, were fixed ways only.

Then came the quantum leap in rail technology during the early 1800's. Steel rails and steam locomotives changed the meaning of railroad: originally a road of rails, it later came to include not just the roadway but also the company which operated carrier service over it. This dramatic structural change was not without its opponents. Many recognized the problems inherent in the then-new structure but chose to accept the problems as the price of progress.

Since that time a number of rail industry analysts have conceded the existence of structure-based difficulties. Some even recognized the railroad industry's structure as the root of industry problems. Nearly all, however, stopped short of calling for the needed structural changes.

Congress proved less bashful in this regard. Prompted in part by the demise of the Penn Central, several legislative proposals were introduced which would have altered the industry's structure. Most of the proposals evidenced an incomplete understanding of railroad economics and operations; many tended to rely too heavily on increased public aid and control. Nonetheless, credit must be given to the legislators for daring to enter where academicians feared to tread.

THE RAILROAD: A PUBLIC HIGHWAY

The roadway/carrier separation concept had supporters even during the Golden Age of Railroading. W. D. Dabney wrote *Public Regulation of Railways* in 1889, a time when railroad companies were the most powerful institutions in America.[1] Rather than extoll the virtues of the status quo or rebuke the robber barons as did most writers of the period, Dabney presented a comprehensive argument for the separation concept.

It has been said concerning the construction of the political constitution of the country, that nothing is so important as a frequent recurrence to first principles. The same remark is applicable to a correct understanding of the relations of the railway system to the public.

There can be no doubt that the system as it has developed, and is now operated, has drifted far away from the principles on which it derived its existence, and to understand fully the right and the extent of public control over the system, an examination of those principles is necessary. The notion upon which railroads came into being, and upon which many early charters were drawn was that any and all persons might have the use of the road, for the transit of their own vehicles by their own motive power, upon the payment of reasonable "tolls" to the owners of the road. The common use of this word "tolls" in respect to railroad charges indicates the prevalent idea entertained as to the character of which railroad transportation would partake—namely, that of the turnpike. And the word is still in frequent use, though as a general thing its original signification no longer applies in this connection.

The modern function of the railroad company as the exclusive carrier upon its own road has become so familiar, that it is somewhat difficult to realize fully the original conception of its function, as a highway upon which numerous carriers might compete for business.

But there is no necessary connection between the two functions of furnishing the road, and carrying upon it. Much less is there any legal reason why the railroad company should be the exclusive carrier over its road. Its right to carry at all, and more especially its exclusive right, depends upon the terms of its charter. This historical view, with the legal relations resulting from it, are clearly recognized in the jurisprudence of the subject. The Supreme Court of the United States has examined the question in this light,* and the fair inference from the remarks of the Court is, that in the absence of provision to the contrary, the railway is, theoretically at least, a public highway, and as such open for the transit of the vehicles of all persons, upon payment of reasonable tolls, and subject to reasonable regulations.

It is undoubtedly true that "in practice, as a general thing, railroads are only operated by companies that own them, or by those with whom they have permanent arrangements for the purpose. The companies have a practical if not a legal monopoly of their use." But "the ascertained impracticability of the general and and indiscriminate use of these great thoroughfares, does not preclude their use by the transportation companies having no interest in the roads themselves." The general course of legislation "sufficiently demonstrates the fact, that in the early history of railroads it was quite generally supposed that they could be public highways in fact, as well as in name."[2]

---

*L., S., & M. Railroad Co. *vs.* United States. 93 U.S., p. 442.

. . . It has also been judicially declared,† that the exercise of the right of eminent domain, in the construction of railroads, and the levy of taxes to raise subsidies in their aid, are justified only by the fact that railroads are public highways. "That railroads though constructed by private corporations and owned by them are public highways, has been the doctrine of nearly all the courts ever since such conveniences for passage and transportation have had any existence." "It has never been considered a matter of any importance that the road was built by the agency of a private corporation. No matter who is the agent, the function performed is that of the State. Though the ownership is private the use is public."[3]

---

†Olcott *vs.* The Supervisors, 16 Wall, 678.

Dabney conceded that opening the roadway to joint use by several carriers would have presented problems, but could offer advantages, even with the limited technology of 1899:

. . . the application upon any railroad line of the theory of free competition, might, in some branches of trade and transportation, be highly beneficial, and might result in a partial solution, at least, of many of the most perplexing problems of railroad transportation.[4]

Next Dabney questioned whether a legislature had the right to grant the public's power of eminent domain for private use by railroads.

Many modern charters and the general railroad laws of some States provide, however, that "the company shall have the exclusive right of transportation over its own road." . . .

The word *"transportation"* suggests two things, namely, motive power, and vehicles for carriage. The language that "the company shall have the exclusive right of transportation over its road," therefore conveys the idea that its own motive power and its own vehicles shall both, exclusively of all others, be used. And to compel the company to haul the vehicles of others, with its own motive power, would be as much of an infringement of the right that language confers, as to compel it to allow others to have the use of its track for their engines and cars.[5]

A railroad was obligated to provide transportation for all who desired it, including the movement of shipper-owned cars in railroad company trains. Dabney argued that a railroad could be compelled by the law to allow the operation of others' trains as well.

In 1949, Charles L. Dearing and Wilfred Owen explored the concept of user fees as a means of assuring equal treatment of each mode and assessed the adequacy of then-existing fees and fee mechanisms in each mode. Structural differences were recognized as the fundamental cause of many railroad industry and transportation policy problems.

The desirability of user charges and their capacity to reflect the relative economy of the various transport agencies would of course be increased if the same method of financing applied to the railroads. We have seen, for example, that the possibilities of achieving an organization of the transportation system based on the economies of full costs is thwarted by the fundamental differences which exist between privately owned rail and publicly provided water, air, and highway facilities. The different manner in which public and private facilities are furnished leads logically to the conclusion that only by uniform methods of providing all basic transportation facilities would it be possible to achieve the environment necessary to attain comparable competitive relationships. It is obvious, because of the public nature and joint use of highways, waterways, and airways, that the goal of uniformity should not be sought by imposing the railroad financial pattern on these undertakings. On the contrary, comparability among transport agencies would suggest that the basic facilities of the railroads—terminals, right of ways, roadbed, and track—be publicly provided, with privately owned equipment operating over the public ways. Such an arrangement would create a situation comparable to that in which the airline company, privately owned and operated, makes use of public airways and airports. Railroad companies, like privately owned airlines, steamship lines, or truck and bus lines, would operate on (and pay for) the public ways.

This possibility suggests a more desirable solution than the alternative of ultimately resorting to complete public ownership of the railroads.[6]

Dearing and Owen did not specify whether rail carriers would share use of the fixed way, but it was implied by the analogies with the other modes.

James C. Nelson's *Railroad Transportation and Public Policy* (1959) supported an economic, full-cost basis for all transportation modes. Roadway/carrier separation was seen as a method for promoting equal government treatment for all modes.

... complete neutrality in treatment of competing agencies will be difficult without government ownership of rail roadways, thereby converting way capital costs and fixed expenses into variable user chargers, making government expenditures available as a source of capital investment as conditions may require, and enabling the railroads also to escape the burden of capital costs merely by curtailing or abandoning operations.[7]

In 1975 Charles P. Zlatkovich proposed "a nationwide network of modernized rail lines similar in scope and function to the Interstate Highway System."[8] The recommended 39,000-mile system of high-density rail transportation corridors would serve the nation's 200,000-mile rail network much as the Interstate highways serve the national and state highway systems. Two methods of implementation were suggested:

One possible method of developing the Interstate Rail System would be for the public sector to provide capital to the various individual railroad companies for improvements to the lines designated for inclusion in the system. Equitable arrangements would have to be made for use of the Interstate Rail System lines by other carriers operating over essentially parallel routes. Such a plan could embody many of the elements of the United States Rail Trust Fund proposal advanced by Governor Milton J. Shapp of Pennsylvania, with the significant difference that rail trust fund use would be limited to use on the Interstate Rail System routes rather than left to the discretion of the individual railroads, as contemplated in the Shapp plan.

Another possible method of developing the Interstate Rail System would be for the public sector to acquire the railroad rights-of-way, tracks, and related facilities designated for inclusion in the Interstate Rail System and to provide funds for their improvement. Public acquisition could also be extended to the entire railroad network, with major improvements restricted to the Interstate Rail System routes. Public ownership of rail rights-of-way and tracks would place rail transportation on the same basis as air, highway, and inland waterway transportation, all of which involve private operation on publicly owned facilities.[9]

The Zlatkovich plan was concerned with the route structure of an Interstate Rail System and the methods of route selection. It did not consider the questions of captive industry (exclusive local service) or service by noncommon carriers. It was significant, because it offered a concrete example of a nationwide joint-use rail system and advocated a structure different from that presently used by the railroads.

D. Daryl Wyckoff proposed roadway/carrier separation in a 1973 article entitled "Public Tracks, Private Users."[10] This proposal was also described in his book *Railroad Management* (1976):

Under this alternative, I propose that the federal government undertake a project to purchase major segments of railroad track and right of way for the purpose of developing a modern, highspeed railroad-track system for public use. This would mean the purchase of some of the existing track and right of way, although that is not mandatory. The railroad would be allowed to continue to own and operate as a private right of way any of its track. Similarly, the federal system would not be obligated to buy undesirable track. The railroads would be responsible for development of classification yards and track connecting their own roads with the federal track system. This feeder track would be analogous with the secondary road that now connects the Federal Interstate Highway System.

Operations on the Public Track System would be in conformance with federal operating regulations. Traffic control through signalling systems would be provided by federal traffic controllers in a role similar to that of the air traffic controllers of the FAA.

Charges for use of this track system would be made on a user-tax basis, again shifting fixed costs of railroading into variable costs, more like the cost structure of the motor carriers.

As it would be a government-provided facility, it makes sense for several operators to use it jointly. In fact, there are several instances in which railroads are already
exchanging trackage rights to each other.[11]

Although Wyckoff recognized roadway/carrier separation as "one of the
most conceptually attractive alternatives," he chose not to pursue the idea.[12]
Wyckoff felt the creation of Conrail averted an outright failure of the
existing railroad structure, removing the immediate need for restructuring.
The expressed opposition of many railroad companies and the Association
of American Railroads to any restructuring led Wyckoff to conclude that
the proposal was politically unacceptable.

CONGRESS ACTS BOLDLY—ALMOST

During the late 1960's and early 1970's academicians and politicians alike
addressed themselves to the Railroad Problem, just as their predecessors
had done for over a century. This time some new proposals were put forth,
prompted by the collapse of the northeastern railroads and the reappraisals
which followed. A common element found in several new proposals was the
roadway/carrier separation concept.

Interstate Railroad Act of 1972

One of the first legislative proposals to incorporate the roadway/carrier
separation concept was the Interstate Railroad Act of 1972, introduced by
Senator Vance Hartke (D-Ind.). Its purpose was

To designate an Interstate Railroad System; to require minimum standards of
maintenance on the railroad lines comprising such system; to establish rights of
access by rail carriers to railroad lines; to provide financial assistance for certain
rehabilitation of railroads; and for other purposes.[13]

The Act found "that the efficiency and quality of railroad service and the
economic utilization of the railroad plant can be improved by freer access
by rail carriers to portions of railroad lines they do not own."[14] Under
provisions of the Act, the Secretary of Transportation would have been
given authority to order a railroad to allow another rail carrier to use its
tracks for reasonable compensation, provided it would "not substantially
impair the ability of the owner or possessor of such railroad line or other
facility to handle its own business."[15] The Act did not explain whether
access for freight carriers meant only through service or both through and
local freight service.

The Interstate Railroad Act of 1972 was unsuccessful. It was introduced
too late for consideration and encountered opposition by the railroad
industry.

Essential Rail Services Act of 1973

Prompted by the continuing problems of the Penn Central, Senator Hartke introduced the Essential Rail Services Act of 1973. It proposed creation of Northeast Rail Line Corporation (NRLC), an independent, not-for-profit public corporation, "to rehabilitate, maintain, modernize, and, where necessary, to restructure rail lines in the Northeast."[16]

The NRLC would have purchased and operated rail fixed ways, or rail lines as they were defined in the Act.

> "Rail line" includes main rail track or tracks; side tracks and yard tracks adjacent to such main tracks; the roadbed supporting such tracks; signalling, communication, and power transmission structures and devices as are permanently installed on or adjacent to such tracks and roadbed; bridges, culverts, fills, tunnels, and other structures occupied by such tracks and roadbed; real estate occupied by such tracks and roadbed; and real estate adjacent to such tracks and roadbed which is used for drainage of, maintenance of, access to, and protection of such tracks and roadbed; but does not include classification yards; station and terminal tracks and facilities, other than running tracks; any structures and devices other than those specified in this paragraph; and does not include air rights over, nor mineral rights under such tracks and roadbed.[17]

The Act would have allowed any rail carrier to use NRLC tracks if the carrier (1) was "fit, willing, and able to properly perform the service proposed"; (2) qualified under the public convenience requirements; and (3) did not "significantly impair the level of performance of the carrier or carriers already using the line who are adequately serving the public."[18] Existing railroad companies would have been granted rights to continue serving routes which they served prior to NRLC's creation, but these rights would not be exclusive.

Like its predecessor, the 1973 Act met stiff opposition from the railroad industry. The most important reason for its failure was the Penn Central bankruptcy. The need for action prompted reliance on the more traditional approach embodied in the Regional Rail Reorganization Act of 1973, which led to the creation of the Consolidated Rail Corporation (Conrail).

Interstate Railroad Act of 1974

Senator Lowell Weicker (R-Conn.) introduced the Interstate Railroad Act of 1974, which was based on the 1972 Act of the same name. The 1974 Act would have empowered the ICC to order the granting of trackage rights "upon application of any rail carrier for the use of any rail line or other facility" if the Commission found that such would not "substantially impair the ability of the owner or possessor of such line or other facility to handle its own business."[19] Senator Hartke observed:

Railroad corporations have been historically reluctant to enter into such arrangements on a voluntary basis for fear that a competitor might get slightly the better part of a bargain. The bill gives the ICC authority to break the impasse when one railroad wants to economize by use of tracks or facilities of another which is not agreeable thereto.[20]

The 1974 Act did not specify whether trackage rights would have included local service or if that service would remain the exclusive domain of the owner railroad company. The Act had no provision for allowing new carriers by rail, implying all rail service would be performed by common carrier railroad companies. Like its two predecessors, the 1974 Act was sidetracked in favor of less controversial, traditional approaches.

Consolidated Facilities Corporation

When the Penn Central led several other northeastern railroad companies into bankruptcy, Congress responded by passing the Regional Rail Reorganization Act. The Act established the United States Railway Association (USRA) to plan the reorganization of the bankrupt railroads.[21]

One of the six preliminary alternative plans drawn by USRA called for the creation of a Consolidated Facilities Corporation (Confac), a government-backed entity which would own rail fixed ways and lease them to Conrail and other carriers.

The Confac approach, federal policymakers say, would head off decades of "government presence" in Conrail and would permit more flexibility in restructuring Northeast-rail operations; the USRA would get more time to negotiate with solvent roads on segments that they might want to buy. . . .

But the Confac idea has implications that frighten many, especially railroaders. It would mean heavy and long-term support by taxpayers for Northeast and Midwest rail operations, at the very least, and additional government intrusion in their business and subsidized competition of some rail lines to the disadvantage of others. Subsidization could spread to rail operations elsewhere in the country and to competing forms of transport such as trucking, many fear. Thinking that the government role won't extend beyond Confac itself may be "wishful thinking," one USRA staff man concedes.[22]

Reaction to the Confac proposal was mixed—even within the railroad industry. As *Trains* magazine observed:

ConFac is the railroad equivalent of the confounding of the language at the Tower of Babel (Genesis 11:9). For in ConFac, both solvents (ICG and N&W) and marginals (MILW) see a way to meld Government and private enterprise without sacrificing the latter; yet other solvents from within and without the region—notably C&O, UP, and SR—see ConFac as a sure, quick lunge toward nationalization. Perhaps as pertinent as the theory of ConFac is the intra-industry dissension which its very mention causes in this troubled 1975.[23]

Debate followed as Confac and the other reorganization alternatives were considered. The Confac alternative was eventually rejected in favor of the Conrail plan. Conrail, the Consolidated Rail Corporation, was to be a traditionally structured railroad with a substantial degree of federal financial involvement.

PROPOSALS AND OPINIONS

Federal roadway takeover and the concept of roadway/carrier separation in general had considerable support even though it did not succeed in Congress. Proposals were made by railroad executives, shippers, and government leaders.

The New England Regional Commission, an agency representing six states, recommended that a federal program be implemented to acquire and maintain rail fixed ways. Railroad companies could sell their roadways voluntarily to a federal agency; the agency would then lease the roadways back to their respective companies on an exclusive-use basis.[24] One of the railroads to support the idea was the Boston and Maine (B&M) Railroad. Alan G. Dustin, President of the B&M, termed federal takeover "the only real alternative. . . . I am basically against the concept, but I consider it as the only acceptable alternative to federalization."[25]

In a survey of shippers taken in 1975, *Railway Age* found support among shippers for federal ownership of rail roadways. Thirty percent of those responding to the poll favored "Federal takeover, rehabilitation and maintenance of roadbeds, with users paying 'rent' to the government."[26]

Just a few years ago, the notion that public money should ever be invested in a private transportation enterprise was anathema to railroad men. "Let the truckers and the airlines and the barge lines do it that way; we'll go it alone," was, for years, the official and profoundly cherished railroad position. A large number of railroad people and railroad shippers still think that's the way it ought to be.

But a growing number are also coming to believe that the way things are and the way things ought to be are not one and the same—and that railroads, having failed in their campaigns to drive competitive modes away from the public fountain, now have no recourse but to get in line.[27]

One of the shippers responding to the poll was A. E. Leitherer, Vice President-Transportation, Allied Mills Incorporated. Leitherer offered a private sector alternative to federal roadway takeover:

. . . railroads should establish a private company assigning to it all railroad track-age on a proper per share basis. Use by more than one carrier should be permitted on an equitable user/charge basis. Essential maintenance should be practiced on a properly agreed upon suitable maximum safe operating speed of agreed upon miles per hour as called for under the FRA. . . .

. . . If this is not done, then I fear absolute nationalization of railroad road bed becomes a necessity.[28]

Four years later, in 1979, the Secretary of Transportation and Construction of the State of Massachusetts, Frederick P. Salvucci, recommended joint use and public ownership of rail fixed ways.

Entry deregulation will work best with public ownership of rights-of-way. Public ownership of airports and highways allows multiple carriers to serve important markets, allows little carriers to compete with big ones, and allows carriers to withdraw (even fail) and be replaced by others without trauma.

Voluntary transfer of rights-of-way to public ownership should be the condition we require in exchange for deregulation and public financial assistance. Any enterprising railroad will prosper under this situation.[29]

Later that same year, the president of a major railroad called for joint use of Conrail trackage in the northeastern United States. John P. Fishwick, President of the Norfolk and Western Railway Company, stated:

. . . A more direct form of rail competition [in the Northeast] could be provided if the federal government merely owned the tracks and facilities, either through Amtrak or another corporation. Conrail, as well as the other major lines connecting with the lines of the facilities corporation, could be given nonexclusive trackage rights to conduct operations over such lines. Similar rights would be given to the D&H, B&M, and perhaps others.

In short, the government would make available rail rights-of-way in the Northeast just as it makes highways available all over the country. The user railroads would pay a charge, perhaps measured by car-miles or by a percentage of revenues. Competition would exist to whatever degree the traffic would support. In the event none of the carriers granted trackage rights was willing to provide service on any lines, the lines could be abandoned, or potential shippers, or others, could provide short-line service to connect with one of the trunk line carriers.[30]

Conrail was viewed as a peculiar situation, and no suggestion was made to open other railroads to joint use. The logic was obvious, however: joint use avoided monopoly, allowed competition, and promoted efficiency.

Fishwick's proposal mentioned that shippers could act as short line rail carriers and operate over branch lines not serviced by the larger rail carriers.

A less modest proposal by C.N.M. Brown of Tesoro Coal Company called for joint use to include private carriers.

As I look at the future, I believe you are going to see increased activity in the formation of energy cooperatives. Many utilities and coal producers already have heavy investments in their transportation facilities. We own rail cars, locomotives, barges, tow boats, and in some cases, railroad rights-of-way. As our needs increase and as common carrier costs escalate, you will see a growing reluctance to leave the management and movement of our equipment in the hands of the common carrier. Just as some members of the petroleum industry determined their need to build and maintain their own pipeline transmission systems, so too, will the coal industry and coal users determine their need to own and maintain their own energy supply routes. This will cause some major disruptions in railroad right-of-way usage and ownership, but there will come a time, when public welfare will demand the divesting of right-of-way ownership, or, at the very minimum, a sharing of that facility.[31]

Arguments for joint use were heard from government officials as well. John P. White, Deputy Director of the federal Office of Management and Budget, "proposed increasing the size of the zone of reasonableness [rate flexibility] for Conrail and other hard-pressed lines provided they are required to sell trackage rights to other railroads and shippers as protection against monopolistic abuses."[32]

The proposals and opinions of these individuals and groups, like the formal legislative proposals, did not result in immediate implementation of the roadway/carrier separation concept. They did help establish the concept firmly as a modern school of thought. The movement toward the roadway/carrier separation concept caused many leaders to reexamine and question the traditional railroad industry structure.

SUMMARY

The concept of railroads as public highways dates from the beginnings of the railroad industry when operation closely resembled that of the turnpikes. Transportation economists over the past forty years have viewed the various modes' structural differences as being the fundamental cause of many general transportation problems and railroad problems in particular. Highways, airways, and waterways function as public highways in fact as well as in theory; the railroads do not.

If the typical transportation industry structure is to be applied to the railroads, two questions must be answered. First, will local service be open to all competing carriers or will it be performed exclusively by one carrier (i.e., monopoly service with captive industries)? Second, will rail carriers other than common carriers be allowed to use the track network?

Addressing these questions cuts to the quick of the Railroad Problem—and to the quick of vested interests inside and outside of the railroad industry. But the issues must be faced squarely and resolved if the railroad is to remain a vital, healthy part of the American transportation machine.

NOTES

1. W. D. Dabney, *Public Regulation of Railways* (New York, 1889).
2. Ibid., pp. 5–7.
3. Ibid., pp. 7–8.
4. Ibid., p. 9
5. Ibid., pp. 9–10.
6. Charles L. Dearing and Wilfred Owen, *National Transportation Policy*, pp. 129–130.
7. James C. Nelson, *Railroad Transportation and Public Policy*, p. 429.
8. Charles P. Zlatkovich, "The Interstate Rail System," Transportation Research Forum, *Proceedings—Sixteenth Annual Meeting*, p. 42.
9. Ibid., p. 45.
10. D. Daryl Wyckoff, "Public Tracks, Private Users," *Transportation and Distribution Management* (April 1973), pp. 38–40.
11. Reprinted by permission of the publisher, from *Railroad Management*, by D. Daryl Wyckoff (Lexington, Mass.: Lexington Books, D. C. Heath and Company, Copyright 1976, D. C. Heath and Company), p. 130.
12. Ibid., p. 133.
13. U.S., Congress, Senate, *Interstate Railroad Act of 1972*, S. 3769, 92d Cong., 2d sess., 1972.
14. Ibid.
15. Ibid.
16. U.S., Congress, Senate, *Essential Rail Services Act of 1973*, S. 1031, 93d Cong., 1st sess., 1973.
17. Ibid.
18. Ibid.
19. U.S., Congress, Senate, *Interstate Railroad Act of 1974*, S. 3343, 93d Cong., 2d sess., 1974, sec. 401(a).
20. U.S., Congress, Senate, *Congressional Record*, April 10, 1974, S. 5590.
21. Those familiar with railroad history will recognize USRA as the initials which were also used by the U.S. Railroad Administration, the federal agency which operated American railroads during the World War I period of nationalization.
22. Albert R. Karr, "Restructuring Northeast Lines May Spur More Federal Involvement Than Expected," *Wall Street Journal*, Volume CLXXXV, Number 38 (February 25, 1975), p. 30.
23. David P. Morgan, "The Sky May Be Falling," *Trains*, Volume 35, Number 9 (July 1975), p. 4. The railroad initials used are ICG, Illinois Central Gulf; N&W, Norfolk and Western; MILW, Milwaukee Road; C&O, Chesapeake and Ohio; UP, Union Pacific; and SR, Southern Railway. Note the different capitalization used during the early stages of the reorganization process, Con-Fac versus Confac.

24. "Governors Back Rail-Plant Takeover," *Railway Age*, Volume 176, Number 15 (August 11, 1975), p. 6.

25. Deborah F. Silver, "Speakers in Wisconsin U. Conference Analyze Midwestern Rail Difficulties," *Traffic World*, Number 2, Volume 175, Whole Number 3716 (July 10, 1978), p. 34; "Tomorrow's Railroads: The View from DOT," *Railway Age*, Volume 178, Number 8 (April 25, 1977), p. 40.

26. "Shippers Back Federal Involvement in Rights of Way," *Railway Age*, Volume 176, Number 8 (April 28, 1975), p. 22.

27. Ibid.

28. Ibid., p. 23.

29. "A Case for Deregulation," *Modern Railroads*, Volume 34, Number 2 (February 1979), p. 71.

30. John P. Fishwick, "The Case for the Firewall," *Railway Age*, Volume 180, Number 22 (November 26, 1979), p. 50.

31. Carl N. M. Brown, "Energy and Transportation: A Time for Decision," *Traffic World*, Number 1, Volume 181, Whole Number 3794 (January 7, 1980), pp. 78–79.

32. "Not All Federal Agencies Comment Favorably on DOT Rail Deregulation Options," *Traffic World*, Number 4, Volume 177, Whole Number 3744 (January 22, 1979), p. 14.

11 | A PROPOSAL

Previous chapters examined the development of the railroad industry and its structure. Particular attention was given to the origins, decline, and recent rebirth of the roadway/carrier separation concept—the idea of a rail fixed way being owned by an entity separate and apart from the carrier companies. The typical industry structure used by the other transport modes was described and compared with the railroads' unique structure. It was concluded that the reasons which originally prompted adoption of the present railroad industry structure are no longer valid: technology no longer demands that a single carrier possess a monopoly of service over each rail line.

Academic and legislative proposals of recent years recognize this fact and promote roadway/carrier separation. However, the proposals vary in quality, scope, and understanding of rail operations. Moreover, none of the proposals directly addresses the two key issues of roadway/carrier separation: (1) exclusive local service, with its captive industries and monopolistic aspects; and (2) the existence of non-common carriers and their use of rail roadways.

The remaining chapters detail a comprehensive proposal for restructuring the railroad industry, based on roadway/carrier separation. This recommended proposal squarely addresses the issues of captive industries and non-common carriers. The greatest advantage of the new structure, though, is that it allows and even *promotes* innovation within the rail industry. Change is encouraged as a positive factor, an asset to a dynamic industry. This is the Free Enterprise Alternative.

A BRIEF DESCRIPTION

The Free Enterprise Alternative is based on the idea of separate roadway and carrier ownership—a concept proven successful in the highway, water, and air transportation modes. Rail roadways would be owned by regional "toll road" companies, unaffiliated with any particular carrier company.

Carriers would be privately owned, and all types of carriers would be allowed to use the roadway network: common, contract, and private. Carriers would share the use of rail roadways, just as carriers share the use of fixed ways in the other modes.

Unlike previous proposals which envisioned government ownership of rail roadways, the Free Enterprise Alternative proposes private ownership of rail roadways in the form of regional roadway companies. All roadways in a given geographic area would be owned, maintained, and operated by a regional rail roadway company. Several roadway companies would serve the nation, much as the regional telephone companies do. Each roadway company would provide maintenance and traffic control for all rail roadways in its area, which could cover all and/or parts of several states. The functions of the roadway companies would be similar to those performed by the state highway departments for highway carriers, except that the roadway companies would be private enterprises. The regional roadway companies would be forced to operate on an economic basis, with each company providing a return to its investors. Private sector ownership with public regulation would provide the combination best capable of serving the needs of carriers, shippers, investors, and the public as a whole with regard to the roadway network.

The railroad company which originally owned a given track would no longer possess a monopoly over that track, although a temporary transitional period would be advisable. Existing railroad companies would become carrier companies by transferring their roadways to the regional roadway companies. As carrier companies, they would be free to enter and leave markets as provided under the new carrier regulatory structure.

Roadway companies and carrier companies would be private sector enterprises. Minimal government regulation would be required, varying with the market structure of each type of company. Roadway companies would be natural monopolies, like utility and telephone companies, and would require stringent yet protective economic regulation. In contrast, the numerous carrier companies would operate in a highly competitive market environment and would be subject to little or no economic regulation.

FREE ENTERPRISE ORIENTATION

Previous proposals for restructuring the railroad industry and implementing roadway/carrier separation usually recommended public sector (government agency) ownership of rail roadways. The Free Enterprise Alternative proposes private sector ownership of rail roadways in the form of regional "toll road" companies. There are several reasons for preferring private sector ownership with public regulation over outright public ownership.

First, public entities have not proven themselves capable of operating large-scale institutions on an economic basis. Public agencies are subject to tremendous political pressure which usually results in politically expedient but highly inefficient operations. Legislators have no qualms about requiring public bodies to provide uneconomic services. This is evidenced by the Postal Service, Amtrak, and many other government-related agencies. Although private sector firms may be required to perform such services on occasion, they can resort to legal action if the legislation requiring the services is confiscatory. This dedication to private property, firmly rooted in the Constitution, acts as a restraint on actions which are politically desirable but economically unacceptable. Private sector operation is inherently more compatible with the nation's capitalistic free enterprise economy.

True, the federal government has the expertise to build and maintain large construction projects like the Interstate highway system and the inland waterway system. These require little active control once they are put in place. The federal airway network is more analogous to the railroads' situation, requiring constant and intensive traffic control. The rail roadway network demands considerable involvement in both fixed way maintenance and traffic control.

Political interference could force inefficiencies on both carriers and roadways if rail roadways were owned by federal or state governments. The quality of facilities, operations, and maintenance of the other modes' fixed ways vary considerably—even under federal direction. Highways, including Interstates, vary in design and maintenance from state to state. Their quality and even their location are often subject to political pressures from interest groups. Waterways and airways have sizeable sporting and recreational lobbies in addition to the political interest of commercial user groups. Highways have a direct impact on a large part of the public as well as truck operators. Rail roadways, if owned by government agencies, would have only their carriers as a lobbying group. Under government control rail roadway budgets would undoubtedly be the black sheep of public transportation. A boxcar of lumber cannot vote; a Volkswagen of people can.

Under private ownership the roadway companies would not be dependent on the legislatures for funding. A properly designed regulatory framework would assure fair economic treatment. Regional roadway companies would be able to best serve the carrier companies on an economic basis, responding to changing traffic demands and other carrier needs.

Private ownership has several advantages, particularly where roadway company-carrier company relationships would be involved. It would be to the advantage of all concerned—carriers, roadway companies, shippers, and the public—to have private sector carriers working with private sector roadway companies. The Free Enterprise Alternative utilizes private sector ownership of all rail industry components as the most effective means for establishing a flexible, dynamic "new" railroad industry.

12 ROADWAY COMPANIES

Most proposals incorporating the roadway/ carrier separation concept utilize government ownership of rail roadways. Under the Free Enterprise Alternative rail fixed ways would remain in the private sector.

Several regional roadway companies would serve the nation, each company owning all rail roadways in its geographic region. Each roadway company would be a corporation, with its stock traded on public exchanges by investors. Roadway companies would not be affiliated with any carrier. Each roadway company would operate its tracks as a toll road for all carriers. Carrier companies would pay published tolls for use of roadway segments. Roadways would be shared by all carriers desiring to use them; there would be no exclusive use of any roadway.[1] In operation, roadways would resemble the fixed ways in the other modes, with the exception that rail roadways would be owned, maintained, and have their traffic controlled by regional roadway companies—not public agencies.

Regional roadway companies would improve roadway maintenance and traffic control. Economic advantages would be obtained through traffic concentration, network utilization, and geographic concentration. By concentrating traffic on the best routes, the roadway company could utilize economies of scale in capital investment, operating flexibility, and maintenance work. Greater network utilization would be possible since the roadway company would own all roadways in its area. Detours, bypasses, and alternative routes could be arranged quickly and easily. Geographic concentration would improve the productivity of maintenance forces, since all of the company's roadways would be located in a compact regional area.

ROADWAYS

The primary asset of each regional roadway company would be its roadways: track, supporting structures, right of way, and traffic control system. The roadway company would own all roadways within its region except (1) tracks and yards owned by shippers and serving shipper-owned facilities; and (2) yards and servicing facilities owned by carriers or independent companies serving the carriers.

Roadways would be classified by traffic volume using four classes:

Class	Annual Traffic Density
Interstate	20 million gross tons or more
Primary	5 to 20 million gross tons
Secondary	1 to 5 million gross tons
Branch	1 million gross tons or less

The volume categories, shown here only as an example, were developed by the Federal Railroad Administration.[2] In many areas the roadway company would consolidate the through traffic of several roadways on one Interstate roadway, so the volumes defining the Interstate and Primary categories might need revision upward as concentration occurs.

The regional roadway company would concentrate traffic as much as possible on the best route between terminals. Route selection would be based on engineering and market factors, not on prior railroad ownership. The selected route could be composed of several segments previously owned by different railroad companies. Joint use would require upgrading of selected routes and downgrading of others. A transition period would allow the planning and making of changes to accommodate the carriers' traffic flows.

Traffic concentration would have its greatest effects and its greatest potential on Interstate roadways, the backbone of the roadway network. Nationally, Interstate routes would account for approximately 30,000 to 50,000 miles of roadway. One example of such a system could be the Federal Railroad Administration's "A" Mainline network.[3] Another example could be the 42,000-mile Interstate Rail System proposed by Charles Zlatkovich.[4]

Regardless of the exact selection method used, several factors must be considered in the selection of Interstate roadways. The distance between terminals by each roadway would be one factor, but minimal grades and curvature would assume major importance due to the predominance of freight traffic. To accommodate the traffic volume previously moving over several parallel routes and to allow for rail traffic growth, the Interstate roadway must have the potential for expansion. Sufficient space should be available for adding sidings and additional main tracks. Horizontal and vertical clearances should accommodate present and future anticipated car sizes. Where possible, clearances should allow for the movement of most oversize loads with minimal traffic disruption. Clearances should provide for eventual electrification with commercial power, leaving room for catenary supports and power-transmission structures. Highway grade crossing elimination would be an important factor for Interstate roadways due to the high volume of rail traffic.

Interstate roadways would usually have two or more main tracks and centralized traffic control (CTC) in both directions on each track. Primary roadways would have single-track CTC with occasional sidings and double track as needed. Some Primary roadways might initially have double track with automatic block signals (ABS), with CTC installed as growth demanded. Secondary and Branch roadways would use track standards and traffic control techniques appropriate to their respective traffic volumes.

The roadway company would provide sidings and train holding yards at various locations as necessary for traffic control. Carriers could use roadway sidings and train yards for a minimal amount of switching and temporary storage, subject to the prescribed fees and at the roadway company's discretion. Carriers must provide their own classification yards, storage yards, and servicing facilities.

TRAFFIC CONTROL

The regional roadway company would control all train movements over its roadway network. Traffic control would have both active and passive elements. It also would include a rules enforcement function.

Centralized traffic control would be the standard method of active control on Interstate and Primary roadways. The signal system would be supplemented by radio communication with all trains and telephone communication with trackside points. Secondary and Branch roadways would be controlled using appropriate types of traffic control: simplified CTC, block signals, train orders (written or radio), staff register system, or radio verbal authority.

Passive traffic control measures would be improved and expanded under the roadway company. Since numerous carriers would be using the same roadways under the new structure, a common set of rules would apply to all roadways and to all carriers using those roadways. In terms of providing traffic control for many users, the roadway company would employ measures used in the other modes—highways, airways, and waterways.

The roadway company would license locomotive engineers, and the different regional roadway companies would honor licenses issued by each other. Licenses would be of several types, varying with locomotive horsepower (total for multiple units) and type of train (freight or passenger). Special licenses would be required for locomotive engineers operating special types of trains, such as trains with mid-train slave locomotives. Examples of licensing procedures include the Federal Aviation Administration's licensing of aircraft pilots, the Coast Guard's licensing of ship and towboat crewmen, and the various state procedures for licensing truck drivers.

Traffic control rules would be established using two books, the *Code of Roadway Regulations* and the *Regional Roadway Charts*. The *Code of Roadway Regulations* (CRR's) would contain fundamental traffic control rules common to all roadway companies plus supplemental rules unique to each region. The CRR's would be revised as necessary and reissued at regular intervals. Periodic license renewal tests would insure dissemination of revisions among all locomotive engineers. The *Federal Aviation Regulations* (FAR's) exemplify how the *Code of Roadway Regulations* might function in practice.

Regional Roadway Charts (RRC's) would contain descriptive information pertinent to specific roadways, much of which is presently contained in railroad general orders, employee timetables, and special instructions. RRC's would be patterned after FAA aeronautical charts, Corps of Engineers navigation charts, and railroad track diagram books, but with additional information. Among the data contained in the RRC's would be:

    Track Diagram Maps
      Grades
      Curvature
      Junctions and Crossings
      Sidings
      Yards and Spurs
        Roadway Company
        Carrier, Shipper, and Independent
    Type of Traffic Control
      CRR's in Effect on Particular Roadway Segments
      Signal Locations
      Radio Frequencies Used
    Speed and Weight Limits
    Roadway Company Facilities
      Trackside Telephone Locations
      Office Locations
      Emergency Services
    Other Facilities and Services
      Carrier Companies
      Independent Firms

The roadway company would not use timetable schedules for traffic control. Trains of all carriers would operate under the regulations (CRR's) in effect on each roadway. On Interstate and Primary roadways, traffic controllers would direct train movements through CTC signal indications. On Secondary and Branch roadways, traffic controllers would use the prescribed control methods. When necessary, train orders could be issued to carrier trains direct by radio or via remote printers at roadway company offices. Unlike existing railroads, the roadway company must place considerably more reliance on trackside signs to communicate speed restrictions, track conditions, and other information.

Under the present structure, a railroad company can rely on administrative methods to convey information to train crews since the crews are all employees of the railroad company. Signs are used infrequently, particularly when compared to highway practice. A stretch of high-speed main track might need repair, have a speed restriction of 10 miles per hour placed on it, and have no signs marking the location. The restriction is communicated to train crews by written train orders or other administrative methods. When a main track has several unmarked speed restrictions, train crews must exercise a high degree of attention in order to observe each one.

With the roadway concept, many different carriers would share use of the roadway. Immediate roadway changes affecting train operations would be conveyed to crews by trackside signs and lights. Use of signs and signals would reduce the possibility of an engineer overlooking a reduced-speed zone and eliminate the need for many written slow orders. Restrictions of a permanent nature would be issued in revised *Regional Roadway Charts* (RRC's) and marked by signs. Roadway signs would be applied thoroughly and would be of standard designs. Highway sign practice could serve as a good example for rail sign applications.

A special police force would enforce roadway regulations as they pertain to carrier and roadway personnel. The police force would be a department of the roadway company, separate from the maintenance and traffic control functions. Roadway policemen would have the authority of state and local agencies in cases of criminal violations. Roadway police would be primarily concerned with carrier observance of roadway rules, but also would report violations of traffic control procedures by roadway company personnel.

Under current practice, railroad company supervisors act as policemen, enforcing the railroad's operating rules. Violations can result in an employee's reprimand, suspension, or dismissal. Local law enforcement agencies can and do enforce laws affecting train operations, such as city speed limits for trains and ordinances against blocking street crossings. More often, enforcement is left to railroad supervisors. Railroad supervisors must also enforce FRA safety regulations. Conflicts of interest can result. When expedient, violations can go unreported even if safety is jeopardized.

Enforcement by roadway police would be fair and impartial. Police would patrol roadways, monitor carrier train operations, license locomotive engineers, and perform periodic weight checks of carrier vehicles. Roadway police would not replace the role of carrier and roadway supervisors in securing conformance with regulations; rather, the police would complement their efforts.

CORPORATE ORGANIZATION

The organization structure of the regional roadway company would be based on the functions of traffic control and roadway maintenance. It would include several commercial and staff-support functions necessary to its role as a business enterprise. (An example of roadway company organization is shown in Figure 10.) Using this plan the company would be comprised of seven major divisions: Traffic Control, Maintenance, Information Systems, Commercial, Finance, Administration, and Police.

Traffic Control Division

The Traffic Control Division would direct the movement of all trains using the roadway company's network. The company's region would be divided into one or more areas, each under the supervision of a traffic control center (TCC). TCC's would be staffed with traffic controllers, service representatives, clerical personnel, and supervisors. The operation of roadway company TCC's would be similar to that of Federal Aviation Administration air route traffic control centers (ARTCC's). Due to the commercial nature of the roadway company, service representatives and their interaction with carrier personnel would assume an important role within the roadway company.

Each traffic controller would direct train traffic over an assigned segment of the roadway network. As necessary, controllers would coordinate their train movements with controllers of adjoining segments and adjacent roadway companies' regions. Roadway company traffic controllers would integrate the train operations of many different carriers as needed for joint roadway use. For individual train movements, contact between the roadway company and carriers would occur at the traffic controller-train crew level. Advance planning of train movements would be handled by the roadway company's service representatives (located at traffic control centers) in conjunction with carrier company personnel.

To describe fully the relationship between the roadway company and the carriers, certain aspects of carrier organization must be noted. Carrier companies would vary in size and complexity from small owner-operators to large corporations. In the typical carrier, supervisors and dispatchers would determine when and where trains should be run, which cars should be moved, and which crews would operate which trains. Train crews would be given work orders with this information. For a through train the work order would be simple; a local train with pickups and setouts could have a sizeable work order. Most of a carrier's trains would originate at that carrier's

Figure 10. Roadway Company Organization Structure

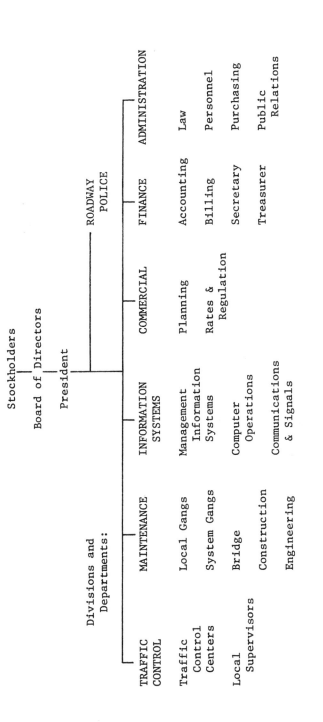

Stockholders

Board of Directors

President

Divisions and
Departments:

TRAFFIC CONTROL	MAINTENANCE	INFORMATION SYSTEMS	COMMERCIAL	FINANCE	ROADWAY POLICE	ADMINISTRATION
Traffic Control Centers	Local Gangs	Management Information Systems	Planning	Accounting		Law
	System Gangs		Rates & Regulation	Billing		Personnel
Local Supervisors	Bridge Construction	Computer Operations		Secretary		Purchasing
	Engineering	Communications & Signals		Treasurer		Public Relations

classification yards. Occasionally, carriers would originate trains at shipper facilities, independent yards, or roadway company train yards.

Using their work orders, the carrier's train crew would file a train movement plan with the roadway company's traffic control center. The train's counterpart of an aircraft flight plan, the train movement plan would include information such as:

Identification
   Type of Train
   Carrier Company
   Engine Number(s)
   Crew Members
Description
   Number of Cars
   Tonnage
   Length
Work Plan
   Origin-Route-Destination
   Pickup/Setout
      Station
      Number of Cars
      Tonnage
      Length
   Servicing Stops
   Other Planned Delays
Desired Schedule
   Estimated Departure/Arrival Times

The movement plan would be filed prior to the train's anticipated departure time. Roadway traffic control would inform the crew of any foreseeable delays and potential problems, in case a revised movement plan would be needed. Although there would be no need to give slow orders—all speed restrictions would be adequately marked by signs, and permanent restrictions would be noted in the *Regional Roadway Charts* as well—traffic control might inform the crew of any major track problems which could be encountered en route.

When ready to depart from the carrier's yard and enter the roadway, the train crew would establish radio contact with the roadway traffic controller. Upon receipt of the proper signal indication or other authorization, the train could move into the roadway's traffic flow. While using the roadway, all trains would monitor the prescribed radio channel for traffic control communications. The carrier company's dispatcher could check on his train's progress by calling a service representative at the traffic control center. A separate radio channel could also be used for the carrier company to contact its trains, but such communications must not interfere with roadway traffic control radio communications.

Should the carrier desire to modify the train movement plan of a train en route, the train crew must contact traffic control and obtain permission to revise its train movement plan. The traffic control interface would be at the train crew-traffic controller level and any changes must be communicated through this channel.

Roadway company traffic control would need to be fair and impartial since the trains of many different carriers, some in direct competition with each other, would be under common authority. Traffic control would seek to move all trains as efficiently and safely as possible, without preference except for type of train as prescribed in roadway company rules and rates. Three types of trains, in order of priority and level of tolls, would be express (fast freight and passenger), regular, and local.

Within the traffic control center, service representatives would provide carrier personnel with information about train locations, arrival/departure times, route conditions, train traffic volumes, alternate routes, and other matters. By having service representatives perform such functions, traffic controllers could devote full attention to directing train movements. Use of a computerized traffic control system such as centralized traffic control with computer-assisted dispatching (CTC-CAD) would allow service representatives to answer many carrier inquiries without disturbing traffic controllers.

Service representatives would play an important role in advance traffic planning by anticipating traffic volumes over the next one- to ten-day time horizon. Carriers would find it advantageous to coordinate their own anticipated train service plans with the traffic control center's service representatives. This coordination, particularly with medium and large carriers having extensive operations in the TCC's area, would reduce peak traffic volumes, reduce traffic interference, and generally improve traffic control. Within the traffic control center, supervisors and staff members would use information from service representatives to anticipate traffic problems. Bypass and secondary routes could be used to alleviate traffic surges; roadway maintenance schedules could be temporarily adjusted. Carriers could be informed of anticipated peak-volume periods and asked to adjust their operations to whatever extent possible. Traffic control planning would be the responsibility of the Traffic Control Division in the short term and of the Commercial Division in the long term. Coordination of efforts between the two divisions and the Maintenance Division would be essential.

In addition to traffic control center personnel, the Traffic Control Division would have field supervisors in each of the company's geographic areas. Field supervisors would work with carrier personnel, roadway traffic controllers, and roadway police to assist train movements and supervise traffic control procedures.

Maintenance Division

The Maintenance Division would be responsible for all of the regional roadways. In terms of function and organization the Maintenance Division would be similar to the engineering and maintenance of way departments of existing railroad companies. Unlike present-day railroads, the roadway company would own all roadways in its region, allowing more effective and efficient deployment of its maintenance resources. Four departments would be included in the Maintenance Division: Roadway Maintenance, Bridge Maintenance, Engineering, and Construction.

The largest maintenance department would be Roadway Maintenance, with several subdivisions reflecting its multiple functions. At the local level section gangs would perform spot maintenance on their assigned track segments. Specialized gangs for tamping, switch repair, crossings, and other work would perform routine maintenance over larger territories within the region. System gangs would perform routine and cycle maintenance such as rail and tie renewal throughout the company's region. A maintenance planning staff would design the maintenance program.

The Bridge Maintenance Department would maintain bridges, trestles, and other supporting structures. The Construction Department would supervise all new roadway construction and expansion projects. The Engineering Department would provide technical and administrative assistance to the other maintenance departments.

Information Systems Division

Data processing, communications, and signaling would be the responsibility of the Information Systems Division. The Signal and Communications Department would install and maintain signal, radio, telephone, and data-transmission systems. Its field personnel would be spread throughout the region; their work would be largely in support of the traffic control system. System design, maintenance planning, and administrative duties would be performed by staff personnel.

The Data Processing Department would provide the roadway company's computerized information system. Much of the system's data base would be generated by traffic control activities. This information would be recorded through manual entry or data transfer from computer-assisted, centralized traffic control. The data base would be used for accounting, toll billing for carriers, commercial systems, and maintenance systems. Computer programs serving other areas, such as personnel and purchasing, would be integrated with the company's information system.

Commercial Division

The primary role of the Commercial Division would be the planning of roadway company profitability. This would be accomplished by (1) forecasting traffic demands; (2) adjusting roadway network capacity to adequately meet those demands; and (3) establishing toll charges sufficient to provide the necessary rate of return while reflecting the costs of individual roadway segments and types of train service. Carrier companies would influence commercial procedures; the setting of tolls would involve approval by the federal regulatory authority.

The Planning Department would forecast traffic levels for the roadway company as a whole and for specific roadway segments. Utilization factors would be applied to determine where expansion or contraction of capacity would be required. Changes in the designation of roadway segments—Primary to Interstate, Secondary to Branch, and so on—would be made by the Planning Department.

The Pricing Department would set tolls based on factors such as roadway segment designation, type of train, and train characteristics. Since cost and utilization factors would also affect tolls, close coordination would be needed between the Planning and Pricing Departments. The Pricing Department would be responsible for obtaining federal approval for toll changes.

Finance Division

The Finance Division would perform the normal corporate financial functions. It would be responsible for the acquisition, investment, and disbursement of funds for the roadway company's operations. The offices of corporate Secretary and Treasurer would be in the Finance Division. The Accounting Department, including the section responsible for billing carriers for roadway usage, would be a major component of the division.

Administrative Division

The Administrative Division would provide support to the other company divisions. Its departments would include those found in most corporations: Legal, Personnel, Purchasing, and Public Relations.

Examples

Other modes of transportation and other industries have organizations similar in form and function to the proposed regional roadway companies. In the other modes—highway, air, and water—government agencies maintain the fixed way, provide traffic control, set operating rules, and license individuals to operate vehicles. These government organizations are similar to the proposed roadway companies, even though the roadway companies would be private corporations.

Utility and telephone companies could also serve as examples for roadway company organization. They are characterized by a large fixed plant which requires considerable maintenance and active operation (the counterpart of roadway traffic control). They also have similar business functions: pricing, planning, financial, and administrative. Furthermore, both utility and telephone companies are typically organized on a regional basis like that envisioned for roadway companies. Although the regional Bell telephone companies are grouped under American Telephone and Telegraph, it is expected that the regional rail roadway companies could achieve the necessary degree of coordination without the use of a national holding company.

ADVANTAGES

With all roadways in a region under the jurisdiction of a single company, the economics of roadway functions could be improved considerably. Regional roadways offer advantages in three areas:

Traffic concentration
Network utilization
Geographic concentration

Traffic concentration would allow the regional roadway company to take full advantage of economies of scale inherent in rail roadways. Network utilization would be improved in terms of traffic flow and track maintenance since all roadways in the region could be used as an integrated system. Common control of all roadways, rather than operation under separate entities, offers greater economies in train operation and track maintenance.

Traffic Concentration

Traffic concentration would make capital investment more productive and maintenance more efficient. Roadway investment increases at a decreasing rate relative to traffic volume capacity. For example, a double-track roadway can handle more traffic than two single-track roadways, yet costs considerably less to construct.

Signal systems also increase traffic capacity. A single-track roadway with centralized traffic control (CTC) can accommodate up to 80 percent more traffic volume than a similar line without CTC. The cost of CTC is much less than that of adding a second track. A double-track roadway with full CTC (allowing trains to use either track in either direction) can provide the traffic capacity of a three- or four-track non-CTC roadway but with a much smaller investment.

Economies of scale are found in the costs of roadway maintenance. As traffic volume increases, maintenance costs increase at a less-than-proportionate rate. For this reason it costs considerably less to maintain one roadway with a traffic volume of ten million gross ton-miles per mile per year than to maintain two separate roadways each with half that volume.

Network Utilization

The regional roadway company could utilize untapped economies of scale in the track network. Under the existing industry structure each railroad must have its own tracks between major cities. The roadways are often operated below their capacity, because each railroad must maintain the minimum-size fixed way, a single-track roadway with occasional sidings, regardless of its traffic volume. Furthermore, each railroad company must have a track able to accommodate its maximum or peak traffic volume. This results in a total excess capacity of substantial amounts, with the consequent costs borne by the various railroad companies.[5]

The single-track roadway with sidings, the mainstay of modern railroading, is comparable in operation to the single-lane highway bridges built early in this century: when train traffic is heavy, trains can spend almost as much time sitting in sidings waiting for opposing trains to pass as they do running. Multiple-track roadways are more efficient, but they are found infrequently, because individual railroad companies seldom have the traffic volume to support them. The traffic does exist, but it is often spread among several railroad companies, each with its own roadway. The Free Enterprise Alternative would concentrate all traffic on the best routes between two terminals, expanding capacity as needed. Redundant routes would be downgraded; some routes could be abandoned.

Maintenance work could be performed more easily and efficiently by the roadway company. Presently, with each railroad operating trains only over its own single-track roadway, trains and maintenance forces compete for on-track time. If maintenance crews work, trains cannot run; if trains run, maintenance must wait. On those railroads with multiple-track roadways train traffic and maintenance work may proceed with minimal interference, but such roadways are only a small portion of the entire rail network. The roadway company could concentrate traffic on the best route, expand it to multiple track as necessary, and take advantage of decreased traffic-maintenance work interference.

The roadway company could easily arrange detours around maintenance work and obstructions such as derailments or washouts. Under the present structure, the detouring of trains of one railroad company over the tracks of another railroad company is done only in emergencies like a major derailment. The railroad desiring to detour its trains must make arrangements with the host railroad. Employees of the host railroad must often act as pilots, guiding detoured train crews who are unfamiliar with the rules and terrain of the host railroad's track. Differences in company attitudes and inability to reach agreement on matters of financial terms, operating procedures, liability for any damages, and other issues often minimize or eliminate the use of detours. It is not uncommon for a railroad company to detour its trains several hundred miles over its own alternate routes rather than use a detour of a few miles over another company's nearby track. In some instances, the Interstate Commerce Commission can intervene and order a company to allow another railroad to use its tracks temporarily as a detour route, but this involves certain legal and administrative procedures and is useful only when track obstruction would continue for some time.

Using all roadways as a system, the regional roadway company could employ detours easily and effectively. In many instances track maintenance could proceed without necessitating a detour, since the roadway company would have many segments of multiple-track roadway. Where detours were necessary, the roadway company could use the shortest combination of Primary, Secondary, and Branch roadways to minimize traffic disruption. By using detours, heavy maintenance work such as rail or tie renewal could proceed without delay. Maintenance forces could work two or three shifts daily, have a given track segment available continuously, and thereby greatly improve maintenance productivity. With all carriers operating under common rules and traffic control, detours would pose no problem to carriers. The flexibilities of common control under a regional roadway company would be a definite advantage to both traffic flow and maintenance work.

Geographic Concentration

Geographic concentration offers many advantages to the roadway company. Geographic divisions would be smaller than those now used by railroad companies due to the relatively compact nature of the regional roadway company's trackage. Whereas a typical railroad company might operate 10,000 or 15,000 miles of track spread over ten states, the roadway company might have that much trackage in one or a few states. Mileage could be comparable to that of the largest railroads now existing but would be much more compact in geographic terms.

For maintenance functions this would translate into numerous savings. Local track forces (section gangs) could be assigned on an area basis instead of a line basis. This would reduce daily travel time between the maintenance base and various work points. At broader levels, even greater economies would be possible in the assignment of tamping gangs, bridge gangs, switch gangs, signalmen, tie gangs, rail gangs, and other forces. Emergency derailment clearing crews (track forces of the roadway company and wrecking crews of carriers or independent firms) would have less distance to travel by serving a radial area instead of a particular linear route or routes.

An example of geographic concentration in fixed way maintenance is found in state highway departments. Each district of the department is responsible for all highways in its area: Interstate, federal, state primary, and secondary roads. This method is more logical and efficient than having one maintenance force assigned to each specific route such as Interstate 57, U.S. 66, or Illinois 127. Route-based maintenance is accepted in the railroad industry, only because different routes are under the ownership of different railroad companies.

SUMMARY

The roadway/carrier separation concept is not new to railroading and transportation. The earliest railroads in England and America employed the concept when they operated as toll roads for horse-drawn wagons. In modern America three major modes of transportation utilize the concept: highways, waterways, and airways. Their fixed ways are used jointly by many carriers, but the ownership, control, and maintenance of the fixed ways is vested in entities separate and apart from the carriers.

The railroads' present industry structure was adopted during the mid-1800's when less advanced technology made it imperative for a single company to provide all rail service over each roadway. Since that time tremendous advancements have been made in technology. Today there is no technological reason for allowing a railroad company to maintain a monopoly of service over a specific roadway, holding all shippers on that roadway captive to a single rail carrier.

Roadway companies offer a means for implementing roadway/carrier separation within a free enterprise framework. Roadway companies would open the rail network to all types of rail carriers, encouraging competition on all roadways. Captive industries would no longer exist. The Free Enterprise Alternative would recognize the roadway as the only element of natural monopoly in railroading and would subject it to appropriate economic regulation. This would allow all carriers to compete while enjoying the economic benefits of joint use. Railroading would be brought out of its nineteenth-century monopolistic-competitive schizophrenia and into the innovative, competitive environment of modern transportation.

NOTES

1. An exception would be the restricted access zones described later in Chapter 14.
2. U.S., Department of Transportation, *Final Standards, Classification, and Designation of Lines of Class 1 Railroads in the United States.*
3. Ibid.
4. Charles P. Zlatkovich, "The Interstate Rail System," Transportation Research Forum, *Proceedings—Sixteenth Annual Meeting*, p. 42.
5. The U.S. DOT *Final Standards Report* cited above identifies several Corridors of Consolidation Potential (CCP's) in which "three or more parallel through-routes, operated by three or more carriers, serve the corridor and the practical traffic-handling capacity of the combined routes exceeds the actual traffic density by 50 percent or more." The CCP's represent only the worst cases of overcapacity. When situations with two parallel railroads are included, and

when parallel non-through routes such as secondary and branch lines are considered, the true extent of consolidation potential becomes apparent.

13 | CARRIER COMPANIES

The Free Enterprise Alternative proposes separation of rail carrier and fixed way functions. All rail roadways in a region would be owned by ¤ regional roadway company, and several roadway companies would form the national roadway network. Many carriers of several different types would share use of the roadway network. Both elements—regional roadway companies and multiple types of carriers—are essential to the Free Enterprise Alternative.

Joint use of roadways offers carriers better routes, lower costs, and improved efficiency. Competition would be enhanced as a constructive market force. Several types of carriers (common, contract, and private) would encourage innovations in rates, service, and equipment.

TRADITIONAL RAIL SERVICE

The highway, water, and air modes all utilize fixed ways which are provided at public expense and made available to all who desire to use them. Joint use of the fixed way facilitates competition among the carriers in each mode.

An industrial plant which ships or receives freight can locate adjacent to a major highway and obtain service from several common and contract carriers. If its shipments are exempt from economic regulation the firm can hire individual owner-operators and other exempt carriers. The firm can lease or buy its own trucks and engage in private carriage.

If the firm builds its plant along a navigable waterway, service is available from a number of common and contract water carriers. Towboats and barges are readily available for charter. The shipper can lease or buy vessels and provide its own private carriage.

If the firm needs air freight service, it can ship by several air cargo and air express common carriers. The firm can contract for air service. The shipper can exercise its private carriage option and fly its own aircraft.

The industrial plant locating next to a railroad is served only by that railroad company. To ship by rail, the firm must deal with that particular railroad company. In contrast to the other modes, each railroad has exclusive use of its own fixed way. No other railroad company has access to that fixed way without the owner railroad company's permission.

A shipper can provide its own freight cars—it can even provide an entire train with cars, road locomotives, and caboose—but the shipment must move in the railroad company's common carrier service.[1] The railroad company has a monopoly of service on its own tracks, and no other carrier—private, contract, or common—is allowed to use those tracks without its permission.

Service Levels

The railroad company decides what level of train service is provided throughout its track network. The railroad determines when and how frequently a shipper will be given switch service. The railroad distributes and places empty cars for loading. Once a loaded car is released by the shipper, movement is at the discretion of the railroad. The railroad decides which trains and yards the car will move through on its journey. Although the shipper may request expedited handling or delivery by a specific date, such a request is not binding on the railroad company and usually involves only monitoring of car movement to prevent excessive delays.

As a rule, a railroad offers only one class of freight service. Carloads of gravel, automobiles, or chemicals all receive the same service. Although a railroad may have local trains, through trains, and variations of the two, they represent complementary components of the railroad's freight movement system and not competing classes of service. A few railroads separate levels of service in the form of all-piggyback trains and unit trains, which operate apart from the general freight system and its train-yard-train process. On most rail routes, however, railroads provide only one class of freight service for shippers.

Provision of a uniform type of freight service is based on (1) the railroad's role as a common carrier; and (2) the need to maximize efficiency at minimum cost. As a common carrier, the railroad has an obligation to serve all customers without undue discrimination. The railroad must serve a broad spectrum of shippers who have conflicting service and price demands. Moreover, the railroad company must serve those shippers efficiently if it is to earn a profit, renew its facilities, and remain in business. To this end, the railroad's trains and yard operations are designed to serve the macro-level needs of shippers as a whole and are seldom tailored to the desires of individual shippers. Unless a shipper has an extremely large volume of traffic, such tailoring is unlikely under present constraints (labor work rules, long trains, and so on). Uniform freight service allows the railroad to serve many customers at a given level of efficiency and cost.

With a uniform level of service available to most shippers, adjustments in the marketing mix must rely heavily on changes in prices (rates). Price flexibility is possible because of the high fixed costs associated with railroads, specifically the investment in the fixed way. Since variable costs represent only a portion of the railroad's total costs, individual prices may vary considerably. "What the traffic will bear" has long been a revered axiom of railroad pricing, and it will continue so long as the present structure's cost relationships are in effect.

Besides service and price, equipment is an important consideration. The railroad may assign cars for use by a particular shipper, and may even provide special types of cars. Special equipment can offer the shipper savings in packaging costs or economies in shipment volumes. With or without changes in price, equipment factors can improve the attractiveness of rail shipment to a customer. However, the uniform level of freight service remains a given in the marketing equation.

The concept of a single service level is applicable to the railroad industry as well as individual railroads. Most shipments originate on the tracks of one railroad and terminate at a point on some other railroad company. Some shipments must move over a series of railroads. Because a railroad company provides all train service on its tracks and, therefore, can provide train service only as far as the extent of its own tracks, railroads must interchange most traffic. The railroad industry's dependence on interchange stems from its basic structure, from the fact that each company has a monopoly of service on its own tracks. Reliance on interchange also means that the railroad industry is often no stronger than its weakest railroad. Alternative rail routes may let a shipper avoid a specific railroad company in some cases, but they cannot provide service to towns and industries served exclusively by that railroad company. The typical level of freight service, including interchange, forms the least common denominator by which the railroad industry's performance as a transportation mode is measured.

The single level of service of most railroads stands in contrast with the other modes. Flexibility in both service and price allows the other modes to fill the different needs of many individual shippers. The shipper can choose from a variety of price/service options offered by many different carriers.

A less obvious but still important consideration in the marketing equation is the degree of control over the transportation process exercised by the shipper. In the highway, water, and air transport modes the shipper can choose from several degrees of control available from the same carrier or from different carriers. In trucking, for example, the shipper can use common carrier service and give the trucking company nearly complete control in the handling of his shipment. The shipper can purchase expedited service involving a pair of drivers and a sleeper-cab tractor to minimize transit time. A contract carrier can be hired to provide service suited to the shipper's special needs. As a final alternative, the shipper can acquire its own trucks and operate as a private carrier. Private carriage gives the shipper complete control over all aspects of service, cost, and equipment. Similar control options are available in air and water transportation.

Avoidance of Captivity

Given the limited range of service offered by the railroads and the fact that most shipper facilities are served by only one railroad, shippers often seek ways to increase their rail service options.[2] There are ways a shipper can avoid being held captive to a railroad's exclusive service, but the methods are generally inefficient or ineffective. The obvious method is to have service by two railroads, either by locating at a junction point or between two nearby tracks and building spur tracks to both railroads. Most heavily industrialized areas are encircled and crossed by the tracks of several railroads for this purpose. Although service by several railroads gives the shipper alternatives, each railroad company still has a monopoly of service over its respective tracks. The shipper must have a track connection to each railroad, and not all shippers can locate at points served by two or more railroads.

The shipper located on only one railroad can minimize its dealings with that railroad by routing its traffic to the nearest interchange and then over another railroad.[3] Still, the shipper must rely on the monopoly service of the railroad serving its plant to provide the initial rail service. If the railroad serving the shipper goes all or part of the way to the destination, and yet the shipper routes its traffic to another railroad at a nearby interchange, the originating carrier receives less than its maximum possible revenue. In return for being "shorthauled" by the shipper, the originating railroad might provide poor service. The shipper might experience problems in switching and empty car supply if it shorthauls the railroad serving its plant. Furthermore, at the interchange point the shipper exchanges one service monopoly for another.

Trackage rights offer a possible means of escaping a railroad's monopoly of service, but they are seldom used in this manner. The railroad company owning the track grants trackage rights to a tenant railroad only if it wishes to do so and, therefore, only on terms it finds acceptable. Trackage right agreements commonly prohibit the tenant from providing any local service: the tenant railroad cannot serve any of the owner railroad's on-line industries. Since local service via trackage rights would require that the owner railroad willingly give up its exclusive service, it is an unlikely alternative.

A simpler means of avoiding a railroad's monopoly of service is to ship by truck. The shipper can truck his shipment to a team track or loading facility located on another railroad. The shipper can use piggyback (trailer on flatcar) service and drive the truck to another railroad's piggyback ramp.

Indeed, many railroads have used piggyback to extend service beyond their traditional market area, invading other railroads' territories by highway. Truck-to-rail and piggyback are usually more expensive than direct carload shipment. Once the shipment is on the other railroad the shipper must contend with that company's monopoly service. Another possibility, selected by an increasing number of shippers, is to move the shipment entirely by truck and avoid rail movement.

TYPES OF CARRIERS

Under the Free Enterprise Alternative, the rail industry would be restructured to resemble the other modes. The rail fixed way network would be owned by private enterprise regional roadway companies. Many carrier companies of different types would share use of the entire roadway network, allowing rail shippers to receive competitive service over the same track from a number of carriers. Shippers would have the option of operating their own trains as private carriers. Common use of all rail roadways would encourage competition while eliminating captive industries and monopolies of service.

Under the new structure three types of rail carrier companies would exist: common, contract, and private. This would reflect the structure of the other modes. With a few exceptions, all carriers would be private sector, free enterprise companies. Many would be transformed descendants of traditional railroad companies; some carriers could be related to carriers in the other modes. Many carriers would be newcomers to the rail industry.

Common Carriers

Rail common carriers would offer for-hire transportation to all shippers who desire to use it. Most would be common carriers of general freight, handling carload freight in the typical move-sort-move manner. Other common carriers would handle traffic only on a trainload basis, with a "train" varying from one to one hundred-plus cars depending on the carrier and the situation. Trainload service would approach that performed by contract carriers, with the exception that the common carriers would provide it without a contract on an as-needed basis to any shipper. When used with a short train of one or a few cars, the trainload common carrier would resemble an irregular route trucking company.

In geographic terms, a rail common carrier could serve different areas at different levels of penetration. The combination of coverage and penetration would vary from carrier to carrier. One group of common carriers might provide service on a national or regional basis but serve only large cities. Another set of carriers might serve both large and small cities in a region and provide local service in a few key areas. Other common carriers might offer extensive local service in a particular area or region. The region served by a carrier would not usually coincide with roadway company regional boundaries.

A general freight common carrier could have local operations in a specific region and through (trunk) service to major cities across the nation. A competitor might provide a more extensive trunk service network while relying on independent connecting carriers for local service. With equal roadway access available to all carriers throughout the roadway network, a carrier's size would have only minor competitive importance. The large trunk carrier might provide local service; so could small carriers which could connect with larger carriers at various cities.

The more specialized trainload carriers could serve areas of larger geographic scope, most likely regional or national. A common carrier might offer both carload and trainload service, using separate subsidiaries, just as many truck lines have special shipment or heavy-hauler divisions.

The ease with which a common carrier could enter and exit a market (city, route, region) would depend on the type and degree of economic regulation imposed. In an unregulated, free enterprise environment, carriers could change their market patterns quickly and easily. If some degree of economic regulation were imposed, it should allow for relatively rapid, short-term market entry and withdrawal. Alternative forms of economic regulation are detailed in Chapter 15.

Contract Carriers

Common carriers and contract carriers provide for-hire transportation, but contract carriers serve only specific customers with whom they have service contracts. Contract carriers usually offer a specialized type of transport operation, handle certain commodities, or otherwise provide services not available from common carriers.

Under the new structure, the geographic scope of contract carriers could range from local to national. The extent of an individual contract carrier's operations would depend on the type of service offered and the location of its customers. Contract carriers might include (1) unit train service linking mine and power plant; (2) train service for oversize or heavy items such as electrical machinery or refinery equipment; and (3) train services for hazardous commodities. Numerous examples are possible.

The contract carrier could be a company in its own right, or it could be a subsidiary of a common carrier if regulation permitted. Dual common/contract carrier operation is allowed to a limited extent in the other modes, and the deregulatory trend implies further easing of existing restrictions. Even though existing railroad companies are common carriers, many operations—particularly unit trains—are candidates for contract status due to high minimum volumes, annual volumes, trainload rates, strict load/unload provisions, and high penalties for non-adherence to service provisions.

Private Carriers

The right of a shipper to transport its own goods is basic to free enterprise. In the final analysis, private carriage acts as the ultimate check on for-hire carrier companies and on their regulation by government agencies when such regulation exists. Private carriage is often used, because it can be suited to the shipper's exact needs. It can be more convenient or less expensive than use of for-hire carriers. Because a common carrier must, by definition, serve any and all customers, an individual shipper's needs may be subordinated so that all shippers can be served at some adequate level of service. Some shippers, however, have transportation needs which common carrier service cannot reasonably provide. These shippers must rely on contract carriers or operate their own service as private carriers.

Under the traditional railroad structure, private carriage is not allowed. Shippers may own freight cars, but the cars must be moved by the common carrier railroad company. Although shippers can operate as private carriers by highway, waterway, and airway, the efficiencies of steel-wheel-on-steel-rail technology are reserved exclusively for those common carrier railroad companies who also own the rail fixed ways. The suboptimizations inherent in any common carriage operation frequently overwhelm the engineered efficiency of rail technology. Many shippers have turned to private truck or barge operations, because private train movements are prohibited under the traditional railroad structure.

The Free Enterprise Alternative allows any carrier to use the rail roadway network, including private carriers. Rail technology can be combined with private carriage operation to provide a highly efficient transportation system tailored to a particular shipper's requirements. A considerable amount of traffic moving in expensive truck operations could be converted to less costly private carrier train services. Private waterway operations of marginal economy (transit time versus transport cost) would be susceptible to rail diversion.

Private carrier trains could range from one car to the maximum length allowed by the roadway company. Short-, medium-, and long-distance runs would be possible. Most private carriers would have their own cars and locomotives. Some private carriers might enter into equipment interchange agreements with one or more for-hire carriers. Private carriers could operate specialized equipment, some of which would not be allowed in national interchange service but could be used in closely controlled, private train operations.

Public Agencies

The Free Enterprise Alternative envisions joint use of the roadway network by numerous common, contract, and private rail carriers. Each regional roadway company would be a private sector enterprise, as would nearly all carriers. Public agencies would be allowed to act as rail carriers only under two circumstances. Government agencies would be able to move their own materials acting as private carriers. Specific government agencies (as defined by statute) would be allowed to act as a for-hire carrier of last resort on a restricted, controlled basis.

A government agency, like any other shipper, would be entitled to provide its own rail transportation as a private carrier. For example, the Department of Defense could operate its own train service over the roadway network between military facilities, suppliers, and other points. The Department of Interior, Tennessee Valley Authority, and other agencies at the federal, state, and local levels might utilize private train service.

Designated government agencies, under the auspices of the Department of Transportation, could provide common carrier train service on roadway segments where no private enterprise found it worthwhile to offer service. Public agencies could provide such politically desirable but uneconomic services, subject to strict limitations designed to (1) protect private enterprise carriers from government agency competition; and (2) assure the overall integrity of the free enterprise rail transportation industry. The government agency could provide train service on a roadway segment only if common carrier service was not otherwise available, and beyond that segment only so far as to obtain the closest connection with a private enterprise common carrier. Government carriers would be restricted to serving only as branch local carriers. It might be desirable to provide by statute that government service must cease if a private sector common carrier offers service over the roadway segment in question. Such a statute would eliminate the possibility of competition between publicly funded government agencies and free enterprise carriers. National policy must recognize that free market competition is the most efficient means of providing rail carrier service, and government common carrier service must be restricted to those few situations where private sector service is uneconomic.

PHYSICAL COMPONENTS

The roadway network would be provided by the regional roadway companies and would be available to all carriers. Carrier companies would supply their own rolling stock (locomotives and cars) through ownership, lease, or rental. Yards, equipment maintenance bases, crew facilities, administrative offices, and other carrier facilities would be provided by carriers (see Chapter 15).

Locomotives and freight cars could be owned by the carrier using the equipment, by another carrier, by several carriers jointly, or by a shipper as a private carrier. Rolling stock also could be owned by an independent firm and be leased or rented to carriers. It would be possible for a carrier to rent a locomotive and cars, load and unload at shipper facilities, use independent servicing facilities, and thereby operate without owning any physical components. The relative ease of entry and exit would enhance competition.

Locomotives, regardless of ownership, would be required to meet standards set by the roadway companies and the federal safety agency. Design standards would govern coupler design, wheel dimensions, wheelbases, body width limits, body height limits, and similar factors. Safety standards would include specifications for brake systems, controls, headlights, horns, bells, and multiple-channel radios.

Most common carriers would continue to interchange freight cars. Private and contract carriers might join the common carriers' interchange agreement on an individual carrier basis, but many would have no need to do so. In some instances a special arrangement between two carriers might suffice, such as a contract carrier delivering cars on a branch roadway for a large common carrier.

Design and safety equipment standards for freight cars would be set by the roadway companies and the federal safety agency.

FUNCTIONS AND ORGANIZATION

Relieved of the responsibility for owning, operating, and maintaining roadways, rail carriers would resemble carrier companies in the other modes. Primary functions of carriers would be the operations of trains and maintenance of equipment. As businesses, carriers would need administrative functions such as data processing, accounting, law, personnel, and purchasing. Commercial carriers—common and contract—would need marketing departments to perform functions like sales, pricing, service planning, and other customer-related activities. Common carriers, serving a great variety of customers with a relatively complex system of train operations, would require relatively large organizations (Figure 11). Private and contract carriers would not need some functions and could perform others on a smaller scale, allowing them to operate with smaller organizations (Figure 12). The size of carriers could range from owner-operators with one locomotive to corporations of national scope.

Carriers would perform all aspects of train operations except roadway traffic control, which would be the regional roadway company's responsibility. This would be similar to an airline which operates its flights subject to FAA air traffic control, or a truck line which dispatches its trucks but does not control traffic on the highway. The carrier's dispatch function does not include roadway traffic control; in this respect it is different from traditional railroad practice. It does, however, follow the practice of the other modes in which carriers dispatch vehicles but do not control fixed way traffic.

The carrier company's dispatchers would assign work among the carrier's crews and equipment. Specific activities would include: (1) keeping track of

Figure 11. Carrier Company Organization Structure, Large Common Carrier

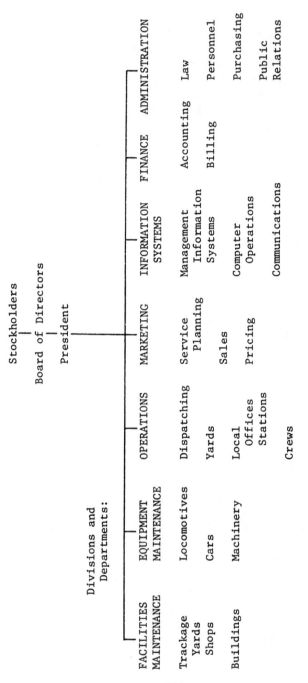

Stockholders

Board of Directors

President

Divisions and Departments:

FACILITIES MAINTENANCE	EQUIPMENT MAINTENANCE	OPERATIONS	MARKETING	INFORMATION SYSTEMS	FINANCE	ADMINISTRATION
Trackage	Locomotives	Dispatching	Service Planning	Management Information Systems	Accounting	Law
Yards						
Shops	Cars	Yards	Sales		Billing	Personnel
Buildings	Machinery	Local Offices Stations	Pricing	Computer Operations		Purchasing
				Communications		Public Relations
		Crews				

156

Figure 12. Carrier Company Organization Structure, Private Carrier

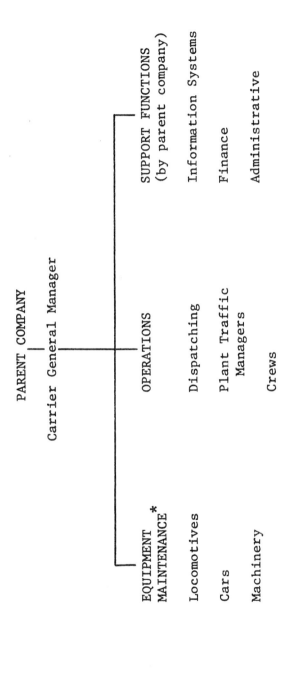

PARENT COMPANY

Carrier General Manager

EQUIPMENT
MAINTENANCE*

Locomotives

Cars

Machinery

OPERATIONS

Dispatching

Plant Traffic
Managers

Crews

SUPPORT FUNCTIONS
(by parent company)

Information Systems

Finance

Administrative

157

*Could be contracted to outside firm.

crews, locomotives, and empty cars; (2) keeping track of cars and trains to be moved; (3) assigning jobs, equipment, and crews; (4) monitoring work performance; and (5) planning train movements in advance and coordinating them with the roadway company's service representatives and traffic controllers.

With the increased competition resulting from joint roadway use and multiple types of carriers, strong marketing efforts would be essential to a commercial carrier's survival and growth. Sales, pricing, and service planning would be important functions for common carriers and, to a lesser extent, for contract carriers. Because train services would be crucial to a carrier's competitive effectiveness and profitability, service planning would be a function of the marketing division. The operations division would assist in service planning and would conduct daily train operations, but both pricing and service would be used as elements of the carrier's competitive marketing strategy.

ADVANTAGES

The Free Enterprise Alternative offers carriers significant advantages over the traditional railroad industry structure. The advantages arise from three fundamental changes: (1) joint use of rail roadways by many carriers; (2) competition among carriers on all roadway segments, including access to local industry; and (3) existence of different types of carriers—common, contract, and private.

Joint Use

The traditional railroad structure, as inherited from the nineteenth century, forced each rail carrier to bear the burden of providing its own separate fixed way. Competition often caused railroads to destroy not only each other but shippers and entire communities as well.

The new structure would utilize competition as a positive innovative force. Maximum reliance on market economics and minimal economic regulation would assure the highest levels of efficiency and service. Rail carriers would operate trains, maintain equipment, and in general produce transportation services as do carriers in the other modes.

Joint use of the roadway network would allow all carriers to benefit from economies of scale and lower costs. Each carrier would no longer need its own fixed way. Instead, carrier companies would pay tolls to regional roadway companies. The toll charges would reflect the economies of concentrating traffic on the best available routes.

Joint use would eliminate exclusive local service, free captive shippers, and remove any semblance of rail carrier monopoly. Aside from the beneficial effects of competition on carrier service and prices, joint use would have other positive impacts on the national economy. Rail carriers would not need special bankruptcy laws, because the failure of a single carrier would not jeopardize the welfare of shippers, cities, and regions. Other carriers serving the same roadways would continue to provide service; carriers from other areas could extend additional service into the affected area quickly and easily.

Just as the bankruptcy of a single carrier would no longer threaten all shippers and communities on a given roadway segment, neither would a strike or work stoppage pose serious harm. With other carriers readily available to serve all shippers, any labor dispute would remain between a carrier and its union—as it should, without harming innocent third parties. By separating carrier service from rail roadway ownership, shippers and communities would no longer be held hostage to rail carrier bankruptcies and strikes.

The Free Enterprise Alternative would eliminate the age-old problem of weak versus strong railroads. Since railroad companies traditionally have been tied to their individual fixed ways and vice versa, certain companies with better routes and service areas have performed better financially over time than their less fortunate competitors. The new structure would not furnish each carrier a reliable revenue base formed by exclusive local markets and captive industries. Instead, the success or failure of a carrier company would depend on its prices, services, and ability to meet shipper needs at a profit. Carriers would not be protected by regulation regardless of their inefficiency. Each carrier would no longer have its existence guaranteed through the threat of a bankruptcy, strike, or other shutdown imperiling the well being of shippers, cities, and the public at large. Less obvious but equally important would be the beneficial effects of competition on many areas long given poor but exclusive service by a railroad company of marginal financial status. Service improvements and service alternatives available under the new structure would aid economic development in those areas.

Competition

With each rail carrier freed of the burden of maintaining its own network of exclusive fixed ways, rail carriers could assume a more competitive posture. Carriers would no longer be burdened by the high fixed costs of roadway ownership and maintenance. The regional roadway company would assume roadway fixed costs, bring about economies of traffic concentration and roadway network coordination, and convert roadway fixed costs into roadway tolls (variable costs to the carriers).

Competition would assure shippers of the lowest economic rate while eliminating the cross-subsidies present in the traditional industry structure. Variable costs would represent a high proportion of a carrier's costs, as is now the case in the other modes. Variable costs could be identified easily for pricing and readily controlled for managerial purposes. Competition would assure that each carrier operates at an optimum level of efficiency or faces the loss of its traffic to more efficient competitors. Optimum efficiency would depend on the carrier's market and price/service strategy. A market demanding fast, frequent service would measure efficiency in terms of transit time and on-time performance; a market demanding lowest possible transportation cost might sacrifice service.

A carrier would be free to pursue any price/service strategy or combination of strategies. The shipping public would have a broader selection of prices and services to choose from. This wide array would be in contrast to existing rail service, which typically offers only one level of service and a limited range of prices.

The new structure would encourage carriers to innovate and utilize their newfound flexibility. Carriers could initiate and terminate service to specific route segments with little or no regulatory constraints. The market would match the demand for rail transportation services and the supply provided by numerous carriers. Since the market would remove any vestiges of monopoly power on the part of carriers, discrimination among commodities, shippers, or communities would not be possible except on the basis of cost of service, which is the only economically acceptable basis for discrimination in a competitive market.

Competition, as enhanced by the new structure, would offer maximum benefits to carriers, shippers, and the public. Rail carriers would be in a better position to compete constructively among themselves and compete effectively with carriers in the other modes at a variety of price and service levels.

Multiple Types of Carriers

The new structure offers the economies of joint use and the benefits of competition, but its effectiveness is not complete without the existence of multiple types of carriers: common, contract, and private. All three types are needed to fill adequately the full range of shippers' needs, as evidenced by the other modes' experience. Although the three types of carriers are competitive within themselves for some movements, there are situations in which one type of carrier cannot substitute for another. For example, a common carrier could physically handle many of a private carrier's shipments, but it is unlikely that the common carrier could provide the level of service (transit time, equipment availability, special stops, extra runs) that a private carrier could provide *and* do so at comparable prices. Likewise, a specialized private carrier designed to serve the peculiar needs of its owner would lose much of its cost and service advantage if it had to serve the broad spectrum of customers which a common carrier must serve.

With different types of carriers engaging in constructive competition, the rail carrier industry would have an environment conducive to innovation. Innovations would be likely in service, rates, operations, labor productivity, and equipment. Many services and train operations not possible under the restrictions of the traditional rail industry structure could be given an unencumbered trial in the marketplace. With the freedom of the new structure, rail carrier innovation should proceed at a rapid pace.

SUMMARY

The Free Enterprise Alternative offers a means for eliminating exclusive carrier service and replacing it with constructive competition. Carrier companies would respond to the needs and demands of the marketplace. Carriers would be given a great degree of freedom in the commercial direction of their operations: services, route structure, market entry and exit. Although this freedom is taken for granted in the other modes, the railroads have never had such latitude because of their exclusive fixed ways and the resultant monopolistic characteristics. By separating carrier and roadway functions, the benefits of both joint use and carrier competition can be obtained.

NOTES

1. In recent years the ICC has given common carrier railroads the approval to implement contract rates for specific situations. Contract rates usually require a minimum annual traffic volume and may place daily, weekly, or monthly maximum volumes in order to improve car utilization. Loading and unloading times may be limited.

   The ICC recently exempted fresh fruits and vegetables from economic regulation when shipped by rail. The railroad remains a common carrier with certain obligations, but rates are not subject to regulatory approval.

   When handling contract shipments or exempt commodities, the railroad company still has the basic common carrier obligations unless modified by specific contracts. The contract and exempt innovations usually relate to price (rate-making) and not service. Exempt and contract shipments can be handled in trains with other regulated common carrier traffic; they share the same yards and tracks. It is the same carrier—the railroad company—which performs the transportation service for all rail shipments.

2. U.S., Department of Transportation, *The Railroad Situation*, pp. 46–48.

3. At some locations, two or more railroads "open" industries to reciprocal switching. The railroad serving an industry will switch cars to and from a nearby connecting railroad(s) for a flat fee rather than a share of revenue as is the case with normal interchange. The connecting railroad(s) at the location reciprocate by switching cars to their industries. If an industry is not open to reciprocal switching, the originating carrier might be able to demand inclusion in the routing to some intermediate interchange point depending on tariff restrictions. In either case, the originating carrier must physically handle the shipment to the connecting railroad.

14 | TERMINALS

The Free Enterprise Alternative separates carrier and roadway functions. A competitive, free market system is used for carriers while regional roadway companies are regulated as natural monopolies. With the roadways open to all carriers, competition is encouraged, captive shippers are freed, and carriers are given the economic benefits of joint roadway use.

The operation of intercity rail roadways and carriers under the new structure is described in the two preceding chapters. The interaction of roadway and carrier companies in terminal areas is more complex. *Terminal* can be broadly defined as any point at which a unit of transportation begins or ends. For the specific purposes of this chapter, a terminal is defined as all rail facilities in an urban area. Adaptation of existing terminals to the new structure poses a challenging opportunity to improve rail service and efficiency.

ROADWAY

All rail roadways in each region would be owned by the regional roadway company. The roadway company would control train traffic and perform roadway maintenance; this would hold true in urban terminals as well as in rural areas. The only trackage not owned by the roadway company would be that in carrier and shipper facilities.

Physical Components

Roadways in terminal areas would be classified as previously described (Interstate, Primary, Secondary, Branch). Although each type would handle local traffic, through traffic would be served mostly by Primary and Interstate roadways. Belt roadways—usually Primary or Interstate—would allow trains to bypass congested areas, just as belt highways do for automobiles and trucks. Local traffic would predominate on Secondary and Branch roadways, which would act as arteries to the many private spurs and yards owned by shippers and carriers.

Functions

Under the traditional railroad industry structure each railroad company usually has exclusive use of its own tracks. In many urban areas this results in duplication of trackage and fragmented traffic control. As different railroads attempt to reach various industries and yards of other railroads, a maze of trackage has developed. It is not uncommon to see the tracks of three or four railroads running side by side through a large city's industrial district.

Traffic control systems vary from simple to complex. Some routes operate under yard limit rules, which require all trains to move slow enough to stop short of a train or other obstacle blocking their paths. Other routes utilize multiple track lines with centralized traffic control. In most terminals the traffic control efforts for different railroads' tracks, yards, and crossings remain largely uncoordinated.

Only in a few cities have railroads made comprehensive efforts to coordinate traffic control, usually through a jointly owned terminal railroad company. Examples include the Kansas City Terminal Railroad and the Houston Belt and Terminal Railroad, both of which allow various railroad companies to operate their own trains over the terminal's multiple-track CTC-signalled routes using trackage right agreements. As a traditional railroad, the terminal company performs local service on its tracks.

Under the Free Enterprise Alternative, the roadway company would perform the functions of traffic control and roadway maintenance throughout its region, including terminal areas. In small towns and some cities roadway functions would be included with those of the intercity routes. In large terminals, a traffic control center (TCC) for the terminal area would be established as a subdivision of the regional TCC's. The terminal TCC would direct the movements of local and through trains, the latter being coordinated with the TCC of the adjoining region(s). Terminal and regional traffic control centers would interact in a manner similar to that of airport control towers and air route traffic control centers.

The roadway company would upgrade and standardize traffic control procedures, signal systems, and signs to accommodate the numerous carriers operating under the new structure. The *Regional Roadway Charts* and the *Code of Roadway Regulations* (described previously) would apply to all roadways including those in terminals. The terminal TCC might require a separate radio channel for train communication in the terminal area, much as airports have assigned radio frequencies. Train movement plans would be required for intraterminal as well as intercity trains.

Concentration of traffic on certain upgraded routes in the terminal and route changes in the surrounding region could improve traffic flow and yield overall cost savings to the roadway company. With more but shorter trains (in most cases) and the general increase in rail traffic expected under the new structure, the roadway companies would need to improve the roadways in their respective terminal areas. Coordinated terminal traffic control, additional main tracks, upgraded bypass belt routes and route connections, and grade separations would be necessary in many terminals. Lead tracks and access roadways to carrier and shipper facilities would need modification in some cases so that local trains would not block through routes while they work. The regional roadway company would make these changes during the transition period and afterward as traffic warranted.

CARRIERS

Carriers would play a vital role in the operation of terminals under the new structure. With many common, contract, and private carriers sharing use of rail roadways, terminal functions would vary in complexity and importance with each carrier. Carrier terminal functions would include the pickup and delivery of cars at shipper facilities, classification of cars, servicing, crew support, interchange of cars between carriers, and loading and unloading of cars. A large common carrier might perform all of these functions. A small contract carrier could simply pick up and deliver cars at shipper facilities, purchase equipment servicing and crew support from commercial firms, and have no need for classification or interchange of cars. The possible variations and combinations are numerous.

Physical Components

Carrier facilities would vary by type, ownership, and user(s). The following outline briefly describes carrier facilities in terminals:

    Types of Facilities
      Yards
        Inbound-Outbound Trains
        Classification
        Storage
      Servicing and Repair
        Locomotives
        Cars
      Crew Support
        Motel
        Restaurant
      Carrier Administration
        Offices

Ownership
  Carrier Company
    Individual Companies
    Several Companies, Joint Ownership
    Shipper (as private carrier)
  Independent Company (non-carrier)
Availability
  Private (owner's use only)
  Commercial (for hire)
    Common (open to all)
    Contract (limited clientele)

Independent companies could make switching yards and storage yards available to all carriers on a commercial basis (by the track, hour, or car). Independent servicing facilities could serve rail carriers much like truck stops and garages in the trucking industry.

The typical service facility (whether carrier-owned or independent) would have a lead track to the rail roadway in each direction. Connected to the leads would be a train yard owned by the service facility and of a size adequate to hold the expected number and length of trains using the facility at any one time. A train's crew would notify the roadway company traffic controller that they wanted to stop at a particular service facility. Notification would be made by radio; the stop could be included in the train movement plan filed at the beginning of the run. The traffic controller would notify the service facility's manager, make certain the facility could accommodate the train, and give the manager an estimated arrival time. Once the train arrived at the facility, the manager would direct the train into the proper track. The train's cars would be inspected and its locomotive serviced while setting in the track. Most facilities would have a restaurant and supply store; train crews could use these while their train was being serviced. The service facility might offer a repair shop and storage tracks for cars and locomotives. The facility would set the prices for its services and products.

Servicing and repair also could be performed by mobile highway trucks. A modified tank truck could bring fuel, water, and other supplies to a locomotive at almost any location. A repair truck, carrying a mechanic and tools, would allow minor repairs to be made on locomotives and cars without bringing them in to a repair shop.

It might prove desirable for some carrier companies to organize their servicing facilities and repair shops as profit centers or separate subsidiaries. The facilities could be open to all carriers on a commercial basis, or limited to a few carriers on a contract basis. Application of the profit-center concept should improve the management and efficiency of the facilities. The sale of products and services to all carriers would allow maintenance facilities to engage in healthy competition.

Loading and unloading facilities could be classified in the same manner as carrier facilities:

Types of Load/Unload Facilities
  General Cargo
    Team Track
    TOFC Ramp
    Warehouse
  Bulk Cargo
    Dry Cargo
    Liquid Cargo
Ownership
  Shipper (industrial firm)
  Carrier Company
    Individual Companies
    Several Companies, Joint Ownership
  Independent Company (non-carrier)
Availability
  Private (owner's use only)
  Commercial (for hire)
    Common (open to all)
    Contract (limited clientele)

Most load/unload facilities would be owned by shippers and operated privately as part of industrial plants. Common carriers might provide some types of general facilities where such services would be profitable.

Interchange

The traditional structure requires interchange among rail carriers, because each railroad company cannot serve beyond its own tracks. Over 80 percent of all rail traffic is interchanged: shipments originating on one railroad must be given to another railroad for forwarding or final delivery.

With the advent of private, contract, and specialized common carriers under the new structure, many trains would move directly from shipper to consignee without interchange. Interchange, although not as important as under the traditional structure, would remain important to many common carriers. Carriers serving different geographic areas and carriers with different levels of geographic coverage (local, regional, national) could benefit from interchange. Since carriers would be free to enter or leave routes and cities, interchange would provide a logical and efficient means by which a carrier could offer service beyond its own market area.

Cars could be interchanged among carriers of different types. A group of shippers could hire a contract carrier to haul cars from a distant origin point to a regional terminal, sort the cars, and forward them to various common, contract, and private carriers for final delivery. Not all carriers would need or desire to interchange cars with other carriers. Many carriers, however, would find circumstances under which it would be advantageous to interchange cars. The option of interchange would provide an important element of flexibility.

SHIPPERS

Trackage in shipper facilities would be connected to the roadway by one or more lead tracks. In size, shipper trackage could range from a single spur track to yards holding hundreds of cars. The shipper would control carrier access to its trackage. Although all carriers could use the roadway, a carrier would have no need to use the trackage of a shipper's facility unless the shipper requested that carrier's services.

RESTRICTED ACCESS ZONE

The existing roadway network was built under the traditional structure and was designed for exclusive service by individual carriers. Some roadway segments in major terminals could not accommodate all traffic which would result under free access for all carriers. Because free access is fundamental to the new structure, every effort must be made to allow its implementation. Trackage could be modified, carrier schedules coordinated, and other measures taken to improve traffic capacity. Still, there might be a few roadway segments in some terminals that could not accommodate free access by all carriers which would desire it. In such situations the federal economic regulatory agency for the regional roadway companies could establish a restricted access zone (RAZ).

The restricted access zone would operate like the remainder of the rail network, with several carriers sharing use of the roadways, except that only a limited number of carriers would be assigned to perform local service in the zone. Depending on the traffic volume and capacity, other carriers might use the restricted roadway segment for through train movements, but only the assigned carriers could provide local service. Unauthorized carriers would interchange cars with an assigned carrier for pickup or delivery in the RAZ.

The restricted access zone would be considered a temporary measure while permanent adjustments were made to permit free access. RAZ's would comprise a small part of roadways in a terminal, if they were used at all. Most terminals would have free access to all industries. Free access would be the norm; restricted access would be the rare exception.

To determine if a restricted access zone would be warranted, the federal regulatory agency would hold public hearings, investigate, and issue its decision. Procedures would involve the regional roadway company, carriers, and shippers. Among the factors to be considered would be: (1) number and type of shippers in the proposed RAZ; (2) traffic generated; (3) track layout and design; (4) number and type of carriers desiring access; (5) frequency and nature of carrier service; and (6) methods available for improving and expanding carrier access.

The regulatory agency would allow carriers to bid on assignments to serve the RAZ for a one-year period. Typically, the agency would select at least two carriers to serve each zone. This would allow a limited degree of competition and promote better service. Bids would be taken on an annual basis and the performance of the assigned carriers would be reviewed. If a carrier decided not to bid again or proved unsatisfactory, another carrier would be selected to replace it. Although this process would not be as efficient as the marketplace, it would provide an administrative form of entry and exit.

Due to the monopolistic restrictions on access, assigned carriers must keep a separate accounting of RAZ operations for regulatory purposes. Assigned carriers might be subsidiaries of larger carriers or small local firms. The regulatory agency would set rates for the pickup and delivery of cars in the RAZ. Each assigned carrier must provide interchange with any and all carriers at one or more locations. Assigned carriers could not discriminate among connecting carriers since they would act as common carriers serving all carriers regardless of type. As on the rest of the roadway network, the assigned carriers in the restricted access zone would pay user fees (tolls) to the regional roadway company for use of its roadways in the terminal, including traffic control. The regulatory agency would approve roadway tolls.

The restricted access zone would be reviewed every two years by the regulatory agency. The RAZ would be a temporary measure of short- to intermediate-term duration while other steps were taken to improve access. The ultimate aim would be to remove RAZ status and provide free access for all carriers as found throughout the roadway network. Review of the RAZ by the regulatory agency would let interested parties comment on plans for implementation of free access, changes in RAZ geographic limits, and changes in access restrictions.

Considerable input for RAZ decisions would come from the regional roadway company. An intentional bias toward free access would result from the fact that free access would allow more carriers to use the roadways in the terminal and thus bring in more toll revenue to the roadway company. Balanced against this tendency would be the roadway company's responsibility for efficient traffic control and provision of capital for roadway trackage expansion. Carriers and shippers usually would favor free access: it would give carriers access to more shippers and give shippers access to all carriers. Only in situations where congestion would make free access truly unworkable would the involved parties support access restrictions. These reasons would tend to reinforce the temporary nature of the RAZ designation.

Access restrictions could be loosened or removed using several methods. If capacity allowed, the number of assigned carriers could be increased. Shippers in the RAZ could be given the option of performing their own service as private carriers or hiring contract carriers, while common carriers would have access only through assigned carriers.

If one or more large industries in a terminal's restricted access zone voluntarily restricted access, free access could be implemented in some cases. A large shipper could use a yard outside the RAZ as its pickup and setout point for all carriers. The shipper's own locomotive or that of a single carrier could move cars between the shipper's yard and plant. Through such a voluntary restriction, the roadway segment in question could remain open for free access to other shippers. Similarly, several shippers might agree voluntarily to use one or two local carriers for most movements, connecting with other carriers at nearby yards, and thereby allow free access on the segment.

If track capacity were nearly adequate on a given segment, train congestion could be managed by traffic control methods. The major carriers using a congested segment of terminal roadway could coordinate their local service schedules through the roadway company's traffic control center. The roadway company could provide yards for holding trains outside the congested area; trains would be allowed to enter as quickly as possible. Traffic control might use one-way movement on the congested segment in coordination with nearby roadways. Techniques used in highway, airway, and waterway traffic control should be considered for easing congestion on terminal roadways.

Expanding and modifying trackage, sometimes in conjunction with changes outside the RAZ, could improve accessibility. By implementing the various changes in facilities and methods, the restricted access zone could be reduced in size or eliminated completely over time.

The restricted access zone concept recognizes that, at least initially, there would be a few terminal roadway segments where traffic capacity would be inadequate. Many methods could be used to improve capacity, but in a few segments the establishment of restricted access zones could prove desirable. The RAZ designation recognizes the monopolistic nature of access restrictions and how they limit carrier competition. Furthermore, it structures the role of the interested parties—roadway company, carriers, shippers—to balance the need for efficient traffic movement against the desire for competitive service among carriers. The structure does encourage a tendency toward competition and toward free access to all shippers by all carriers. Review of the RAZ on a periodic basis would assure that all possible steps were taken to improve access and that removal of all restrictions would occur as soon as feasible.

SUMMARY

The distinction between roadway and carrier would be maintained in terminals the same as it would throughout the newly restructured rail industry. Application of the roadway/carrier separation concept would provide the efficiencies of joint use and the benefits of competition. The new structure would encourage flexibility and innovation.

Nearly all terminals would employ the free access principle characteristic of the Free Enterprise Alternative: any carrier could use the roadway network to reach any shipper. In a few cases, access might need to be restricted temporarily while adjustments were made to permit eventual free access. Since all terminals would be structured like the rest of the rail industry with regional roadway track ownership and traffic control, the changeover to free access would be relatively simple. In fact, the relationships under the new structure would encourage the removal of access restrictions as soon as it would be practical.

Even in the rare circumstance where access would be restricted for a terminal roadway segment, two or more carriers would share use of the roadway. Competition and efficiency would be promoted but in a regulated, limited manner. The preferable course would be to remove access restrictions and let all carriers operate throughout the terminal in a free market, free access environment.

15 ║ REGULATION

Government plays a legitimate role by providing any necessary economic and safety regulation. It is equally important, however, for the government to provide no more regulation than is absolutely necessary. In some cases no regulation is needed.

Two distinct forms of regulation exist: economic and safety. The need for economic regulation is determined by market structure. A free, competitive market requires no regulation, but a monopolistic market needs regulation to prevent abuse. Safety regulation is intended to protect the public from unreasonable hazards and commonly involves technical standards and engineering specifications.

The free market is the best form of economic regulation. It is automatic, efficient, and fair to both producers and consumers. It rapidly equates the needs of individual participants with those of the entire market. In some instances a minimal degree of policing is needed to assure that the market remains free. In other markets, such as natural monopolies, economic regulation is required due to the absence of free competition. It is axiomatic, though, that economic regulation achieves nothing in and of itself. Regulation can only facilitate or hinder the functioning of producers and consumers.

To be effective, economic regulation must complement industry structure. Neither regulation based on competition nor regulation based on monopoly can be effective for the railroads' traditional industry structure, which has elements of both competition and monopoly. The Free Enterprise Alternative separates monopolistic and competitive elements. Economic regulation must recognize these distinctions if the industry is to function properly. The regional roadway companies would be natural monopolies and would require a high degree of regulation. Carrier companies would compete in a free market and need little or no economic regulation.

ROADWAY ECONOMIC REGULATION

Economic regulation of the regional roadway companies must address their natural monopoly structure. It must protect the interests of both the roadway companies and their customers, the carriers. A basic premise of roadway company regulation would be that the rail roadways are a national asset like highways, airways, and waterways. Although the roadways would be owned by regional private enterprise companies, they would exist for the benefit of all carriers—the entire nation—and not for the benefit of any particular group. Fair and impartial regulation would be needed to balance the needs of the carriers and the roadway companies. Economic regulation would encompass three areas: tolls and services; extensions and abandonments; and financial matters.

Tolls and Services

Each train would be charged a toll for its use of each roadway segment. Tolls would be determined by the roadway company based on cost, service, and market criteria. Tolls would vary for individual roadway segments, class of roadway, and type of train.

As a natural monopoly in its own region, each roadway company would be subject to federal economic regulation. Regulation would consider not only specific tolls but also the adequacy of toll revenues for roadway company needs. Since the roadway company would own all roadways in its region—a true monopoly—regulatory procedures could assure more effectively a specific level of return on investment.

Regulation of tolls would be flexible enough to allow rapid response to traffic changes. The roadway company would publish all of its tolls in a monthly or quarterly tariff. The tariff would list fees for other services such as use of storage tracks and use of roadway-owned yards for carrier switching. It could be used for other purposes as well. For example, if a roadway segment were to be out of service for planned maintenance, advance notice could be given in the tariff so carriers could plan for detours via alternate routes. When advance notice was not given, the roadway company would be allowed to charge only the normal route's tolls and not the higher tolls of a detour route.

Abandonments and Subsidy Program

Extension and abandonment of rail roadways would be subject to federal regulation. Extensions—the construction of new roadways—would be rare occurrences since existing roadways could be modified to accommodate increased traffic in most cases. Abandonments would result from changes in traffic patterns and local economies, though the new structure's flexibility would allow some segments to remain viable which otherwise would not. Operating over the roadway network in a competitive environment, carriers could enter and leave markets with little or no regulatory restriction. The roadways, as a natural monopoly, would serve not only the carriers but also industries, cities, and rural areas. The effect of a roadway abandonment on these interests must be considered; however, the roadway company should not be compelled to provide a roadway at a financial loss.

Most abandonments would involve Branch roadways with little or no traffic volume. When toll revenues from a segment drop below its direct costs (maintenance, traffic control) the roadway company must seek either higher tolls or abandonment. In some cases carriers (and ultimately shippers) could absorb higher tolls and thereby allow the roadway segment to remain economically viable. In other instances, higher tolls could reach a point at which traffic would start to decline and abandonment would have to be requested.

Should the roadway company request abandonment, the federal regulatory agency would examine the accounting data and hold public hearings. Involved governments—federal, state, regional, local—would be notified as would interested shippers and carriers. If the regulatory authority found that toll revenues did not cover direct costs, abandonment would be approved automatically subject to a ninety-day waiting period. During the waiting period any interested party or group (governments, shippers, and/or carriers) could initiate a subsidy program and thereby postpone abandonment for the duration of that subsidy program. Subsidy would cover only the difference between toll revenues (at some maximum level) and direct costs.

In some circumstances changes in traffic patterns might make a Primary or Secondary roadway redundant. The roadway would be relegated to Branch status; and, if traffic were insufficient, toll increases or abandonment would be considered.

If the abandonment of a roadway segment conflicted with the needs of the Defense Department, that department could intervene as an interested party and provide subsidy to keep the roadway in existence. The Strategic Rail Corridor Network for National Defense (STRACNET) and roadways serving specific defense installations would be of greatest concern to the Department of Defense.

Even with the possibility of subsidy from interested parties, the existence of a roadway does not mean it necessarily will be used by one or more carriers. Carriers, as competitive enterprises, would be free to enter and leave roadway segment markets. If a segment could not generate traffic sufficient to attract a carrier's services, then it might be without service. Shippers could act as private carriers or hire contract carriers. In a few cases, local governments might act as carriers subject to the restrictions described in Chapter 13. Acting as a private carrier and providing roadway subsidy could prove uneconomic for a shipper, depending on the situation, and might force the shipper to change to another mode of transportation or another system of distribution. The new structure would not eliminate branch roadway abandonments, but it would offer more flexible alternatives along with the abandonment option.

Subsidy would be unnecessary if the roadway company could operate in a completely economic environment, setting tolls and abandoning segments based on economic factors only. Since other factors do affect abandonments—and are affected by the abandonments—the subsidy option allows political, social, defense, and other goals to be met without disrupting the roadway company's economic balance. Economic incentives are preserved as a whole in the roadway company and the rail industry.

The subsidy option identifies uneconomic roadway segments—segments incapable of covering their direct costs. All involved parties know exactly which segments are subsidized and to what extent. This allows realistic appraisals and rational decision-making by interested parties. Outright subsidy is preferable to internal cross-subsidy, under which a regulatory authority forces profitable segments to support unprofitable but politically desirable segments. Internal cross-subsidy only serves to hide segment losses and lower overall roadway company profitability. It can lead to the inability to fund needed expansion and modernization efforts while unneeded segments drain resources. Cross-subsidy also penalizes carriers not using uneconomic segments by raising the general toll level, using it as a private tax to benefit those few parties with interests in the uneconomic segments. Outright subsidy of roadway segment direct losses is preferable since it readily identifies the funds spent and whom they benefit. The subsidy option would be applicable only to a small portion of the roadway network; by far most roadway mileage would be self-sustaining in the economic sense.

Financial

Because each roadway company would be a natural monopoly in its own region, regulatory authority would extend to company financial matters as well as tolls and abandonments. Accounting procedures, stock and bond issues, and investments outside the roadway company would be subject to regulatory approval. The roadway company would not be allowed to have subsidiaries, holding companies, or other outside investments except short-term items normally associated with cash flow procedures. Roadway company profits could be used only to improve roadway assets or reduce toll levels: the roadway company must operate as a closed-loop financial system so profits are not used to support ventures in unrelated businesses.

CARRIER ECONOMIC REGULATION

Chapter 13 describes the three types of carriers found in all modes: common, contract, and private. These types are defined by the clientele each serves. Common carriers offer their services to all. Under the traditions of common law a common carrier must serve all who desire its services and do so without undue discrimination.[1] Contract carriers serve specific customers and provide services as set forth in a written contract. The contract describes the duties of both parties: for example, in return for a lower rate or specific services the shipper might guarantee the contract carrier a definite volume of traffic. Private carriers are available only to their respective owners and do not offer services on a commercial for-hire basis.

The Free Enterprise Alternative envisions all three types of carriers sharing use of the rail roadway network. The new structure is designed so carriers operate in a competitive, free market environment and therefore need no economic regulation. With all roadways open to every carrier upon its payment of the prescribed tolls, free entry and exit is provided. Joint use of the roadway gives shippers and communities competitive rail service. Absent the burden of fixed way ownership, rail carrier rates can be set effectively by the marketplace. The carrier component of rail industry structure is thus oriented toward operation without government economic intervention under the strictest regulator of all, the competitive free market.

Economic regulation of carriers is needed only when an element of monopoly power exists, such as the exclusive service associated with the fixed way ownership of traditional railroad companies. With the monopoly element of carrier fixed way ownership replaced by competitive joint use, regulation becomes arbitrary and artificial, serving only as a poor substitute for market forces. However, two alternative regulatory schemes for rail carriers are presented in addition to the more effective unregulated, free market format.

Truck-style Regulation

The most restrictive, most comprehensive form of economic regulation for rail carriers under the new structure would generally duplicate that currently applied to the trucking industry. Although this alternative would be less restrictive than traditional rail regulation, the absence of exclusive fixed way usage would make even this form of economic regulation an unnecessary burden for all concerned. However, truck-style regulation could be useful in the rail industry as part of the transition from the traditional structure to the new structure. As such, truck-style regulation would be part of a program leading to an unregulated competitive market.

Truck-style regulation would recognize the three types of carriers: common, contract, and private. Common carriers would be required to obtain a certificate of public convenience and necessity. The certificate would impose a definite obligation to serve and would grant specific route authority to the carrier. Route authority could possibly limit the number of carriers competing on a roadway or route but would not grant exclusive use. The certification process would provide a means to limit entry; exit would also be controlled. Common carriers could be classified as carriers of general or specialized cargo. Carriers could also be characterized by regular or irregular route services. Rates would be published in tariffs subject to regulatory approval. In some instances common carriers might be exempt from regulation, following the example of agricultural commodity exemptions in the trucking industry.

Contract carriers would have to obtain permits approving their respective operations as consistent with the public interest. Rates would be reviewed only as part of the contracts themselves. Route approval would not be necessary for contract carriers, though the permit process would constitute a form of entry restriction. Private carriers would be exempt from economic regulation since their services would not be available on a for-hire basis.

Truck-style regulation would be applicable as a means for controlling the changeover from the traditional rail structure with exclusive use of fixed ways to the new structure with joint use and greater freedom of entry and exit.

Flexible Minimal Regulation

The second alternative would exempt both contract and private carriers from economic regulation. Common carriers would be subject to a minimal level of regulation characterized by flexibility and reliance on competitive market forces.

Any carrier which proved itself fit, willing, and able to perform common carrier service on a specific route or area could obtain the required certificate. The certificate would obligate the carrier to serve for a period of one year, renewable at the carrier's request. The carrier's rates would not be regulated, but the rates must be published in a tariff.

The simple certification procedure would not restrict entry since any carrier could qualify if the "fit, willing, and able" criteria were met. A carrier could exit a market prior to the expiration of its certificate if more than one additional carrier served the market. If one or no other carrier served the market, the carrier could not leave until its certificate expired. The ability to set rates and the freedom to exit after the certificate period would minimize the risk facing the common carriers.

Flexible, minimal regulation would provide a certain level of stability, particularly to shippers in small markets. Market forces could act upon common carriers with little regulatory interference. Even in the situation where the remaining common carrier(s) elected not to renew the certificate, shippers would have sufficient advance notice to make arrangements for contract or private carriage. Flexible, minimal regulation would approach deregulation, and it would be a political decision whether the benefits of minimal regulation would justify the expense of its administrative organization.

Deregulation

Except as a transitory phenomenon, economic regulation of rail carriers is not needed under the Free Enterprise Alternative. Traditional railroad regulation, truck-style regulation, and even flexible, minimal regulation cannot provide the efficiency of the marketplace. A market without economic regulation does not mean the market is without restraint, for competition is the most effective and most efficient form of regulation. Its automatic operation, unimpeded by artificial restraints, is preferable to any bureaucratic surrogate. A competitive, free market for rail carriers is a fundamental element of the Free Enterprise Alternative.

The new structure encourages competition on each roadway through joint use. Contract and private carriage offer further competition, acting as the ultimate regulator of common carrier prices and services. A wide variety of unregulated competitive markets exist in the other modes and can serve as models for rail carriers.[2]

TRANSITION PERIOD

Transition from the traditional railroad industry structure to the Free Enterprise Alternative would be accomplished through a multiple-stage metamorphosis. Initially each railroad company would split into two parts, a carrier subsidiary and a roadway subsidiary.

During the second phase the roadway subsidiaries would be combined to form the regional roadway companies. In return for roadways the railroad companies would receive non-voting stock and/or bonds issued by the roadway companies. Roadway companies would receive tolls from the railroads-turned-carriers, and the roadway companies would begin the process of integrating, consolidating, and expanding the roadway network into a unified whole. Operating rules, signals, and signs would be standardized. Traffic control centers would be established. *Regional Roadway Charts* and the *Code of Roadway Regulations* would come into force, as would the licensing of carrier locomotive engineers.

Having reached the minimal level of standardization required in Phase 2, roadway integration and improvement would continue under Phase 3. Ex-railroad rail common carriers would begin to exercise limited freedom of entry and exit under truck-style regulation. Joint use would receive widespread application. With the advent of competition on individual roadway segments, carrier rate regulation would become unnecessary.

Phase 4 would see the entry of contract and private carriers. With private carriage a viable option, common carriers would be given complete entry and exit freedom—initially under the flexible, minimum regulation format, later evolving into a free, competitive market with no government regulation.

The transition process should follow a planned schedule so that the ultimate end would be achieved as rapidly as possible. Although the transition would present problems, as does any type of change, the problems must be seen in terms of the permanent benefits of the new structure.

SAFETY REGULATION

Safety regulation is necessary to protect the public, rail industry employees, carrier companies, and roadway companies from exposure to unreasonable risks. At the federal level, the Department of Transportation (DOT) would establish safety standards for carriers and roadways. Enforcement and inspection responsibilities would belong to DOT, except when it chose to delegate its duties to state agencies. The National Transportation Safety Board would continue to function as an independent body, investigating transportation accidents and recommending regulatory improvements.

For roadway companies, safety regulation would encompass minimum standards for track, signal systems, and traffic control procedures. Roadway traffic control personnel would be examined over traffic control procedures and licensed.

Carrier safety regulations would cover operating personnel, equipment, and traffic control procedures. Locomotive engineers would be licensed as are truck drivers, airplane pilots, and waterway personnel. Licensing examinations would cover train operation and traffic control procedures. Equipment standards would cover items such as brake systems, couplers, wheels, and vehicle weight. Roadway and carrier standards would function as an integrated system of safety regulation.

Safety regulation would be separate from economic regulation; roadway companies, as regulated monopolies, could pass along safety costs through increased tolls. Carrier companies would be subjected equally to safety costs, so safety requirements would not adversely affect the competitive market. The safety regulatory agency would determine if the benefits of a particular standard justified the imposition of its costs on the involved parties.

SUMMARY

Regulation serves two distinct purposes under the new rail industry structure. Safety regulation protects persons from unreasonable risks of physical harm and is typically implemented through the establishment of technical standards. Economic regulation is used to balance conflicting financial interests in markets where such balance cannot be obtained through the workings of normal economic forces. In markets where economic forces can operate successfully, the market itself provides the most efficient form of economic regulation and renders government intervention redundant if not detrimental.

Chapter 9, "Economics and Structure," described the traditional railroad industry structure as having both monopolistic and competitive aspects. Government economic regulation of railroads has proven largely unsuccessful due to the structure's dualistic nature. In contrast, electric utilities and telephone companies adhere closely to the classic natural monopoly model and have been regulated with a far greater degree of success.

The Free Enterprise Alternative would apply the concept of roadway/carrier separation to the rail industry, separating carrier and fixed way functions as in the other modes (highway, water, and air). Regional roadway companies, each owning all rail roadways in its region, would be true natural monopolies and would be regulated as such. Numerous carriers, sharing use of the roadway network, would constitute a free, competitive market in which government regulation would be unnecessary. The functions, structure, and regulation of each industry segment—roadways and carriers—would be properly matched, maximizing efficiency and effectiveness. The Free Enterprise Alternative would provide economic regulation only where necessary and eliminate it where unnecessary.

NOTES

1. Donald V. Harper, *Transportation in America: Users, Carriers, Government* (Englewood Cliffs, New Jersey, 1978), pp. 112–121. With economic regulation removed, carriers would still be subject to certain requirements. Common law defines the common carrier by the carrier's offering of its services to the public on a continual basis. The common carrier must accept shipments to the limits of its service capacity; however, the carrier can restrict the types of commodities it moves. The common carrier is held liable for loss or damage to shipments, except for loss or damage caused by acts of God, acts of public enemy, negligence of the shipper, inherent nature of the goods, or acts of public authority. There is also a duty to deliver the shipment to the right person. Interstate commerce regulations have further defined these obligations, but the basic law applies as well to common carriers outside the realm of economic regulation.

2. Market mechanisms for truck transportation such as rate clearinghouses, brokers, and auction markets are described in U.S., Department of Transportation, *A Long Term Study of Produce Transportation, Volume 2, General Summary, Final Report* (Washington, D.C., 1977), pp. 66–84.

   Descriptions of the barge transportation auction market include (in chronological order): "Barge Freight Trading Auction to Begin August 1," *Waterways Journal*, Volume 92, Number 17 (July 22, 1978), p. 5; "St. Louis Barge Freight Trading Begins," *Waterways Journal*, Volume 92, Number 19 (August 5, 1978), p. 5; "Open Auction for Fertilizer Transport in Offing," *Waterways Journal*, Volume 93, Number 9 (June 2, 1979), p. 29; "Fertilizer Call Session," *Waterways Journal*, Volume 93, Number 12 (June 23, 1979), p. 31; Dan Layton, "Trading Sessions to Open for Upbound River Freight," *Waterways Journal*, Volume 93, Number 22 (September 1, 1979), p. 6; "Merchants Exchange Reports Gains," *Waterways Journal*, Volume 93, Number 42 (January 19, 1980), p. 7; "Exchange Expands Scope of Barge Freight Trading," *Traffic World*, Number 5, Volume 183, Whole Number 3824 (August 4, 1980), pp. 28–29.

16 | OPPORTUNITY FOR INNOVATION

Innovation is essential to the health of any industry. The Free Enterprise Alternative encourages innovation by placing rail carriers in a free, competitive market. Carriers are given the freedom and flexibility to try new ideas. They are given the opportunity to succeed and the opportunity to fail.

Under the traditional railroad structure innovation typically follows a slow and torturous path. Because each railroad company provides exclusive service over its own tracks, any innovation must meet not only the physical requirements of the railroad company but also its commercial standards. A proposal must adhere to that particular company's business philosophy, profitability objectives, and operating procedures.

Innovation also faces formidable obstacles at the industry level. The railroad industry is highly interdependent, because each railroad has access only to its own tracks, and the commercial philosophies of a few conservative companies often dominate the rail industry. To be effective, innovations usually must be accepted by several railroads, if not the entire industry. This slow process involves considerable second-guessing by other railroads and brings any innovation down to the least common denominator level. The committee approach to creativity stifles many new ideas in the railroad industry.

The burden of proof traditionally has been upon those desiring change, so many worthwhile ideas have been denied a trial in the rail marketplace. The new structure would promote innovation by opening the roadway network to any carrier. As long as basic safety standards were met, any commercial concept would be fair game for the competitive marketplace. New ideas could be tried easily with complete freedom to fail or to succeed.

The market would reward those carriers which met shipper needs; carriers which ignored shipper needs could not survive. Innovation would be imperative, not optional. New ideas, once proven, would be quickly accepted and move all competitors ahead. Improvements in efficiency would prompt other carriers to follow suit, thereby lowering prices and increasing productivity. For those carriers which did not adopt proven innovations the penalty would be reduced profits and eventual failure. The market could not guarantee success, but it would offer the opportunity for an unencumbered trial of new ideas. Through the application of proper industry structure, the Free Enterprise Alternative would foster innovation and bring dynamic growth to the static railroad industry.[1]

This chapter examines several areas of innovation and the possible effects of the new structure. The change in structure itself would not solve most problems, but it would make it easier for carriers, roadway companies, shippers, and others to find, test, and implement innovative solutions.

SHORT-HAUL TRAFFIC

The average rail shipment moves about 600 miles, and the average truck shipment moves about half that distance. Railroads pride themselves on handling long-haul traffic—the farther the better—and generally regard short-haul traffic as a nuisance. Since 1947 the average rail haul has increased roughly 30 percent, from approximately 410 miles to 540 miles in 1976.[2] In contrast, the average length of haul for all modes (excluding pipeline and domestic deep sea) has increased only 11 percent. As the railroads have moved toward longer hauls they have given up sizeable amounts of traffic in short- to medium-distance movements, principally to truck competition.[3]

The railroads' exit from the short-haul market is not due to any flaw in that traffic; trucks survive and flourish on it. Rather, the flaw is in the railroads' inflexible operating methods and the traditional industry structure which promotes those methods.

It would be unreasonable for a postman to deliver letters house to house using a highway tractor-trailer rig; yet this level of overkill is essentially how railroads serve short-haul business (defined here as distances under 250 miles). To move any shipment requires a minimum of a four-man crew; a 115-ton, 1500 horsepower locomotive; and a 30-ton caboose under current operating practice. The short-haul shipment moves through the same system of trains and yards which serves as the pickup and delivery system for long-haul traffic. Short-haul traffic usually moves in local trains which operate on a once-daily basis, so transit time is measured in days, not hours. Consequently, a railroad frequently takes longer to move a freight car 200 miles than 700 miles. The Appendix following this chapter describes the schedules of a hypothetical shipment moving by rail and highway.

Aside from inflexible operating methods, short-haul service is hindered by the railroad companies' geographic nature. For many decades railroads have been oriented toward regional and national traffic flows. The routes of a specific railroad company are usually lines between major cities and branches feeding those lines. A given area can be served by several railroads whose routes cross and overlap, but the track network is operated as separated fragments, because each railroad has exclusive service on its own tracks. Even if two railroads cross at a certain point and a connecting track exists, they cannot transfer cars unless an interchange agreement is in effect. Furthermore, tariffs and rates may be effective only over specific routes and interchanges for a given type of shipment.

Although railroads have strived to conform to long-distance linear traffic patterns, short-haul shipments often require a radial pattern.[4] The gathering of agricultural commodities and other raw materials—wheat, soybeans, pulpwood, ores—is usually done by trucks operating to a mill, elevator, or other central processing plant. Distribution of products such as fertilizer, food, construction materials, machinery, and petroleum also assumes a radial pattern, except the flow is outward from a central point. Trucks dominate both gathering and distribution segments of the short-haul market.

The railroads' orientation toward long-haul traffic is evidenced (1) physically, through the removal over time of branches, connecting tracks, and interchange tracks; (2) commercially, through tariff route restrictions; and (3) operationally, in the design of train services and operating procedures. When short-haul traffic is handled, it is handled as an adjunct to "normal" rail traffic. Given the proper type of service, however, a considerable amount of short-haul traffic presently moving by truck could be moved profitably by rail. The Minitrain experiments conducted in 1969 by the Illinois Central Railroad proved that a train could be truck-competitive for hauls over *two* miles.[5] To be competitive, a train must operate like a truck, with changes from traditional railroad work rules and operating methods. The IC's experiments focused on the 50- to 75-mile market and could have formed the basis for a new type of rail service if negotiations with labor unions had been successful.

The necessity for special labor agreements has restricted innovation in short-haul service, but more important has been the lack of enthusiasm among railroad managements. The overwhelming tendency has been to adhere to the status quo and let the trucks have the short hauls. If it were not for the traditional rail operating methods, the trucks' advantage would be far less. The organizational impediments created by the railroads themselves prevent the technical energy efficiency of the rail mode from being converted into competitive economic advantage.

The Free Enterprise Alternative would open the rail system to effective short-haul transportation. Since all rail roadways would be owned by regional roadway companies, all roadways in an area would form a true network. Radial traffic patterns could be accommodated as easily as linear ones. Sharing use of the roadways common, contract, and private carriers could provide efficient short-haul operations tailored to market demands. Trains could operate like trucks, ranging from a small locomotive and a few cars to a single car propelled either by its own motor or by a four-wheel power unit (a true rail "truck"). Larger trains could be used in short-haul volume movements.[6]

The new structure would offer the opportunity and flexibility for innovative short-haul services. Advantages would include the availability of (1) a regional roadway network; (2) a competitive carrier market; (3) the option of private carriage; and (4) the acceptance of new equipment designs made specifically for dedicated short-haul services. In contrast to the traditional railroad structure, the Free Enterprise Alternative would create an environment which encourages rail carriers' penetration of short-haul markets.

NEW SERVICES

By opening the rail roadway network to all carriers the new structure would promote the development and growth of new, innovative services. The short-haul services discussed in the previous section are only one form of innovation. Small minitrains, equipped with sleeper-cab locomotives and operated by a two-person team, could provide the service needed for long-distance, highly time-sensitive traffic. A self-propelled vehicle or a locomotive and one or more cars could serve many types of traffic currently abandoned to the trucks, because it did not fit the railroads' traditional system of yard-train-yard-train movements. With the new structure's flexibility, the type of carrier, equipment, service, and crew could be tailored to fit almost any transportation need.

Although small trains would offer much potential for innovation, long trains could also be used in new ways. Unit trains of 80, 100, or more cars could be operated by common carriers, contract carriers, and private carriers (industrial firms). These bulk haulers could move grain, coal, rock, oil, chemicals, and many other commodities in trainload quantities. In some instances the unit train could be barge-competitive; in fact, some might be owned and operated by barge line companies. John Kneiling has proposed new designs and operating schemes for unit trains, his most advanced concept being the integral train.[7] Characterized by minimal tare weight and motive power throughout the train, the integral train's operation would be a land-based version of ocean freighter ships.

Innovation would be likely in piggyback (trailer on flatcar, TOFC) services. Many rail common carriers would handle TOFC traffic as part of their routine carload operations; some might give it special service, perhaps as a separate subsidiary carrier. Specialized carriers for TOFC might also develop.[8] Carrier services would vary in price, transit time, and frequency. Train length could range from one car to over one hundred. Equipment types could also vary, from conventional locomotives and cars to advanced concepts like the RoadRailer and Kneiling's integral train for containers.[9]

The new structure would encourage more growth in piggyback traffic by giving carriers the flexibility necessary to fill various market demands. One study has shown railroads presently have 10 to 35 percent of the long-haul TOFC market and only 2 percent of the short-haul TOFC market.[10] The need for service frequency increases as the length of haul decreases; yet few railroads have offered the frequent TOFC services needed to enter such markets. Instead, they prefer "normal" train operations and an insignificant share of the total truck market.

Under the new structure, the carrier's resources could be deployed in the most effective manner. Competition from other carriers would provide strong incentive for innovation. Some TOFC carriers, for instance, could be trucking companies operating as rail private carriers (hauling their own trucks) or as rail common carriers (hauling any trailer, for a fee). This possibility would encourage use of the most efficient mode as well as the most efficient method of operation within each mode. The advent of new types of carriers, increased competition, and greater flexibility would prompt the creation of a wide range of carload freight services.

MULTIMODAL

Intermodalism, multimodalism, integrated transportation—the operation of a transportation company in several modes—has been a perennial avant-garde favorite for debate among industry experts. Historically, the discussion has been limited to the expansion of railroads into other modes (highway, water, air, pipeline). Should railroad companies be allowed to compete with carriers in another mode, on that mode's fixed way, but not vice versa? With multimodal restrictions removed, a railroad company could use any public highway, waterway, or airway. The reverse would not be true since, unlike the other modes, each railroad company traditionally has exclusive use of its own fixed way. A barge line could not provide its own locomotives, cars, and crews and operate over railroad tracks, because the tracks are the private property of an individual company and are not available for public use. Trucking companies and air carriers would be prohibited from rail operations for the same reason. In short, the railroads have always had much to gain and little to lose by promoting the multimodal concept.

Recognizing this inequality, legislation and regulation have placed numerous restrictions on the operation of carriers in the other modes by railroad companies. The Panama Canal Act of 1912 prohibited the ownership of water carriers by railroads. The Motor Carrier Act of 1935 and its subsequent amendments have restricted rail ownership of trucking firms to rail-related operations, though there has been some easing of restrictions in recent years. The Civil Aeronautics Board prohibited ownership of air carriers by carriers in other modes. Railroad intermodal ventures have been limited to specific types of truck service and pipelines. The few railroads which do own pipelines have found them to be of minor transportation importance since they are restricted to a small group of commodities moving between a few points.

D. Philip Locklin discusses the advantages and disadvantages of multimodal companies in the book, *Economics of Transportation*:

> . . . it seems likely that in most instances nonrail operations would be secondary to rail operations, and rail interests would become dominant in the integrated company.
>
> Probably the most crucial question to be raised in considering the desirability of so-called integrated transportation companies is their effect on competition. The integrated company would certainly have an advantage over independent motor and water carriers, particularly on shipments that originated or terminated on the rail line and moved partly by rail. The independents would have little chance to compete for such traffic.
>
> Theoretically there could be competition between integrated transportation companies but, on intermodal traffic, only if the rail lines themselves were competitive. Two integrated companies could hardly be said to be competitive with each other on intermodal shipments, unless the rail services of both companies were competitive, i.e., unless both provided rail services at the same points. Competition between integrated companies would therefore only be effective where there was considerable duplication of rail lines.
>
> In view of the limited extent to which integrated transportation companies would be competitive with each other, it seems likely that the most important result of their creation would be to stifle independent nonrail carriers and allow the integrated companies to dominate a major part of the transport system. If it should be considered desirable, in the interests of economy or of transport coordination, to encourage integrated transportation companies, strict control would be necessary to protect the public from abuses. Competition could not be relied upon as much as at present to provide that protection.[11]

Under the traditional railroad industry structure, multimodal ownership would extend the railroads' inherent structural and regulatory problems into the other modes. The Free Enterprise Alternative, by eliminating exclusive use of rail fixed ways and creating a rail industry structure basically identical to the structures of the other modes, would eliminate most complications arising from multimodal ownership. The rail roadway network would be available to all carriers, so carriers in the other modes could establish rail carrier subsidiaries. Multimodalism would no longer be a unilateral process—a "one-way street." With access available to all fixed ways—rail, highway, waterway, and airway—and with competitive markets in each mode, neither single-mode carriers nor multimodal carriers would be disadvantaged.

True, a multimodal carrier could benefit from coordination by using the most efficient mode or combination of modes for each shipment, but it would also incur the costs of coordination. As evidence of these costs consider (1) the marginal profitability of many railroad-owned trucking subsidiaries; (2) that these "integrated" trucking subsidiaries often spend as much effort competing with their railroad-owners as they do coordinating; and (3) that some of the most profitable rail-owned truck lines are those which have been given a large degree of independence from the railroad. A large-scale, widespread, multimodal carrier's operation would be difficult to control from a managerial standpoint, especially in the dynamic competitive environment of each mode under the new structure. Furthermore, multimodal companies would compete with each other as well as with single-mode carriers. A good portion of a multimodal carrier's traffic might move via only one of the modes, competing directly with single-mode carriers. Some types of traffic might tend to favor multimodal carriers, some might favor single-mode carriers, but most traffic would be open to competition by both types of carriers. With the new rail industry structure in place, the market could determine the value of the multimodal concept—a concept which has been the subject of much theory and little practical experience.

WORK RULES

Work rule and labor productivity problems which plague railroads under the traditional structure would not be solved directly by application of the new structure. It would, however, create an environment with incentives for flexibility and improvements by both management and labor.

As outlined previously, a single carrier would no longer have a monopoly of service over each roadway segment. Instead, carriers would have access to any and all roadways, sharing the network in a competitive market. Since each roadway would be available to all carriers, a single carrier company or a single carrier union (or group thereof) could not monopolize service over any roadway. Employees of a particular carrier company could elect to be represented by the traditional rail craft unions, by a single rail union, by a non-rail industrial union, or by no union. In this manner the rail industry under the new structure would resemble the highway, water, and air transportation modes.

Innocent third parties such as shippers and communities would be treated with fairness since they would have access to alternative rail carriers during labor disputes. Any dispute would remain between the carrier company and its employees, as it should.

Under competitive pressure inefficient practices would be eliminated eventually and innovative procedures would be given objective consideration. A healthier attitude toward change would evolve. Carrier companies would have greater incentives to seek changes and share the benefits of such changes with their employees.

ELECTRIFICATION

An indirect effect of the energy crisis has been a renewed interest in railroad electrification. Railroads can be converted to electric power with relative ease using available technology, whereas highway, water, and air transportation cannot. Electrified railroads can be powered by any energy source convertible to electric current. Electric locomotives offer many efficiencies not available in diesel locomotives.[12]

The reason why electrification has not been pursued on a large scale is the requirement for extensive capital investment in power-distribution systems and electric locomotives. Although rising oil prices favor electrification, inflation has affected capital costs and economic justification has remained illusory. The high capital investment can be justified only for roadways with high traffic density, and such densities are not common under the traditional structure. Electrifying the few high-density segments would be difficult to justify since their operations must be integrated with low-density, non-electrified routes. Dual-mode locomotives which operate as either electric or diesel do exist but are more expensive than simpler single-mode models.

Federal assistance through grants, loans, or loan guarantees has been suggested as a means for promoting electrification but such assistance is difficult to justify. First, electrification would not save enough oil to justify federal assistance strictly as an energy-saving measure.[13] Second, it would be seen as public funds aiding private interests (railroad stockholders) with little benefit to the general public. Third, to be fair, federal assistance must be available to competing railroads on an equal basis.[14] Since each railroad company has its own tracks under the traditional structure, electrification of competing routes—a duplication in itself—could result in the upgrading of inefficient roadways, simply because the railroads involved will not share the best roadway. In some cases sufficient traffic density can be achieved to justify electrification without federal assistance by merging competing railroads, but then efficiency is achieved at the expense of competition.

The new structure achieves high levels of traffic density while increasing competition. Interstate roadways would be prime candidates for electrification, as would some other roadways. Not all carriers would use electric power, but many could find it economical if it were available. With the overall growth of rail traffic envisioned under the new structure, combined with traffic concentration on the best routes, electrification could be justified even though it would go to private roadway companies since any carrier would have access to the roadway network. Federal loans to the roadway companies for electrification could be repaid using the proceeds from toll increases and/or part of the amounts charged to carriers for their electric power consumption.

AUTOMATION

At the present time it is technologically feasible to operate road freight trains automatically between terminals using a radio control link, centralized traffic control, and a small computer. It is even possible to operate local switch trains in the same way, but is more practical to have one person operate the switcher. A radio control pack would allow the person to act as both brakeman and engineer. Industrial firms are far ahead of railroad companies in applying these techniques.

Advancements like automation and remote control are *not* dependent on a single carrier having exclusive use of the roadway. Automation of road trains would connect traffic control directly to train operation, bypassing the human link in the control chain. Several carriers using the same roadway could "tune in" to roadway traffic control through automated train control devices. Traffic control would provide for both automated and manually operated trains.

Automated rail operations could resemble the operation of instrument landing systems (ILS) at airports. While ILS is a guidance system, not traffic control, several characteristics would be applicable. ILS ground equipment is part of the fixed way provided by the Federal Aviation Administration, which also provides air traffic control. Any carrier can use ILS if its aircraft have the necessary equipment. FAA safety regulations require some aircraft to have ILS equipment; it is optional for other types such as small aircraft for private use.

The rail roadway traffic control system could offer automated train control for through trains as an option on certain routes. Those carriers choosing to use automated control could equip their locomotives with the proper devices, or the devices could be placed in separate control cars. A control car could be coupled ahead of a locomotive and connected to it with multiple-unit cables. Railroads have used control cars with mid-train slave locomotives, with the slave units being operated by the engineer via radio control from the lead locomotive on the front of the train. For automated operations the control car would be placed on the front of the train, controlled via radio by the traffic control system. The important point is that separation of roadway and carrier functions does not preclude automation or use of other advanced technology. In fact, the new structure would encourage such improvements by concentrating traffic, promoting traffic growth, and spreading the costs of improvements over a greater traffic base. Automation would be an extension of normal traffic control functions through a different physical medium: instead of a trackside signal's light waves being translated by a human operator into locomotive control actions, radio waves would convey the information directly to the locomotive. When viewed from this perspective, the option of automated operations on certain routes would be an evolutionary change readily accommodated by the new structure.

SUMMARY

In terms of innovation, the Free Enterprise Alternative has two advantages: it gives carriers immense flexibility in arranging their resources and provides incentives through a competitive free market. These two factors create an optimal level of resource use in a dynamic sense throughout the rail industry.

Without economic regulation and with rail roadways open to all carriers, the free market would guide and regulate all carriers. Carriers could use their resources in the most effective and most efficient manner. Carriers could decide which markets to serve, defining their respective markets by geography, commodity, type of service, type of customer, and other factors. Carriers could change markets and market strategies as desired. In short, there would be nothing to keep a carrier company from succeeding—or failing—except the carrier company itself.

NOTES

1. Peter F. Drucker, *Management: Tasks, Responsibilities, Practices*, pp. 47, 65–67, 782–803 (particularly p. 786).
2. U.S., Department of Transportation, *The Railroad Situation*, p. 109 (see also pp. 26–28, 107–109).
3. There is no established definition for short, medium, or long hauls. As a rule of thumb, *long-haul traffic* can be considered as that above the average rail haul, generally over 500 miles. *Short hauls* can be those movements under 250 miles, or roughly below the average haul for all trucks. *Medium-length hauls* would then be approximately in the 250- to 500-mile range.
4. Chapter 12 describes the advantages of a unified roadway network and geographic concentration with respect to maintenance work.
5. Chapter 8 describes several short-haul service experiments, including the Illinois Central Railroad's Minitrain.
6. John G. Kneiling has written a number of articles concerning innovations in rail service. Among them are the following: "A Tale of Three Trains—1. How to Make Money Hauling Gravel," *Trains*, Volume 35, Number 3 (January 1975), pp. 36–39; "A Tale of Three Trains—2. Get the Stuff Out of Town," *Trains*, Volume 35, Number 4 (February 1975), pp. 44–46; "A Tale of Three Trains—3. Pulpwood Trains Can Be Profitable," *Trains*, Volume 35, Number 5 (March 1975), pp. 26–28; "The Professional Iconoclast: Bits and Pieces from the Trade," *Trains*, Volume 37, Number 7 (May 1977), p. 5; "The Professional Iconoclast: Innovations and Quality," *Trains*, Volume 33, Number 8 (June

1972), p. 5; "The Professional Iconoclast: Win Some, Lose Some," *Trains*, Volume 35, Number 2 (December 1974), p. 5.

7. John G. Kneiling, *Integral Train Systems*; John G. Kneiling, "The Professional Iconoclast: We Progress—A Little," *Trains*, Volume 39, Number 9 (July 1979), p. 5.

8. U.S., Department of Transportation, *National Intermodal Network Feasibility Study*.

9. David P. Morgan, "Roadrailer, nee Railvan," *Trains*, Volume 37, Number 12 (October 1977), p. 7; John G. Kneiling, "How to Switch from Boxcars to Containers Without Wasting Money on TOFC," *Trains*, Volume 36, Number 10 (August 1976), pp. 40–47; John G. Kneiling, "The Roadrailers Come Back," *Trains*, Volume 38, Number 4 (February 1978), p. 5; "ICG Inaugurates RoadRailer Service," *Modern Railroads*, Volume 36, Number 11 (November 1981), p. 9.

10. "Growth Through Improving Productivity," *Modern Railroads*, Volume 34, Number 11 (November 1979), pp. 73–78; "The New Ballgame," *Modern Railroads*, Volume 34, Number 11 (November 1979), pp. 67–72.

11. D. Philip Locklin, *Economics of Transportation*, 7th ed. (Homewood, IL, Richard D. Irwin, Inc. 1972), pp. 870–871. Copyright Richard D. Irwin, Inc. 1972.

12. Robert Roberts, "Electrification," *Modern Railroads*, Volume 33, Number 6 (June 1978), pp. 56–59. The typical railroad diesel locomotive in the United States is actually a diesel-electric, using a diesel engine to drive an electric generator powering electric motors on the axles (an electrical transmission system). Some locomotives have been built which can operate either as a conventional diesel-electric or as a "straight" electric, obtaining power from an overhead wire or third rail. These are known as dual-mode locomotives.

13. U.S., Department of Transportation, *A Prospectus for Change in the Freight Railroad Industry*, pp. 179–186.

14. "Catenary in the South," *Modern Railroads*, Volume 34, Number 2 (February 1979), p. 11.

SERVICE ALTERNATIVES
FOR
SHORT-HAUL TRAFFIC

Using the hypothetical area illustrated in Figure 13, four service alternatives are explored and compared. The shipments originate at point "A" and terminate at point "D."

Under the existing rail structure, demurrage rules apply without respect to length of haul. Shippers are given, usually, one free day for loading a car and two free days for unloading; demurrage charges begin after that time. A car must be spotted at the unloading point before 7:00 A.M. for that day to count, otherwise free time starts at the following midnight.

ALTERNATIVE 1: RAIL ROUTE A-EAST RR-C-NORTH RR-D

This route is most likely if the East RR, the origin carrier, pursues its longest haul and greatest division of revenue from the shipments.

Day 0 Empty car spotted by East RR local train at A.
    1 Free day for loading.
    2 East RR local train takes loaded car to B and lines it to move in next day's local train from B to C.
    3 East RR local train takes loaded car to C and sets it to interchange with North RR.
    4 North RR local train takes loaded car to D and spots it for unloading.
    5 Free day for unloading.
    6 Free day for unloading.
    7 North RR local train takes empty car to C and sets it to interchange with East RR.
    8 East RR local train takes empty car to B and lines it to move in next day's local train from B to A.
    9 East RR local train takes empty car to A and spots it for loading.

Since local trains often do not operate on Saturdays or Sundays, the cycle should include:

6-day week, add 1/7 or 14%: 9 days × 14% = 1.3 days
5-day week, add 2/7 or 29%: 9 days × 29% = 2.6 days

Figure 13. Hypothetical Area, Short-Haul Traffic Example

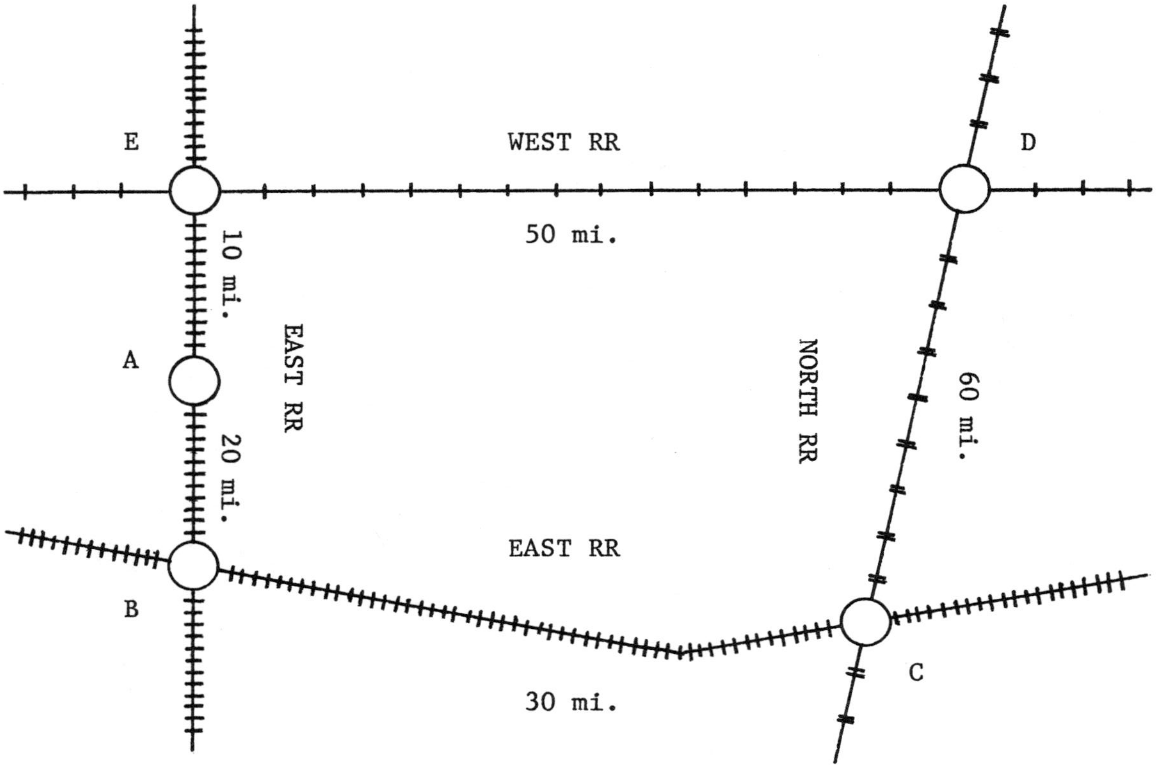

D

60 mi.

C

NORTH RR

WEST RR

50 mi.

EAST RR

30 mi.

EAST RR

10 mi.   20 mi.

E   A   B

Allowing extra time for missed connections, total cycle time would be about 12 days per carload, resulting in 30.4 round trips per year (5-day week). A typical railroad car of 80 tons capacity would haul 2,432 tons in one year.

ALTERNATIVE 2: RAIL ROUTE A-EAST RR-E-WEST RR-D

This route is likely only if the customer insists on it since it would shorthaul the East RR which is the originating carrier. It would be proper if the car were provided by West RR for the shipment.

Day 0 Empty car spotted by East RR local train at A.
     1 Free day for loading.
     2 East RR local train takes loaded car to E and sets it to interchange with West RR.
     3 West RR local train takes loaded car to D and spots it for unloading.
     4 Free day for unloading.
     5 Free day for unloading.
     6 West RR local train takes empty car to E and sets it to interchange with East RR.
     7 East RR local train takes empty car to A and spots it for loading.

Adding the allowance for Saturdays and Sundays:

6-day week, add 1/7 or 14%: 7 days × 14% = 1.0 days
5-day week, add 2/7 or 29%: 7 days × 29% = 2.0 days.

Allowing extra time for missed connections, total cycle time would be about 9 or 10 days. Using 9.5 days per cycle, a car could make 38.4 trips annually (5-day week). A typical railroad car of 80 tons capacity would haul 3,072 tons a year.

ALTERNATIVE 3: TRUCK SERVICE A-D DIRECT

Day 0 7:00 A.M. Load at A.
       8:00 A.M. Drive from A to D.
       9:30 A.M. Unload at D.
      10:30 A.M. Drive from D to A.
      12:01 P.M. Load at A.
       1:00 P.M. Drive from A to D.
       2:30 P.M. Unload at D.
       3:30 P.M. Drive from D to A.
       5:00 P.M. Arive at A.

At 2 trips per day, a tractor-trailer truck could make 520 trips annually (5-day week) or 312 trips (6-day week). A typical truck with 15 tons capacity could haul 7,800 tons a year (5-day week).

ALTERNATIVE 4: RAIL, OPERATED LIKE A TRUCK WITHOUT REGARD TO RAILROAD COMPANY TRACK OWNERSHIP

Using the same schedule as Alternative 3, but substituting a single railroad car and a small locomotive for the tractor-trailer truck, the railroad could haul 41,600 tons annually. If the loading and unloading capacity was adequate, the train could likely handle five or ten cars as easily as the single car.

SUMMARY

Although the above examples do not attempt to apply cost or investment factors, they do indicate how drastically structural differences can affect productivity. The difference between a single car in routine rail freight service and in a truck-style service is roughly 39,000 additional tons or an increase of 12-to-16 times depending on the days per week it operates. Put another way, it would take 17 cars in the routine service to produce the same transportation as one car in a truck-style service. The highway truck in the example, with only 15 tons capacity, produces the transportation of three railroad cars in routine service, because it operates more efficiently. It is readily apparent that inflexible, traditional rail operating methods are unsuitable for the short-haul market, and that to compete effectively in that market the rails must assume the flexible methods used so successfully by the trucks.

17 | THE PROMISE AND THE PROSPECTS

The Free Enterprise Alternative harnesses private sector economic forces to create a dynamic, flexible, innovative, and efficient rail industry. Basic to this structure is the separation of carrier and roadway functions, which allows each to be structured in the most appropriate manner: carriers participate in a free market governed by competition, and the roadway network exists as a regulated natural monopoly available for use by all carriers. Joint use of roadways provides both competition and efficiency. The new rail industry structure offers many advantages over the existing traditional industry structure. Despite its benefits, the new structure would doubtless encounter opposition.

GOVERNMENT OWNERSHIP OF ROADWAYS

Many previous proposals for restructuring have called for government ownership of rail roadways. Some proposals have viewed government ownership as a means for addressing inequalities between the railroads and the other modes. Other proposals have envisioned government ownership as simply a means for subsidizing railroad companies.

Government ownership of rail fixed ways would not resolve inequalities among the different modes. The disparity is in the structure, not merely who owns what components. Fixed ways in the other modes are available to any and all carriers, but rail fixed ways are not. Government ownership of rail roadways cannot correct the inequalities, particularly if the government grants individual railroad companies exclusive-use leases.

Government ownership, as a conduit for subsidy to existing railroad companies, would not address the structurally rooted inequities. No method exists to determine a fair or equal amount of subsidy for each mode. Subsidy subverts market economics; equality cannot be obtained through subsidization. Equality can only be achieved through an economic environment which requires each mode to shoulder its own full costs, including user fees based on the most accurate allocation of costs from multipurpose facilities.

RESTRUCTURING

Since government ownership of rail roadways would not produce equality with the other modes, restructuring is the essential course. Equality requires that the other modes' user fees reflect the fully allocated costs of publicly provided fixed ways. Just as important, the rail industry structure must be compatible with that of the other modes.

There are arguments which have been raised in opposition to previous restructuring proposals, not on the basis of government ownership but on the basis of the restructuring itself. Opposition to restructuring centers on two concepts, roadway/carrier separation and joint use of roadways.

Roadway/Carrier Separation

Many railroad companies object to roadway/carrier separation, because it would diminish somewhat the carrier's ability to influence fixed way functions. A carrier might have greater difficulty in setting schedules and service priorities when another entity—the roadway company—performs the traffic control function.[1] Some fear that passenger trains or even track maintenance work would be given undue preference over freight operations.[2]

Although roadway/carrier separation would require coordination between carriers and the respective roadway companies, schedules and priorities could be established as needed. With centralized traffic control (CTC) on Interstate and Primary roadways, traffic control would be flexible enough to readily accommodate carriers' schedule needs. Note that the airlines set schedules and achieve satisfactory performances without acting as traffic controllers. In some instances, performance could be improved—for example, when trains could be detoured around track work by using nearby roadways not normally available under the traditional structure.

Another objection to the separation concept is that it would harm efforts to integrate locomotives, cars, track, and operations into a single, efficient system.[3] A traditional railroad company can design and operate all physical components with engineered precision, or so the argument goes. In fact, railroads interchange cars and even locomotives on a routine basis, so the optimization is not as perfect as some contend. Industry standards promulgated by the Federal Railroad Administration, American Railway Engineering Association, Association of American Railroads, and other groups usually govern the design of rolling stock and track components. The new structure would have standards and procedures for integrating the designs of rolling stock, track, and operations.

The cost of acquiring the roadways is cited as a disadvantage of the roadway/carrier separation concept.[4] Rail roadways are a vast asset of unique character. Their value for nonrail uses is often minimal (at or near salvage value); yet they would be prohibitively expensive if not impossible to reproduce. Some roadways have a high value because, under the traditional structure, their owner has exclusive access to certain shipper facilities. With joint use eliminating these monopolies under the new structure, roadway values would lie between scrap value and replacement cost.

The rail industry has been earning a meager return on its assets in recent years, and roadways are a major asset. Obviously, if the rail industry cannot earn a normal return from these assets, another entity cannot purchase the assets, operate them in the same way, and expect a higher return. Roadway companies would operate roadways differently—and increase returns by pursuing the economies of joint use and the benefits of traffic increases resulting from the broader range of services available to shippers.

The regional roadway companies would be in an excellent position to utilize rail rights of way for nonrail uses. Communications companies and utilities could negotiate with a roadway company and gain access to corridors over an entire region. Since roadway companies could not divert profits to other business ventures, nonrail roadway income would be available for roadway expenses, thereby possibly reducing toll levels for all carriers.

Joint Use

Opposition to joint use of rail roadways is twofold. One argument promotes exclusive use; one opposes the advent of contract and private carriers.

The argument favoring exclusive use is, simply, the argument for monopoly. In theory, a monopoly can be highly efficient but practice rarely bears this out. The United States has generally rejected the pro-monopoly view in favor of competition and free enterprise. The only exception has been for a few industries categorized as natural monopolies. As shown in Chapter 9, only the rail *roadway* qualifies as a natural monopoly: carriers can operate in a competitive market if exclusive service is replaced with free access. The Free Enterprise Alternative recognizes this fundamental distinction and, in so doing, invalidates the argument for exclusive service.

The joint use concept is opposed by those who fear the entry of contract carriers, private carriers, and even specialized common carriers.[5] Critics charge that these carriers would "skim the cream" by taking certain highly profitable types of rail traffic and leave common carriers with a small base of marginal traffic. Common carriers, it is argued, would be denied the economies of scale possible with large traffic volumes; the resulting inefficiency would force rates higher for the remaining common carrier shippers. The Association of American Railroads states that joint use

opens up the use of railroad fixed plant to private and restricted-commodity carriers, who will enter into rail operations under the guise of providing "competition" for existing common-carrier railroad operating companies. These new carriers will skim the cream (heavy, long-haul, base-load traffic) off of the railroad common carrier market; all to the direct benefit of the largest industrial corporations (e.g., General Motors, Consolidation Coal, Cargill).[6]

Railroad companies have functioned traditionally as regulated common carriers, and they have no desire to see their traffic, revenues, size, or influence diminished. Rail contract and private carriers could create operations to meet a shipper's individual needs, providing better service and/or lower rates in many instances. Firms of all sizes—not just industrial giants—could avail themselves of private and contract carriage, as is done in the other modes.

Under the new structure, rail common carriers would play a diminished but important role. Subsidiaries of common carriers might offer specialized common carrier services and might also act as contract carriers. Once carrier and roadway functions have been separated, the size of a carrier would have relatively little bearing on its efficiency. The other modes have shown that a carrier need not be large to be efficient, and that small firms can compete effectively with large ones. Ultimately, efficiency is how well the carrier fills the market's needs. As market share statistics show, the other modes with a spectrum of common, contract, and private carriers are doing a better job of filling shipper needs than the mode with only common carriage, the railroads.

Once regulation is removed, experience in the other modes has shown that some rates would fall, and others would increase. No doubt this would happen in the rail industry as carriers convert to a competitive market posture. On the whole, rates eventually would move to a lower level reflecting the economies of joint use, the greater efficiency demanded of carriers by the competitive market, and an increase in total rail market share (traffic volume) due to the improved responsiveness of rail carriers to shipper needs. Since the competitive market would guide carrier prices, and since carriers would be free to enter and leave markets as they chose, a carrier would handle marginal traffic only if it chose to do so.

D. Daryl Wyckoff summarizes the case for joint use in his book *Railroad Management*.

There are certainly those who would argue that opening the railroad fixed plant to competitors would restore *vigorous* railroad competition to the industry. With the separation of the track ownership and operating company ownership, the barriers to entry for the protection of the existing natural monopolies are no longer as justified. So this may only be a disadvantage to the existing business entities that certainly would like to perpetuate themselves.[7]

... In many respects, it is the ownership, construction, and maintenance of private rights of way by railroads that make them natural monopolies and drive them towards increasingly larger, but less manageable, enterprises. Once the ownership of the right of way is separated from the operations, it appears that many markets can support several competitors because of the reduced fixed costs.[8]

THE PROSPECTS

The challenges associated with restructuring are not insignificant, nor are they insurmountable. The Free Enterprise Alternative possesses a considerable net advantage over the traditional industry structure. It would benefit shippers, carriers, and the public.

Despite its promise, the new structure would likely encounter opposition. This is the product of an industry structure which places the self-interests of certain groups at odds with the public interest.

The new structure would disadvantage existing railroad companies by removing their exclusive service monopolies and opening captive shippers to competitive rail service. The rise of contract and private carriage would further threaten the status now enjoyed by railroad companies. The existing structure, with exclusive service over each roadway, promotes monopolistic action by both individual railroad companies and by the rail industry as a whole. It encourages restraint of competition. For these reasons, most railroad companies would prefer the security of the traditional structure to the competitive opportunities of the new structure.

Like railroad management, rail unions tend to be conservative and favor the status quo. This attitude is apparent in the lack of modernization in work rules. Although other modes have a great diversity in labor practices, the railroads have a long history of domination by powerful craft unions. Consequently, precedence and historical tradition carry more importance than innovation in rail labor relations. The relative decline in influence of the rail industry and the decline in rail employment over recent decades have further encouraged the unions' conservative inclination.

Under the new structure, rail unions would risk some decline in membership as new carriers entered the market. The possible entry of unions from other industries and non-union carriers would not be welcomed by railroad unions, even though the practices are common in the other modes. The employees of roadway companies and many rail carriers would constitute a field of opportunity for responsive, dynamic rail unions. There is no reason why the existing rail unions could not fill such a role; still, it is a question of security in a stagnant industry versus demanding opportunities in a growing restructured industry.

Government—federal, state, local—would usually prefer to let the rail industry solve its own problems, but the events of recent years have forced the government to play a greater role in the rail industry. Government has sought direction in addressing rail problems; however, this situation has created occasional conflicts between the railroads' interests and the public interest. Moreover, the tendency has often been to take the path of least political resistance and seek short-term remedies instead of long-term solutions to basic problems. This is why subsidy is such a popular answer to railroad ailments: it is simple—and it is ineffective as a long-term solution.

By relying on guidance from within the railroad industry, government has failed to adequately address the issues of joint use and roadway/carrier separation. Therefore, most proposals have sought to prop up the existing structure and patch over its deficiencies. It has been expedient to do so.

Government involvement, specifically at the federal level, would be necessary to implement the Free Enterprise Alternative. At a minimum, economic and safety regulatory agencies would need to be realigned to reflect the new structure. In all likelihood, legislation would be needed to implement conversion since the rail industry would not be able to complete reformation under its own volition. The new structure, to be most effective, must include all railroads. Roadway companies must control all roadways in their respective regions, and carriers must have access to all roadways. It would be difficult for the rail industry to operate part under the traditional structure and part under the new structure.

Since government action, particularly legislative action, would be required to implement the new structure, public approval would be an essential element of the implementation process. The national preference for free enterprise and competitive markets should favor the Free Enterprise Alternative once its benefits become known.

Under what conditions would the new structure be a candidate for implementation? In the short term, the new structure can serve as an alternative to nationalization. If one or more large railroads should fail, the new structure would provide a private sector option.

Over the long term—a period of years and even decades—the Free Enterprise Alternative could gain wider acceptance, evolving as did the concept of regulation over a century ago and, more recently, the concept of deregulation. The academic community will play an important role, providing objective examination and critical evaluation not possible in settings dominated by special interests.

With time, the novel and somewhat radical first impression of the new structure can be replaced with studied appraisal. Time will also allow problem areas to be identified and solutions determined. Only through such impartial, objective appraisal can the Free Enterprise Alternative find its proper place, either as a theoretical curiosity or as the blueprint for tomorrow's rail transportation industry.

NOTES

1. Robert G. Lewis, "Let's Keep Our Rights-of-Way," *Railway Age*, Volume 174, Number 5 (March 12, 1973), p. 54; "Tomorrow's Railroads: The View from DOT," *Railway Age*, Volume 178, Number 8 (April 25, 1977), pp. 40–41.

2. "N.D. Transport Official Asks Abandonment 'Cure' for Ailing U.S. Railroads," *Traffic World*, Number 5, Volume 177, Whole Number 3745 (January 29, 1979), pp. 20–21.

3. Association of American Railroads, *Government Ownership of Railroad Fixed Plant*, p. 4; Don Byrne, "Union Pacific Chief Calls for Caution in Approach to Railroad Deregulation," *Traffic World*, Number 7, Volume 176, Whole Number 3734 (November 13, 1978), p. 28.

4. John W. Barnum, "Midwest Railroads and Northeast Lessons," *Railway Age*, Volume 179, Number 17 (September 11, 1978), p. 59 (reprinted from July–August 1978 issue of *Regulation* magazine); Association of American Railroads, *Government Ownership of Railroad Fixed Plant*, pp. 6–8.

5. Lewis, p. 54.

6. Association of American Railroads, *Government Ownership of Railroad Fixed Plant*, p. 5.

7. Reprinted by permission of the publisher, from *Railroad Management*, by D. Daryl Wyckoff (Lexington, Mass.: Lexington Books, D. C. Heath and Company, Copyright 1976, D. C. Heath and Company), p. 133.

8. Ibid., p. 130.

18 | A LOGICAL CONCLUSION

Railroads in America are built for a single avowed purpose; namely, to make money.[1]

Private enterprise is justified, in the defense long offered by economists, by the service it renders to people in their capacity as consumers. Private enterprise seeks profit. But, to obtain profit, it must serve consumers, for this is the only way to profit that competition will allow. It is thus on the foundation of competition that the case for private enterprise is built.[2]

Each railroad company provides its own fixed way and has exclusive use of that fixed way. In contrast the highway, water, and air transport modes use publicly provided fixed ways which are available to all carriers. This distinction is the root of the Railroad Problem.

The present railroad industry structure was implemented during the early nineteenth century when two technological developments, the iron rail and the steam locomotive, pushed the railroad beyond the realm of then-existing communications and management capabilities. The complexities of the steam-and-iron railroad mandated adoption of the exclusive service concept under which only one railroad company used each rail fixed way.

During the late 1800's and early 1900's the railroads dominated the national transportation scene. Exclusive service meant many shippers were served by only one railroad company. Only those shippers at junction points, terminals, and a few other locations received competitive service. The competitive-monopolistic dichotomy often led to destructive competition. Shippers in monopolistic markets were commonly charged high rates so that low rates could be charged in competitive markets. This situation caused the railroads to try to control and minimize competition through techniques like pooling, mergers, and even economic regulation.

The railroads' aversion to competition placed them at a disadvantage. Vigorous competition within each of the other modes demanded responsiveness and efficiency from their carriers. The complete absence of economic regulation from large segments of the highway and water modes further encouraged competition among their respective carriers. When the non-rail carriers applied the same aggressiveness to intermodal competition that they did to competition within their own modes, the railroads found themselves in a foreign environment. In the years which followed, the railroads suffered prolonged, dramatic loss of market share. To this day the structural disadvantage persists, evidenced by the railroads' feeble attempts to cope with competition increased by deregulation in the other modes and in the rail industry itself.

Standardization efforts made joint use of rail fixed ways possible by the late 1800's, but the success of the railroad industry had firmly entrenched its structure. Since that time, technological progress has completely eliminated the need for exclusive service. The traditional railroad industry structure and its inherent shortcomings have been rendered obsolete by economic developments—most notably, by the success of the typical transportation industry structure in the highway, water, and air modes.

It is not possible nor desirable to impose the outdated railroad structure on the other modes. It is possible to apply the typical transportation industry structure to the railroads. With the aid of modern technology, the rail mode can readily accommodate the typical structure. This is the premise of the Free Enterprise Alternative.

Applying the typical structure to rail transportation would give consistency among the modes. Economic equality would require, in addition to structural consistency, that adequate user fees be imposed for carriers which use publicly provided fixed ways (highways, waterways, and airways). Carriers in different modes could then compete fairly on an equal basis.

The fundamental principles of the Free Enterprise Alternative—roadway/carrier separation, joint use, open access, multiple types of carriers—are radical only when compared to the traditional railroad structure. Compared to the other modes or to the earliest railroads (the toll tramroads), the new structure is intrinsically logical.

The new structure uses the private sector environment to construct a system of economic checks and balances. Components of rail transportation are structured by function to provide the greatest effectiveness. Rail roadways would be organized as regional roadway companies, each one a natural monopoly subject to public regulation. Carrier companies would compete in a free market with access to the entire roadway network.

Each roadway company would own all rail roadways in its region and could take full advantage of the economies of traffic concentration, network utilization, and geographic concentration. Economic regulation would be essential for roadway companies since they would be natural monopolies. Rail roadways, while owned by private sector companies, would function as public highways available to all carriers on an equal basis.

⊲ With open access to all roadways, rail carriers could engage in true competition. Shippers would be given a choice among numerous rail service alternatives as well as among those of the other modes. Economic regulation would not be necessary for carriers since the ultimate regulator, the free market, would govern carrier competition. Common, contract, and private carriers would compete while sharing use of the roadway network. The special advantages of each type of carrier would be available in the rail mode as they are in the other modes.

The advent of true competition among rail carriers would signal a new day for transportation. Competition would be a constructive force, encouraging rail carriers to utilize the flexibility and freedom of the new structure. The "stern disciplinarian," competition would require continual innovation and ever-increasing efficiency. Competition would be intense, not to the liking of special interests which enjoy the fruits of monopoly under the existing structure. For those carriers bold enough to seize it, ample opportunity would be offered by the new structure's dynamic market.

Free entry and exit would play an important role by assuring a ready supply of carriers' services. New companies and new services would enter constantly while obsolete services and inefficient carriers were weeded out. The traditional structure does not have this natural selection capability, since the exclusive service concept ties the well-being of shippers, communities, and regions to individual railroad companies. The failure of a conventional railroad company therefore threatens serious economic dislocation. The new structure, with joint use and open access to the roadway network, eliminates this threat and easily accommodates change. It recognizes that the right to fail is just as important as the right to succeed; one cannot exist without the other.

Free enterprise is successful, because it offers choices to consumers. Choice is the embodiment of freedom, the ultimate economic power of the people. It is the foundation of democracy as well as free enterprise: the political process and market activity are reflections of the same idea. The Free Enterprise Alternative, like free enterprise itself, is founded on the principle of choice as expressed through competition. Built into the new structure, choice demands responsiveness to the needs and wants of shippers. Choice, through the market mechanism, delivers the optimal level and mix of transportation services for individual shippers and for the nation.

The Free Enterprise Alternative structures rail transportation to assume a role of importance long denied it by the rigid traditional structure. By discarding exclusive service and applying the typical structure which has proven successful in over a half century of use by the highway, water, and air transport modes, the rail industry could experience real growth, expanding its market share in a growing economy. Most of all, the Free

Enterprise Alternative creates a responsive, efficient, and innovative rail industry capable of meeting the dynamic transportation needs of this nation through the twenty-first century—and beyond.

NOTES

1. William G. Raymond, *Elements of Railroad Engineering*, p. 1.
2. Clair Wilcox, *Public Policies Toward Business*, rev. ed. (Homewood, IL, Richard D. Irwin, Inc. 1960), p. 11. Copyright Richard D. Irwin, Inc. 1960.

BIBLIOGRAPHY

BOOKS AND REPORTS

Armitage, Merle. *Operations Santa Fe.* New York: Duell, Sloan & Pearce, 1948.

Armstrong, John H. *The Railroad—What It Is, What It Does.* Omaha, Nebr.: Simmons-Boardman Publishing Corporation, 1979.

Association of American Railroads. *Government Ownership of Railroad Fixed Plant,* Staff Studies Group Working Memorandum 74-10. Washington, D.C., October 22, 1974.

_____ . *Yearbook of Railroad Facts.* Washington, D.C., annual issues.

Barriger, John Walker. *Super-Railroads for a Dynamic American Economy.* New York: Simmons-Boardman Publishing Corporation, 1956.

Baxter, Bertram. *Stone Blocks and Iron Rails.* Newton Abbot, Devon, Great Britain: David & Charles (Publishers) Ltd., 1967.

Burkhardt, Robert. *Federal Aviation Administration.* New York: Frederick A. Praeger, Publishers, 1967.

Conant, Michael. *Railroad Mergers and Abandonments.* Los Angeles: University of California Press, 1964.

Dabney W. D. *Public Regulation of Railways.* New York: G. P. Putnam's Sons, 1889.

Dearing, Charles L., and Wilfred Owen. *National Transportation Policy.* Washington, D.C.: The Brookings Institution, 1949.

Droege, John A. *Freight Terminals and Trains.* New York: McGraw-Hill Book Company, 1912.

Drucker, Peter F. *Management: Tasks, Responsibilities, Practices.* New York: Harper & Row, Publishers, 1974.

Fair, Marvin L., and John Guandolo. *Transportation Regulation,* 7th ed. Dubuque, Iowa: Wm. C. Brown Company Publishers, 1972.

Haines, Henry S. *American Railway Management.* New York: John Wiley & Sons, 1897.

_____ . *Problems in Railway Regulation.* New York: The Macmillan Company, 1911.

_____ . *Railway Corporations as Public Servants.* New York: The Macmillan Company, 1907.

Haney, Lewis Henry. *A Congressional History of Railways in the United States,* Volume I: *Congress and the Railway Down to 1850,* Book I: *Rise of the Railway Question.*

Madison: University of Wisconsin, 1908. Reprinted in New York: Augustus M. Kelley, Publishers, 1968.

Harper, Donald V. *Transportation in America: Users, Carriers, Government.* Englewood Cliffs, N.J.: Prentice-Hall, Inc., 1978.

Hay, William W. *An Introduction to Transportation Engineering,* 2nd ed. New York: John Wiley & Sons, 1977.

Illinois Central Railroad Company, Research and Development Bureau. *Organization and Traffic of the Illinois Central System.* Chicago, 1938.

Inland River Guide, 1977 Edition, ed. Dan Owen. St. Louis: *The Waterways Journal,* Inc., Publisher, 1977.

Joy, Stewart. *The Train That Ran Away—A Business History of British Railways 1948-1968.* London: Ian Allan Ltd., 1973.

Kneiling, John G. *Integral Train Systems.* Milwaukee, Wis.: Kalmbach Publishing Company, 1969.

Kolko, Gabriel. *Railroads and Regulation 1877-1916.* New York: W. W. Norton & Co., Inc., 1965.

Lederer, Eugene H. *Port Terminal Operations.* New York: Cornell Maritime Press, 1945.

Leftwich, Richard H. *An Introduction to Economic Thinking.* New York: Holt, Rinehart and Winston, Inc., 1969.

Leilech, Robert H. *The Economics of Short Trains.* New York: Peat, Marwick, Mitchell and Company, 1974.

Lewis, Edward A. *American Short Line Railway Guide.* Strasburg, Pa.: The Baggage Car, 1975.

Liebhafsky, H. H. *American Government and Business.* New York: John Wiley & Sons, Inc., 1971.

Locklin, D. Philip. *Economics of Transportation,* 7th ed. Homewood, Ill.: Richard D. Irwin, Inc., 1972.

McConnell, Campbell R. *Economics: Principles, Problems, and Policies,* 3rd ed. New York: McGraw-Hill Book Company, 1966.

Martin, Albro. *Enterprise Denied.* New York: Columbia University Press, 1971.

Mayer, H. M. *The Railway Pattern of Metropolitan Chicago.* Chicago: University of Chicago, 1943.

Nelson, James C. *Railroad Transportation and Public Policy.* Washington, D.C.: The Brookings Institution, 1959.

Phillips, Edmund J., Jr. *Railroad Operation and Railway Signaling.* New York: Simmons-Boardman Publishing Corporation, 1953.

Railway Systems and Management Association. *Railroad Terminal Strategy.* Chicago, 1967.

———. *Terminal Operations.* Chicago, 1960.

Raymond, William G. *Elements of Railroad Engineering.* New York: John Wiley & Sons, 1917.

Saunders, Richard. *The Railroad Mergers and the Coming of Conrail.* Westport, Conn.: Greenwood Press, Inc., 1978.

Taff, Charles A. *Commercial Motor Transportation,* rev. ed. Homewood, Ill.: Richard D. Irwin, Inc., 1955.

Transportation Association of America. *Transportation Facts and Trends.* Washington, D.C., annual issues.

U.S., Bureau of the Census. *Historical Statistics of the United States, Colonial Times to 1970*, Bicentennial ed. Washington, D.C., 1975.

———. *Statistical Abstract of the United States*. Washington, D.C., annual issues.

U.S., Department of Transportation. *A Prospectus for Change in the Freight Railroad Industry*. Washington, D.C., 1978.

———. *Final Standards, Classification, and Designation of Lines of Class 1 Railroads in the United States: A Report by the Secretary of Transportation, Volume II (Interim)*. Washington, D.C., 1977.

———. *National Intermodal Network Feasibility Study*. Washington, D.C., 1975.

———. *The Railroad Situation: A Perspective on the Present, Past and Future of the U.S. Railroad Industry*. Washington, D.C., 1979.

U.S., General Services Administration, National Archives and Records Service, Office of the Federal Register. *United States Government Manual 1974-1975*. Washington, D.C., 1974.

Waterways of the United States, ed. Harry O. Locher. New York: National Association of River and Harbor Contractors, 1961.

Wyckoff, Clair. *Public Policies Toward Business*, rev. ed. Homewood, Ill.: Richard D. Irwin, Inc., 1960.

Wyckoff, D. Daryl. *Railroad Management*. Lexington, Mass.: Lexington Books, D. C. Heath and Company, 1976.

———, and David S. Maister. *The Owner-Operator: Independent Trucker*. Lexington, Mass.: Lexington Books, D. C. Heath and Company, 1975.

ARTICLES

"Air Freight Leader Says Deregulation Producing Gains for Shipping Public." *Traffic World*, Number 10, Volume 175, Whole Number 3724, September 4, 1978, pp. 37-38.

Alexander, Tom. "The Surge to Deregulate Electricity." *Fortune*, Volume 104, Number 1, July 13, 1981, pp. 98-105.

Armstrong, John H. "Industrial Car Movers: New Power in an Old Package." *Railway Age*, Volume 181, Number 5, March 10, 1980, pp. 25-26.

"Barge Freight Trading Auction to Begin August 1." *Waterways Journal*, Volume 92, Number 17, July 22, 1978, p. 5.

Barnum, John W. "Midwest Railroads and Northeast Lessons." *Railway Age*, Volume 179, Number 17, September 11, 1978, pp. 58-60.

Bartley,Robert D. "OSHA: What It's All About, How Railroads Are Complying." *Railway Age*, Volume 174, Number 24, December 31, 1973, pp. 31-33.

Beers, David M. "Short Line, Bridge Carrier, Marine Operator, Terminal Road." *Trains*, Volume 38, Number 12, October 1978, pp. 48-57.

Beyer, Morton S. "Elephants on Thin Ice: The Coming Crisis in Airline Yields." *Air Transport World*, Volume 15, Number 11, November 1978, pp. 22-25.

"The Big Push into Shortline Railroads." *Business Week*, Number 2302, October 20, 1973, p. 104.

Blabey, E. H., II. "Rutland Revival—Part 3: Ogdensburg Bridge & Port Authority." *Railfan*, Volume 1, Number 4, Fall 1975, pp. 30-32.

"BM&LP: First 50Kv Electrification." *Railway Age*, Volume 175, Number 5, March 11, 1974, p. 9.

"BN's Bid to Scrap Merger Conditions Meets Opposition from Competitors." *Traffic World*, Number 11, Volume 187, Whole Number 3882, September 14, 1981, p. 58.

"BN to Fight ICC Grant to C&NW for New Coal Line in Wyoming." *Modern Railroads*, Volume 36, Number 9, September 1981, p. 15.

Breen, Terry. "Labor Pains." *Modern Railroads*, Volume 33, Number 12, December 1978, pp. 63–64.

Brown, Carl N. M. "Energy and Transportation: A Time for Decision." *Traffic World*, Number 1, Volume 181, Whole Number 3794, January 7, 1980, pp. 78–79.

Burck, Charles G. "Truckers Roll Toward Deregulation." *Fortune*, Volume 98, Number 12, December 18, 1978, pp. 74–85.

Byrne, Don. "Union Pacific Chief Calls for Caution in Approach to Railroad Deregulation." *Traffic World*, Number 7, Volume 176, Whole Number 3734, November 13, 1978, p. 28.

"Can Rails Win a Bigger Share of Aggregates Traffic?" *Railway Age*, Volume 172, Number 8, April 24, 1972, pp. 30, 39.

"A Case for Deregulation." *Modern Railroads*, Volume 34, Number 2, February 1979, p. 71.

"Catenary in the South." *Modern Railroads*, Volume 34, Number 2, February 1979, p. 11.

"C&NW Adds Commoditrains." *Railway Age*, Volume 172, Number 11, June 12, 1972, p. 12.

"C&NW/UTU Agreement." *Railway Age*, Volume 171, Number 9, November 8, 1971, p. 24.

"Coal Operator Solves L&N Problem." *Modern Railroads*, Volume 33, Number 12, December 1978, p. 13.

"Commoditrain Gets Union Go Ahead." *Railway Age*, Volume 171, Number 5, September 13, 1971, p. 16.

"Conrail, UTU Sign Crew Consist Pact." *Railway Age*, Volume 179, Number 8, September 25, 1978, p. 14.

Corns, John B. "Ohio's Robot Railroad." *Trains*, Volume 39, Number 5, March 1979, pp. 22–28.

Curry, Bruce P. "Rutland Revival—Part 1: The Vermont Railway." *Railfan*, Volume 1, Number 3, Summer 1975, pp. 18–27.

————, and Donald Valentine, Jr. "Rutland Revival—Part 2: Green Mountain Railroad." *Railfan*, Volume 1, Number 4, Fall 1975, pp. 23–29.

"Deregulation Begins as Kahn Resigns." *Air Transport World*, Volume 15, Number 11, November 1978, p. 7.

Dick, M. H. "What Really Happened on the Black Mesa & Lake Powell." *Railway Age*, Volume 172, Number 1, January 12, 1976, pp. 26–29.

"East-West Rail Merger Predicted." *Modern Railroads*, Volume 36, Number 11, November 1981, p. 27.

"Exchange Expands Scope of Barge Freight Trading." *Traffic World*, Number 5, Volume 183, Whole Number 3824, August 4, 1980, pp. 28–29.

"Fast On-and-Off at the FEC." *Progressive Railroading*, Volume 21, Number 11, November 1978, p. 43.

"The FEC Story: Survival Without Unions?" *Railway Age*, Volume 157, Number 4, July 27, 1964, p. 34.

"Fertilizer Call Session." *Waterways Journal*, Volume 93, Number 12, June 23, 1979, p. 31.

"First Crewless Freight Train." *Railway Age*, Volume 153, Number 10, September 3, 1962, p. 12.

Fishwick, John P. "The Case for the Firewall." *Railway Age*, Volume 180, Number 22, November 26, 1979, p. 50.

"Florida East Coast Strike: Beginning of the End." *Railway Age*, Volume 172, Number 1, January 10, 1972, p. 11.

Ford, Nancy. "Can FEC Go It Alone?" *Modern Railroads*, Volume 18, Number 5, May 1964, p. 61.

———. "Florida East Coast: Still Struck, Still Operating, Still Militant." *Modern Railroads*, Volume 20, Number 3, March 1965, p. 67.

"FRA Proposes Equipment Inspection Standards." *Railway Age*, Volume 173, Number 6, September 25, 1972, p. 40.

"FRA Publishes Proposed Track Standards." *Railway Age*, Volume 170, Number 12, June 28, 1971, p. 12.

"FRA Revises Track Standards." *Railway Age*, Volume 173, Number 5, September 11, 1972, p. 20.

"FRA Will Draft Operating Rules." *Railway Age*, Volume 175, Number 21, November 11, 1974, p. 12.

"Governors Back Rail-Plant Takeover." *Railway Age*, Volume 176, Number 15, August 11, 1975, p. 6.

"Growth Through Improving Productivity." *Modern Railroads*, Volume 34, Number 11, November 1979, pp. 73–78.

Harwood, Herbert H., Jr. "Horse-Era Railroading at the Harborside." *Railfan*, Volume 2, Number 2, February 1978, pp. 50–58.

"House, Senate Conference Agrees on Terms of Airline Deregulation Bill." *Traffic World*, Number 3, Volume 176, Whole Number 3730, October 16, 1978, p. 37.

"ICC Acts to Permit Contract Rates Between Railroads and Shippers." *Traffic World*, Number 8, Volume 176, Whole Number 3735, November 20, 1978, pp. 44–46.

"ICC Evaluating Chairman's Scheme for Wide-Spread Truck Deregulation." *Traffic World*, Number 7, Volume 176, Whole Number 3734, November 13, 1978, pp. 13–14.

"ICG Inaugurates RoadRailer Service." *Modern Railroads*, Volume 36, Number 11, November 1981, p. 9.

Ingles, J. David. "For a Diesel Medley." *Trains*, Volume 34, Number 12, October 1974, pp. 46–53.

———. "We Are Now Able to Compare Conrail with Conrail." *Trains*, Volume 37, Number 12, October 1977, pp. 42–50.

"Innovative and Inventive." *Modern Railroads*, Volume 34, Number 6, June 1979, p. 56.

Karr, Albert R. "The Deregulator: CAB Chairman Kahn Leads Agency Activists Spurring Competition." *Wall Street Journal*, Volume LVIII, Number 182, July 3, 1978, p. 1.

_____ . "Major Cuts in ICC Control over Truckers Are Proposed by Commission's Chairman." *Wall Street Journal*, Volume LIX, Number 17, November 7, 1978, p. 3.

_____ . "Restructuring Northeast Lines May Spur More Federal Involvement Than Expected." *Wall Street Journal*, Volume CLXXXV, Number 38, February 25, 1975, p. 30.

Keefe, Kevin P. "How Michigan Got into the Railroad Business." *Trains*, Volume 36, Number 12, October 1976, pp. 46–49.

Kneiling, John G. "How to Switch from Boxcars to Containers Without Wasting Money on TOFC." *Trains*, Volume 36, Number 10, August 1976, pp. 40–47.

_____ . "The Professional Iconoclast: Bits and Pieces from the Trade." *Trains*, Volume 37, Number 7, May 1977, p. 5.

_____ . "The Professional Iconoclast: Innovations and Quality." *Trains*, Volume 33, Number 8, June 1972, p. 5.

_____ . "The Professional Iconoclast: We Progress—A Little." *Trains*, Volume 39, Number 9, July 1979, p. 5.

_____ . "The Professional Iconoclast: Win Some, Lose Some." *Trains*, Volume 35, Number 2, December 1974, p. 5.

_____ . "The Roadrailers Come Back." *Trains*, Volume 38, Number 4, February 1978, p. 5.

_____ . "A Tale of Three Trains—1. How to Make Money Hauling Gravel." *Trains*, Volume 35, Number 3, January 1975, pp. 36–39.

_____ . "A Tale of Three Trains—2. Get the Stuff Out of Town." *Trains*, Volume 35, Number 4, February 1975, pp. 44–46.

_____ . "A Tale of Three Trains—3. Pulpwood Trains Can Be Profitable." *Trains*, Volume 35, Number 5, March 1975, pp. 26–28.

Kraemer, Ken, and Devan Lawton. "Buffalo Terminal." *Trains*, Volume 36, Number 4, February 1976, pp. 29–43.

Layton, Dan. "Trading Sessions to Open for Upbound River Freight." *Waterways Journal*, Volume 93, Number 22, September 1, 1979, p. 6.

Lefer, Henry. "Air Traffic Control System for the 1990's and Beyond Is Gestating at FAA." *Air Transport World*, Volume 17, Number 4, April 1980, pp. 30–33.

Lewis, Robert G. "Let's Keep Our Rights-of-Way." *Railway Age*, Volume 174, Number 5, March 12, 1973, p. 54.

Loving, Rush, Jr. "Ed Ball's Marvelous, Old-Style Money Machine." *Fortune*, Volume XC, Number 6, December 1974, pp. 170–185.

_____ . "Michigan's Wacky Ride on the Railroad That Couldn't." *Fortune*, Volume 98, Number 8, October 23, 1978, pp. 48–57.

McDonald, William J. "Railview: UP's McDonald: Are We Expecting Too Much from Mergers?" *Railway Age*, Volume 179, Number 19, October 9, 1978, pp. 48–51.

"Marketing Effort Aims at Aggregates." *Railway Age*, Volume 174, Number 20, October 29, 1973, p. 17.

"Meet a Heretic." *Trains*, Volume 30, Number 3, January 1970, p. 8.

"Merchants Exchange Report Gains." *Waterways Journal*, Volume 93, Number 42, January 19, 1980, p. 7.

Miller, Jay H. "Houston's Belt." *Railfan*, Volume 2, Number 8, January 1979, pp. 20–26.

Miller, Luther. "As the Editor Sees It." *Railway Age*, Volume 167, Number 18, November 10, 1969, p. 32.

_____. "Florida East Coast: We Dared to Be Different." *Railway Age*, Volume 180, Number 22, November 26, 1979, pp. 26–30.

"Milwaukee: A Breakthrough on Crew Consist?" *Railway Age*, Volume 179, Number 7, April 10, 1978, pp. 10–12.

"Mini-Train an Operating Success." *Illinois Central Magazine*, Volume 61, Number 2 (July 1969), pp. 2–3.

"Mini-Train Lives." *Railway Age*, Volume 166, Number 23, June 30, 1969, p. 11.

Mitchell, F. Stewart. "Loosening the Grip." *Modern Railroads*, Volume 36, Number 4, April 1981, pp. 34–35.

"More Regulation?" *Modern Railroads*, Volume 36, Number 11, November 1981, p. 16.

Morgan, David P. "The Cabooseless Trains." *Trains*, Volume 36, Number 3, January 1976, pp. 3–4.

_____. "FEC: The Metamorphosis Road." *Trains*, Volume 30, Number 8, June 1970, p. 3.

_____. "The FEC of Appalachia." *Trains*, Volume 39, Number 3, January 1979, p. 3.

_____. "Roadrailer, nee Railvan." *Trains*, Volume 37, Number 12, October 1977, p. 7.

_____. "The Sky May Be Falling." *Trains*, Volume 35, Number 9, July 1975, p. 4.

_____. "Where Did the Railroad Go That Once Went to Sea?" *Trains*, Volume 35, Number 4, February 1975, pp. 22–28.

"N.D. Transport Official Asks Abandonment 'Cure' for Ailing U.S. Railroads." *Traffic World*, Number 5, Volume 177, Whole Number 3745, January 29, 1979, pp. 20–21.

"The New Ballgame." *Modern Railraods*, Volume 34, Number 11, November 1979, pp. 67–72.

"Not All Federal Agencies Comment Favorably on DOT Rail Deregulation Options." *Traffic World*, Number 4, Volume 177, Whole Number 3744, January 22, 1979, p. 14.

Novas, Peter P. "Profitability in Intermodalism." *Progressive Railroading*, Volume 21, Number 11, November 1978, pp. 29–31.

"Now, This Is the Way to Run a Railroad." *Business Week*, September 7, 1974, p. 66.

Oates, Joseph L. "The Creatures of Bone Valley." *Railfan*, Volume 2, Number 7, November 1978, pp. 46–55.

"Open Auction for Fertilizer Transport in Offing." *Waterways Journal*, Volume 93, Number 9, June 2, 1979, p. 29.

Overbey, Daniel L. "Trackage Rights: Advantages and Disadvantages." Transportation Research Forum, *Proceedings—Sixteenth Annual Meeting*, Oxford, Indiana, 1975, pp. 339–347.

_____, and Patrick D. Hiatte. "SY: 03-08-80." *Trains*, Volume 41, Number 3, January 1981, pp. 22–31.

Panza, Jim. "Union Pacific into Chicago." *Railfan*, Volume 2, Number 3, April 1978, pp. 18–24.

Pinkepank, Jerry A. "When (and Where and Why) Railroads Share Track." *Trains*, Volume 39, Number 3, January 1979, pp. 20–29.

"Possibility of a Profitable D&H Line Held Out in Study Made for FRA." *Traffic World*, Number 11, Volume 182, Whole Number 3817, July 16, 1980, pp. 25–27.

"P&W: New England's Newest." *Railway Age*, Volume 174, Number 4, February 26, 1973, p. 14.

Quinby, Gilbert F. "Anticipating Avionics Evolution." *Air Transport World*, Volume 17, Number 4, April 1980, pp. 36–41.

"Radio Controls Plant Switcher." *Modern Railroads*, Volume 17, Number 3, March 1962, p. 97.

Railway Systems and Management Association. "The Design and Management of Railroad Yards." *Railway Management Review*, Volume 72, Number 2, 1972, pp. A1–A119.

"Remote Control." *Trains*, Volume 19, Number 3, January 1959, p. 21.

"Remote Control Aids Fast Coal Transfer." *Railway Age*, Volume 152, Number 10, March 12, 1962, p. 12.

Roberts, Robert. "Electrification." *Modern Railroads*, Volume 33, Number 6, June 1978, pp. 56–59.

———. "Hustling for Traffic." *Modern Railroads*, Volume 33, Number 12, December 1978, p. 69.

———. "Insight: Mr. Lang Sees Trucker Gains." *Modern Railroads*, Volume 36, Number 4, April 1981, p. 25.

———. "Service Is Golden." *Modern Railroads*, Volume 33, Number 6, June 1978, pp. 44–47.

"Runthrough Trains: The Proof Is in the Bottom Line." *Railway Age*, Volume 175, Number 4, February 25, 1974, pp. 28–29.

Saillard, Louis. "Last of the Cane Haulers." *Rail Classics*, Volume 3, Number 2, May 1974, pp. 18–27.

"St. Louis Barge Freight Trading Begins." *Waterways Journal*, Volume 92, Number 19, August 5, 1978, p. 5.

Shaffer, Frank E. "The Elusive Goal." *Modern Railroads*, Volume 34, Number 11, October 1979, pp. 68–69.

———. "Profits in Aggregates by Rail Depicted in A. T. Kearney Study." *Modern Railroads*, Volume 27, Number 6, June 1972, p. 56.

Shedd, Tom. "Energy: What Role for the Rails?" *Modern Railroads*, Volume 34, Number 11, November 1979, pp. 37–42.

———. "Mine Railroad Previews Future Electrification." *Modern Railroads*, Volume 24, Number 9, September 1969, p. 75.

———. "The Savior?" *Modern Railroads*, Volume 32, Number 7, July 1977, p. 55.

———. "Understanding and Trust." *Modern Railroads*, Volume 30, Number 1, January 1975, pp. 58–60.

"Shippers Back Federal Involvement in Rights of Way." *Railway Age*, Volume 176, Number 8, April 28, 1975, pp. 22–23.

"Shippers Form Groups to Buy Lines the Big Railroads Are Seeking to Unload." *Wall Street Journal*, Volume CLXXXII, Number 126, December 23, 1973, p. 11.

Silver, Deborah F. "Speakers in Wisconsin U. Conference Analyze Midwestern Rail Difficulties." *Traffic World*, Number 2, Volume 175, Whole Number 3716, July 10, 1978, p. 34.

Spencer, Harold E. "Deregulation of Railroads: The Road to Nationalization." *Traffic World*, Number 6, Volume 189, Whole Number 3903, February 8, 1982, pp. 89–93.

"The Story Behind Arizona's New Railroad." *Railway Age*, Volume 170, Number 12, June 28, 1971, p. 14.

Strauss, Edwin. "The P&W Rolls Again." *Rail Classics*, Volume 3, Number 1, February 1974, p. 40.

"Tomorrow's Railroads: The View from DOT." *Railway Age*, Volume 178, Number 8, April 25, 1977, pp. 40–41.

"Union Pact with Small Providence Road Grants Concessions Denied Penn Central." *Wall Street Journal*, Volume CLXXXI, Number 34, February 16, 1973, p. 8.

Uttal, Bro. "How to Deregulate AT&T." *Fortune*, Volume 104, Number 11, November 30, 1981, pp. 70–75.

Welty, Gus. "Crew Consist: The New Pacts Are Paying Off." *Railway Age*, Volume 181, Number 6, March 31, 1980, pp. 48–50.

———. "Lines on Labor." *Railway Age*, Volume 176, Number 23, December 8, 1975, p. 14.

———. "Wallflowers at the Merger Ball." *Railway Age*, Volume 182, Number 17, September 14, 1981, pp. 35–37.

"Will 'Sprint' Finish in the Money?" *Railway Age*, Volume 180, Number 20, October 29, 1979, pp. 26–27.

Wyckoff, D. Daryl. "Public Tracks, Private Users." *Transportation and Distribution Management*, April 1973, pp. 38–40.

Yates, Jeff L. "Delayed VTS Popular Topic at Annual Maritime Seminar." *Waterways Journal*, Volume 91, Number 26, September 24, 1977, p. 4.

Zimmerman, K. R. "Big Little D&H." *Trains*, Volume 37, Number 2, December 1976, p. 12.

Zlatkovich, Charles P. "The Interstate Rail System." Transportation Research Forum, *Proceedings—Sixteenth Annual Meeting*, Volume XVI, Number 1, Oxford, Indiana, 1975, pp. 42–45.

———, and E. H. Enochs. "Short-Line Railroads of Texas." *Texas Business Review* , Volume XLIII, Number 9, September 1969, reprint.

U.S. CONGRESS

U.S., Congress, Senate, *Essential Rail Services Act of 1973*, S. 1031, 93d Cong., 1st sess., 1973.

———, *Interstate Railroad Act of 1972*, S. 3769, 92d Cong., 2d sess., 1972.

———, *Interstate Railroad Act of 1974*, S. 3343, 93d Cong., 2d sess., 1974.

———, *National Transportation Rehabilitation and Modernization Act of 1975*, S. 2027, 94th Cong., 1st sess., 1974.

INDEX

About the Author

DANIEL L. OVERBEY is a senior transportation analyst for a major American railway company. He is the author of "Trackage Rights: Advantages and Disadvantages" and "SY 03-08-80: Twenty-Four Hours at the Crossroads of Frisco."